SILENT
THEFT

DAVID BOLLIER

SILENT THEFT

THE PRIVATE PLUNDER OF OUR COMMON WEALTH

ROUTLEDGE
New York and London

Published in 2003 by
Routledge
29 West 35th Street
New York, NY 10001

Published in Great Britain by
Routledge
11 New Fetter Lane
London EC4P 4EE

Routledge is an imprint of Taylor & Francis Group.

Printed in the United States of America on acid-free paper
Design and typography: Jack Donner

10 9   8   7   6   5   4   3   2   1

Library of Congress Cataloging-in-Publication Data

Bollier, David.
      Silent theft : the private plunder of our common wealth
    / by David Bollier.
          p. cm.
    Includes bibliographical references and index.
      ISBN 0–415–94482–1 (pbk) 0-415-93264-5 (hbk)
        1. Public goods. 2. Commons—United States. 3. Capitalism—United States.
    I. Title.
    HB846.5 .B65 2002
    333.2—dc21

                                                        2001045727

To my parents

CONTENTS

ACKNOWLEDGMENTS

A project of this ambition and breadth requires many friends, facilitators, supporters and advisors. I have been blessed with a generous community of such people.

Norman Lear, an irrepressible student of our political culture, quickly recognized that the commons is one of the great, neglected issues of our time. I am grateful for his support of this project, his advice on various drafts, and his wonderful friendship.

The New America Foundation also played an indispensable role in the inauguration and completion of this book. Ted Halstead, Steve Clemons, Sherle Schweninger, and Michael Calabrese each offered advice, helpful conversation, and a welcoming work space when I visited Washington, D.C.

My thanks as well to Edward Skloot and the Surdna Foundation for recognizing the long-term importance of this topic and providing generous financial support just when it was needed. I am also grateful to Eric Nelson, my editor at Routledge, for his many insightful suggestions that improved the final manuscript.

As I attempted to pull together the disparate threads of research and activism dealing with the commons, I realized anew how certain activists and thinkers have greatly inspired and informed me. This book stands on the shoulders of giants, among them Ralph Nader, who was a first mover on many issues in this book, Peter Barnes, James Boyle, Larry Lessig, James Love, John Richard, Jonathan Rowe, Gary Ruskin and Gigi Sohn.

Many other people have provided me with valuable insights as the manuscript progressed. For this, I am indebted to Richard Behan, Lara Bergthold, Harry Boyte, John Seely Brown, Paige Brown, Bill Curry, Brian Dabson, Ned Daly, John Echeverria, Brett Frischman, John Herron, Jennifer Horney, Michael Kazin, Joanne Kliejunas, Gene Karpinski, Emily Levine, Ansje Miller, Jane Pratt, Laurie Racine, Jed Shilling, Ed Stanek, Jim Stodder, Jennifer Washburn, and Helen Payne Watt.

None of these people, needless to say, bears any responsibility for how I've made use of their contributions.

Jeanne Shu of Routledge supervised production of the book with great care and aplomb. And for research and production support of early versions of the manuscript, I am indebted to Nikolai Slywka, Tina Sherman, Nathan Haga, Andrew Harig, and Hannah Fischer. A special thanks to David Kusnet, who wielded a blue pencil with great skill and judgment.

My deepest appreciation goes to my wife Ellen and sons Sam and Thomas. While living in close proximity to a working writer, they have been heroically indulgent and great company besides.

David Bollier
Amherst, Massachusetts

They hang the man and flog the woman
That steal the goose from off the common,
But let the greater villain loose
That steals the common from the goose.

The Law demands that we atone
When we take things we do not own
But leaves the lords and ladies fine
Who take things that are yours and mine.

The poor and wretched don't escape
If they conspire the law to break;
This must be so but they endure
Those who conspire to make the law.

The law locks up the man or woman
Who steals the goose from off the common'
And geese will still a common lack
Till they go and steal it back.

English folk poem, circa 1764

INTRODUCTION

It was a close call, but the West Publishing Company almost won its claim to *own* the law. Yes, until 1998, the law of the land, as set forth in *Brown v. Board of Education*, *Roe v. Wade*, and tens of thousands of other federal cases, actually belonged to a privately held company based in Eagan, Minnesota.

Technically, of course, all of the opinions rendered by the U.S. Supreme Court and lower federal courts belong to the public domain and can be republished by anyone. But as a practical matter, West enjoyed a lucrative monopoly control over the nation's legal rulings because it claimed a copyright on the *pagination* of the cases. The only acceptable way for attorneys to cite cases in legal proceedings has been to use West's proprietary page numbers, which effectively prevented any potential competitor from arising to offer its own, cheaper version of federal court rulings.

This meant that West Publishing had a pretty sweet deal: access to a huge, well-heeled market, an endless supply of new product financed by taxpayers, the ability to charge premium prices, and an impregnable wall against competition—in perpetuity![1] For the American people who finance the federal judiciary and must be governed by its rulings, the situation might be charitably described as a travesty.[2]

A century ago, when there was no centralized or comprehensive method for the courts to compile their rulings, West performed a valuable function in organizing access to the law and offering minor editorial enhancements. But even before the arrival of the World Wide Web in the 1990s, a number of critics argued that West's *de facto* monopoly ought to be replaced with a uniform citation system that would allow legal opinions to be more broadly disseminated. After all, if access to our society's body of *law* is not available to all, and the official rulings of our judicial system can be exploited as a cash cow, what then of the moral authority of the law? It was Franz Kafka, prophet of the legal labyrinth, who admonished that "the Law . . . should be accessible to every man and at all times. "[3]

Yet the struggle to wrest public control of the law from the grip of West Publishing (1998 revenues: $1.3 billion) proved how difficult it is to protect a commons in our market-dominated society, even when the issue is as utterly central as the rule of law. Over the decades the U.S. court system had settled into a cozy partnership with West Publishing. Federal judges and their clerks enjoyed unlimited access to West's online compilations. They enjoyed the company's help in assuring the accuracy of final opinions and the lavish gifts and trips to exotic locales that West sponsored for federal judges, including at least seven Supreme Court justices. Politicians from Al Gore to Newt Gingrich to key congressional committee chairmen also enjoyed warm relationships with West Publishing, thanks to generous campaign contributions. Such favors were only too helpful in West's attempts to sneak through stealth amendments to defend its hammerlock on access to the law. In effect, West was claiming private ownership of the commons, the collectively owned resources that are fundamental to a democratic commonwealth.

Few of these facts might have received much visibility to the wider world but for the activism of James Love, director of the Ralph Nader-founded Taxpayer Assets Project. In 1993, he began to debunk West's arguments, expose its ethically dubious lobbying, and mobilize law librarians, bar associations, legal publishers and the press to take their own initiatives.[4] After years of legal and public relations skirmishes, in 1998 a small New York CD publisher, HyperLaw, successfully challenged in a federal lawsuit West Publishing's copyright control over court opinions.[5] In coming years, many companies will publish federal cases in various formats, including on the Web for free. The struggle between public rights and private control will persist, however. Under pressure from West and Lexis, an online vendor of legal cases licensed by West, the U.S. federal courts have to date refused to adopt a public domain, technology-neutral citation system.[6]

What Is the Commons?

West Publishing v. The People may be a parable for our times. It is but one of dozens of cases that pose the question: *Who shall control the commons?* In ways that are variously egregious, subtle, clever, and obscure, business interests are gaining ownership and control over dozens of valuable resources that the American people collectively own. The American commons include tangible assets such as public forests and minerals, intangible wealth such as copyrights and patents, critical infrastructure such as the Internet and government research, and cultural resources such as the broadcast airwaves and public spaces.

We, as citizens, own these commons. They include resources that we have paid for as taxpayers and resources that we have inherited from previous generations. They are not just an inventory of marketable assets, but social institutions and cultural traditions that define us as Americans and enliven us as human beings—public education, community institutions, democratic values, wildlife and national forests, public spaces in cities and communications media.

Astonishingly, Americans are losing the right to control dozens of such commons that they own. While business and technology tend to be the forces animating this silent theft, our government, as we shall see, is complicit in not adequately protecting the commons on our behalf. When not being seduced by what has been called the legalized bribery of campaign contributions, politicians may gamely try to defend our common assets, and occasionally succeed. But even well-meaning government leaders are often overwhelmed by the pace of technological change and the complications of consensus-building and due process. The public, for its part, is often clueless and thus politically moot in many battles over the commons. (Throughout, I will use the collective noun "commons" instead of the more archaic term "common.")

This trend raises serious questions about the future of our American commonwealth. In an age of market triumphalism and economistic thinking, does the notion of "commonwealth"—that we are a people with shared values and control over collectively owned assets—have any practical meaning? Or have we lost sight of our heritage as a commonwealth and lost control of our assets, and perhaps our democratic traditions, as private interests have quietly seized the American commons?

Business, let it be said, is no more a villain than a lion whose metabolism needs gazelles. Companies are in the business of maximizing competitive performance in the market, and use of the commons simply represents an available resource and frequently a path of least resistance. That is why fortifying the commons is not equivalent to attacking the market, which clearly generates many important benefits for our society.

It should be stressed that protecting the commons is about maintaining a balance, not bashing business. It is self-evident that we need markets. It is far less clear—particularly to businesses operating within markets—that we also need commons. A society in which every transaction must be mediated by the market, in which *everything* is privately owned and strictly controlled, will come to resemble a medieval society—a world of balkanized fiefdoms in which every minor grandee demands tribute for the right to cross his land or ford his streams. The flow of commerce and ideas—and the sustainability of innovation and democratic culture—will be seriously impeded. Furthermore, such a market-dominated society is not likely to cultivate the sense of trust and shared commitments that any functioning society must have.

So the issue is not market versus commons. The issue is how to set equitable and appropriate boundaries between the two realms—semi-permeable membranes—so that the market and the commons can each retain integrity while invigorating the other. That equilibrium is now out of balance as businesses try to exploit all available resources, including those that everyone owns and uses in common.

Of course, the creative tension between business interests and our democratic polity is nothing new.[7] It may be one of the central organizing principles of our political culture. Clashes between the two have shaped the very framing of the Constitution, numerous Progressive-era campaigns, the labor movement, and many New Deal and Great Society initiatives. But today we live in a troubling new stage of this struggle that differs in scope and ferocity from previous ones.

The market's role in American society has exploded. It now penetrates into nooks and crannies of daily life that could not have been imagined in an earlier generation—video ads at gas pumps, marketing disguised as education in the public schools, and Broadway theaters named after airlines. Companies now obtain patents on genetic structures of life and on mathematical algorithms, and universities urge their students to consider themselves "the President of Me, Inc."

The floodgates of commercialization in American culture really opened up in the 1980s, as powerful new electronic technologies—computers, cable television, the VCR, new telecommunications systems, and others—began to take root. Businesses began penetrating more deeply into nature, knitting together new global markets, and colonizing our consciousness and public culture. As the government agencies that set socially acceptable boundaries for market activity were slowly sabotaged by budget cuts and curbs on their authority, a wide array of commons in American life became open game for market exploitation: public lands, government R&D, information resources, and ethical norms for safety, health, and environmental protection.

Still, the privatization of the commons has crept up slowly and quietly, in fits and starts. It has not been an identifiable juggernaut with a single battlefront or defining moment. It has had scores of manifestations, some prominent, most of them obscure, which helps explain the wicked insight of the nursery rhyme: Why do we "hang the man and flog the woman/ That steal the goose from off the common,/But let the greater villain loose/That steals the common from the goose"? Because, I fear, we no longer *see* the commons, and thus no longer understand its meaning.

Stealing the Commons from the Goose

The nursery rhyme comes from the period of the English enclosure movement, which flourished at various points from the fifteenth to nineteenth centuries, but especially from 1750 to 1860. In order to exploit emerging markets and aggrandize their power, the aristocracy prevailed upon Parliament to allow the ruthless seizure of millions of acres of commonly used forests, meadows, and game. As economic historians such as Karl Polanyi have shown, enclosure helped lead to the creation of modern industrial markets while inflicting devastating social, environmental and human costs on once-stable rural communities.

With similar dynamics today, many business sectors are finding it irresistible to enclose common resources that were once commonly shared. If the mineral resources on federal lands can be mined for $5 an acre under an archaic 1872 law, a lucrative windfall that the mining industry can preserve through well-deployed campaign contributions, *why not?* If commonly used agricultural seedlines can be genetically reengineered to be sterile, rendering them artificially scarce and thus suitable for market control, *why not?* If new software technologies can lock up information that was once readily available to all, and if information vendors can convince Congress to allow compilations of *facts* to be owned through copyright law, *why not?*

It is no wonder that businesses find exploitation of the commons so easy and attractive. Most common resources are largely unrecognized by the American people *as* common resources. Not surprisingly, they have few legal protections or institutional defenders.

Such enclosures of the commons are aided by a Washington officialdom increasingly captive to business and indifferent to ordinary citizens; a journalism profession that has grown soft now that it competes with entertainment and marketing; and the dominion of market culture over our civic identities. We have become a nation of eager consumers—and disengaged citizens—and so are ill-equipped even to perceive how our common resources are being abused.

The abuse goes unnoticed also because the theft of the commons is generally seen in glimpses, not in panorama, when it is visible at all. We may occasionally see a former wetlands paved over with a new subdivision or acres of tree stumps on federal lands that timber companies leased for a pittance. If we listen closely through the cacophony of the media, we may hear about the breakthrough cancer drugs that our tax dollars helped develop, the rights to which pharmaceutical companies acquired for a song and for which they now charge exorbitant prices. It is not easy to connect the dots among these complicated, seemingly unrelated events and recognize the larger pattern of enclosure.

The truth is, we are living in the midst of a massive business-led enclosure movement that hides itself in plain sight. Government R&D laid the groundwork for some of the most significant innovations in computing—the original Internet architecture and protocols, e-mail, the Mosaic software that gave rise to the Netscape browser, among others—but these investments have essentially been privatized and recast as the singular product of entrepreneurial vision. Our government has given commercial broadcasters large portions of the public's electromagnetic spectrum, worth tens of billions of dollars, in return for token gestures of public service. The public domain in intellectual property—the information and creative expression that everyone must draw upon to make anything new—is rapidly being carved up by proprietary interests through radical extensions of copyright and patent law.

Some invasions of the commons, while quite egregious, are sanctioned because we no longer can muster a spirited commitment to the public sector—hence the widespread acquiescence to Channel One, a pseudo-educational TV news program whose advertisements are forced upon millions of children in public schools every morning; hence the naming of beloved sports stadia after corporate sponsors that have few valid claims to our civic respect beyond the payment of sponsorship fees. Sports itself, while always a business endeavor, has been radically transformed, as companies such as Nike successfully market themselves as sources of transcendent meaning.

What makes this moment so different from many earlier ones in our history is the gross imbalance between the market and our democratic polity. The market and its values assert dominion over all, and in so doing, erode the sinews of community, undermine open scientific inquiry, weaken democratic culture, and sap the long-term vitality of the economy. If we are to arrest this trend, I believe we must begin to develop a new language of the commons. We must recover an ethos of *commonwealth* in the face of a market ethic that knows few bounds. This not only means reasserting democratic control over the "common wealth"—the vast array of publicly owned resources and traditions of social cooperation that constitute a vast reservoir of wealth. It also means recognizing the intrinsic importance of the commons as a sovereign realm whose integrity and subtle fecundity must be respected.

Honoring the common is not a matter of moral exhortation. It is a practical necessity. This book aspires to explain why.

The Effects of Market Enclosure

The increasing pace of market exploitation of the commons is troubling for five reasons.

First, enclosure needlessly siphons hundreds of billions of dollars away from the public purse every year that could be used for countless varieties of social investment, environmental protection, and other public initiatives. The public's assets and revenue streams are privatized, with only fractional benefits accruing to the public in return.

Second, enclosure tends to foster market concentration, reduce competition, and raise consumer prices. The power to enclose generally belongs to the largest companies, which have the market clout and political influence to acquire public resources on favorable terms. These gains are often leveraged by industry leaders, in turn, to extend their market dominance even further. Large ranchers are the heaviest users of federal grazing lands, for example. Biotechnology firms use proprietary seeds to dominate the market for a given crop. Pharmaceutical companies use federally sponsored drug research to gain control over specific drug treatment markets.

Third, enclosure threatens the environment by favoring short-term exploitation over long-term stewardship. The familiar result is greater pollution of the earth, the air, and the water. Leading companies find it strategically useful to displace health and safety risks onto the public or shift them to future generations. The flagrant abuses of public lands by timber, mining, and agribusiness companies are prime examples.

Fourth, enclosure can also impose new limits on citizen rights and public accountability, as private decision-making supplants the open procedures of our democratic polity. Consider the privatization of Internet governance through the creation of ICANN, the Internet Corporation for Assigned Names and Numbers. Instead of a democratic process of open standards, openly arrived at through public participation, a quasi-private replica of democratic governance was invented to manage domain names in the interest of commercial users. Large companies have also learned that they can freeze out democratic and market accountability by using sophisticated proprietary technologies. Microsoft's Windows operating system and Monsanto's bioengineered foods are two cases where companies have used exceedingly complicated technologies to confound democratic oversight and effectively prevent consumer choice.

And fifth, enclosure frequently imposes market values in realms that should be free from commodification. The character of community values, family life, public institutions, and democratic processes should not be blindly dictated by the market. Yet that is the effect when public schools sell their captive audience of youngsters to junk-food vendors; the

Smithsonian Institution lets corporate donors determine the content of its museum exhibits; and cost-benefit equations are used to dictate acceptable levels of contaminants in food. The problem, too often, is that economic gains tend to be measurable and culturally esteemed (Gross National Product, rising quarterly profits), while the larger societal impacts are fuzzy and diffuse (community dislocations, ecological stress, public health risks). There are no simple yardsticks, no "bottom lines," for evaluating the pernicious effects of market enclosures. This naturally makes it easy to ignore them or dissociate them from market activity.[8]

Reclaiming the Commons

Developing a discourse of the commons—the burden of this book—is especially important at a time when our market culture encourages us to believe that we have little in common and can accomplish little when we work together. Talking about the commonwealth reminds Americans of the things we share: the forests and minerals that we all own, the miraculous technologies that we all have helped finance, and the values—belief in equal opportunity, say, and due process of law—that we share.

A reckoning of what belongs to the American people is a first step to recovering control of common assets and using them either to generate new revenues for public purposes or to protect them from market exploitation. At a time when the public purse is raided for all manner of "corporate welfare," an analysis based on the "common wealth" offers some powerful ways to leverage assets that we, the American people, already own.[9]

Talking about the American commons has important strategic value too. It helps reassert public control over public resources without necessarily triggering the familiar dichotomy of the free market ("good") versus regulation ("bad"). Too often, attacks on regulatory shortcomings have been used to justify a return to the era when business was not regulated at all. Talking about the commons can help the American public identify both its distinct interests as well as policy options that include, but go beyond, traditional regulation. As we will see in Chapter 13, the commons can be preserved through stakeholder regimes that give citizens equity ownership, government auctions of the right to use common assets, new extensions of legal principles such as public trust doctrine (environmental law) and the public domain (copyright law), and Internet vehicles that enable collaboration.

Finally, the idea of the commons helps us identify and describe the common values that lie beyond the marketplace. We can begin to develop a more textured appreciation for the importance of civic commitment, democratic norms, social equity, cultural and aesthetic concerns, and ecological needs. They need no longer be patronized as anecdotal and subjective, misconstrued through bizarre economic theories that purport to monetize human pleasure ("hedonics") or human choice ("contingent value"). The idea of the commons helps us restore to center stage a whole range of social and ecological phenomena that market economics regards as sideshows—"externalities"—to the marquee events of the marketplace: economic exchange. A language of the commons also serves to restore humanistic, democratic concerns to their proper place in public policy-making. It insists that citizenship trumps ownership, that the democratic tradition be given an equal or superior footing vis-à-vis the economic categories of the market.

This is not just a moral argument but also an intensely pragmatic one. Any sort of creative endeavor—which is to say, progress—requires an open "white space" in which experimentation and new construction can take place. There must be the *freedom* to try new things. There must be an unregimented work space in which to imagine, tinker, and execute new ideas. When all the white space is claimed and tightly controlled through commercial regimes that impose quantitative indices and quarterly profit goals and that insist upon propertization and control of all activity, creativity is bureaucratized into narrow paths. There simply is no room for the visionary ideas, the accidental discoveries, the serendipitous encounters, the embryonic notions that might germinate into real breakthroughs if only they had the space to grow. An argument for the commons, then, is an argument for more white space.

▪ ▪ ▪

The story of the myriad commons in our midst—and their relentless enclosure—traverses a wide terrain of subject matter. We will start by examining some basic ideas that will recur throughout: the notion of the commons as a counterpoint to the market, the workings of the gift economy, and the dynamics of market enclosure (Part I). These concepts offer a fresh, insightful way of understanding the market's role in a range of disparate arenas: the exploitation of nature, the abuse of federal lands, the privatization of the Internet, the overmarketization of knowledge and creative expression, the corporatization of academic research, the giveaway of the public airwaves, and the commercialization of public spaces and institutions (Part II).

An inevitable question, after reviewing this gauntlet of disturbing enclosures, is whether anything useful can be done. What larger conclusions about the commons might we make, and how might the commons be reclaimed? How might we invent the commons we need for the twenty-first century?

Perhaps the preeminent lesson is that a commons need not result in a "tragedy." Through the right structures, a commons can use social and democratic means to manage a resource effectively. Indeed, certain commons, particularly in the Internet milieu, can even produce a *cornucopia* of shared wealth. The robust, innovative character of many commons stems from a key strength: the diversity and social equity of participants in a commons. Also, when "ownership" of resources in a commons is not alienated but controlled by a stable, defined community, environmental sustainability and democratic accountability are more easily achieved.

What, then, can be done to preserve and fortify the commons?

The answer varies, of course, from one resource domain to another and one community of interest to another. But here are some of the more useful initiatives (explored in Part III) that could be taken:

- New policy structures must be invented to assure a fair economic return on public assets and the protection of gift economies.
- More effective regimes must be devised to oversee and manage the private use of government lands and natural resources.
- New sorts of stakeholder trusts should be created to give ordinary citizens an equity interest in public assets, as the Alaska Permanent Trust does for that state's oil revenues.
- Congress should work to stop the enclosure of the Internet commons and public knowledge by fortifying the public domain and fair use rights. It should also refuse to grant sweeping new intellectual property rights to book publishers, film studios, the recording industry, and software makers.
- Our government should insist upon some meaningful forms of public access to the airwaves, which have been surrendered wholesale to commercial broadcasters for virtually nothing.
- The fruits of federally sponsored research must be recovered for the American people and not forfeited for fire-sale prices, and the independence and integrity of academic inquiry must be assured.
- The overcommercialization of public spaces, community institutions, childhood experience, and culture should be stoutly resisted through public policy and social protest.

Our government is supposed to act as a steward for the public's economic, civic, and environmental interests. It is revealing that our government has not even compiled a comprehensive inventory of common assets, the prerequisite for any accounting of lost revenues, lasting harm to the assets, and damage to gift economies. Business critics often cry that environmental regulations amount to unconstitutional "takings" of their private property. But as a commons analysis makes clear, the actual "takings" are often committed by the victors of our Darwinian market, and the victims are the unorganized public: the commoners. This book, then, is a first rough draft of that much larger project, the reclamation of the common wealth—and the reinvigoration of the commonwealth.

Part I.

The Commons,

Gift Economies,

and Enclosure

1.

Reclaiming the Narrative
of the Commons

It takes thirty leaves to make the apple.

—Vietnamese monk Thich Nhat Hanh[1]

"The commons" is a concept that many Americans have trouble comprehending. We are so accustomed to thinking about the individual and so focused on "property" as tangible things owned by individuals—this is *mine!*—that we have trouble understanding that some of the most important wealth we own is collective and social in character.

The leaves, the roots, the trunk, the orchard, and the ecosystem? It is our Western conceit to focus on the apple. This may be why so many of our commonly owned resources are abused. Fixated on the fruit, we only belatedly come to see that a vast, complex apparatus of collective wealth lies behind even the simplest outputs. "The thing that troubles us about the industrial economy," writes Wendell Berry, "is that it tends to destroy what it does not comprehend, and that it is *dependent* upon much that it does not comprehend."[2]

Learning to see and understand the dozens of commons in our very midst is one of the preeminent challenges of our times. The commons is not the relic of some pastoral age or a quaint throwback practiced by villagers in Africa and Indonesia. Even in high-tech America, home to the biggest, most muscular market system in the world, the commons is ubiquitous. It is an underrated, much-ignored reservoir of valuable resources, system of social governance, and crucible for democratic aspiration that is only now starting to be recognized for what it is.

Why does the commons live in the shadows, virtually ignored? Let us start with a parable from one of the most market-obsessed sites on the globe, New York City.

New York City's Improbable Community Gardens

A few years ago, the newspapers of New York City were ablaze with a controversy about dozens of plots of derelict land that had been slowly turned into urban oases. Should hundreds of beautiful community gardens that neighborhoods had created on trash-filled lots be allowed to stay in the public domain? Or should the mayor and city government, heeding the call of developers, try to generate new tax revenues on the reclaimed sites by selling them to private investors?

The community gardens emerged in a realm that the market had written off as worthless. Throughout the 1970s and 1980s, the New York City real estate market had abandoned hundreds of buildings and city lots as unprofitable. Investors stopped paying taxes on the sites, and the City became the legal owner of most of the properties—some 11,000 nontaxable vacant lots by the late 1990s. Many soon became rubble-strewn lots for trash, junked cars, drug dealing, and prostitution—with predictable effects on neighborhoods.[3]

Distressed at this deterioration, a group of self-styled "green guerillas" began to assert control over the sites. "We cut fences open with wire cutters and took sledgehammers to sidewalks to plant trees," said Tom Fox, an early activist. "It was a reaction to government apathy."[4] Soon, the City of New York began formally to allow residents to use the sites as community gardens, with the understanding that the property might eventually be sold.

Over 800 community gardens sprang up throughout the five boroughs, and with them, an economic and social revival of the neighborhoods. Although no economist would have predicted it, neighborhood groups were able to deliver what the private market alone could not—the civilizing of blighted neighborhoods—through noneconomic means at minimal cost. "What were once marginal neighborhoods have become more stable and valuable, in part because of their green spaces and the sweaty, collective, imaginative effort that greening took," wrote one journalist.[5]

In both the Lower East Side and Harlem in Manhattan, and Coney Island in Brooklyn, neighborhoods came together to clean up the discarded tires and trash, and plant dogwood trees and vegetable gardens. Over time, hundreds of cool, green oases in the asphalt cityscape emerged—places that helped local communities see themselves as communities. Families would gather in some gardens for baptisms, birthday parties, and weddings. Other gardens were sites of poetry readings and performances, mentoring programs, and organic gardening instruction.

"Ten years ago, this community had gone to ashes," said community advocate Astin Jacobo of his community garden. "But now there is a return to green. We're emerging. We're seeing things return to the way it should be. Green. For joy. For humanity."[6] More than 200 of the community gardens have been maintained for over ten years.

The way that the community gardens combined cost-efficiency with community-building was especially notable. One study found that the average price of constructing a city park was $50 a square foot, while the cost of a community garden was only $5 a square foot.[7] Moreover, maintenance was a matter of sweat equity, not City expenditure. What economist would have predicted that impoverished neighborhoods could create such beauty and liveliness at so little cost?

Perhaps more importantly, the community gardens gave neighborhood residents a chance to govern a segment of their lives. A City bureaucracy was not needed to "administer" the sites and users; a self-selected neighborhood group shouldered the burden. Moreover, these volunteers did not treat the sites as interchangeable units of land without history, personality or context. They made the sites organic expressions and possessions of their communities.

By the 1990s, it was becoming clear that the community gardens were generating some significant externalities. The greenery and social vitality were boosting the rents of storefronts and apartment buildings—which, ironically, only alerted the City to the growing economic value of the sites. In 1997 Mayor Giuliani proposed auctioning 115 of the gardens in order to raise between $3.5 to $10 million (at a time when the City had a $2.1 billion budget surplus). Although affordable housing was one possible use of the sites, there was no assurance of that result. Defenders of the gardens saw the auction as a privatization of public resources, a government seizure of community-created economic value that would benefit chiefly investors and speculators.

For the mayor, the myriad benefits of community gardens were essentially a nullity. Officially, the sites were considered vacant lots: underutilized sources of tax revenue that should be sold to private investors. "These properties should go for some useful purpose, rather than lying fallow," said a city official, in support of the mayor.[8] The mayor's plan ignited an uproar, as hundreds of citizens demonstrated, some through civil disobedience, in numerous attempts to save the gardens. "We're all for development," said one activist, "but when community gardeners go in and make a neighborhood livable, I think that needs to be respected and rewarded."[9]

Determined to eke maximum revenue from the sites, the City rejected an offer by the Trust for Public Land (TPL) to buy 112 garden lots for $2 million. Then, one day before a planned auction of the sites in May 1999, actress Bette Midler donated $1 million to help the TPL and other organizations consummate a purchase of the lots for $3 million.[10] While the fate of dozens of other gardens remains unclear, the actual value of the sites, beyond the strict market reckoning, had been forcefully asserted.

How you interpret the story of New York City's community gardens depends a great deal upon the narrative you choose. Under the traditional narrative favored by Mayor Giuliani, the sale of the community garden sites is a case of using the market to maximize wealth and exploit under-utilized resources more efficiently: an open-and-shut case of neoclassical economics. But to a large segment of the City's residents, the community gardens exemplify the power of the gift economy. A gift economy is not so much a physical resource as a social and moral system by which sharing, collaboration, loyalty, and trust are cultivated within certain commons.

Does that mean that the many benefits that city-dwellers received from the gardens offset the revenues the City would otherwise have gained through auctions of the sites? This is the kind of question an economist asks. It implicitly assumes, even insists, that a price be attached to every human satisfaction, even to the aesthetic and social enjoyment that the gardens provided in an oppressive cityscape. The benefits of the gardens are *incommensurate* with an economic matrix and can no more be plugged into a cost-benefit analysis than can the joy of raising one's children. While the City had every *legal* right to reclaim the vacant lots, the point of this story is that the unorganized public—the participants in public gift economies—also have strong *moral* claims that conscientious governments would do well to accommodate. Governments, after all, are not chartered to cater solely to investors and market needs but to the *commonweal* in the broadest sense of the term.

There is some irony, perhaps, that in the end, the gift economies that arose through the community gardens could be protected only by encasing them in conventional property rights: the Trust for Public Land had to buy the sites. While market champions might seize upon this outcome as a vindication of the market and the impotence of gift economies, there is a more thoughtful way to interpret the purchase of the gardens. The trust-owned land represents "property on the outside, commons on the inside," a term coined by Yale law professor Carol Rose to describe "a regime that holds some resource as a commons among a group of 'insiders,' but as an exclusive right against 'outsiders.'"[11]

While the commons may need to be protected through conventional (and imaginative) legal mechanisms, the inner life of the commons makes it a different creature from anything imagined by Adam Smith or Milton Friedman. Internally, the logic of a commons does not resemble that of the utility-maximizing automaton of neoclassical economic theory, but that of a living, evolving organism whose integrity must be assured in order to meet its diverse needs. In terms of its external effects, a commons is the source of a rich variety of social and economic benefits. Strangely, the wealth generated by the commons is barely appreciated. Why?

Reclaiming the Narrative of the Commons

For at least a generation, the archetype of "the commons" has been tainted by the narrative that a commons is invariably a tragedy. This view was popularized by Garrett Hardin in a famous essay, "The Tragedy of the Commons," which described how a scarce resource open to all comers would be depleted and left to ruin; he used the example of herders using a common meadow.[12] The commons would fall apart, Hardin argued, because every herder would enjoy direct benefits from overexploiting the commons while suffering only indirect costs. Eventually, overuse would destroy the resource.

Even though Hardin used the tragedy-of-the-commons paradigm to inveigh against overpopulation, the metaphor soon took on a life of its own in public policy circles. In the hands of conservatives and economists, it began to be an all-purpose metaphor to denigrate collectively managed property and champion the efficiencies of private-property regimes. In practice, Hardin's metaphor has been a Procrustean rack; circumstances that do not fit its premises must be stretched or slashed to fit, or ignored.[13] The many domains in which the commons actually works, and works well, are not seriously considered.

Two other metaphors have purported to show the severe barriers to collective solutions to common problems, notes political scientist Elinor Ostrom.[14] The "prisoner's dilemma" is a formal, game-theory version of the tragedy of the commons in which two prisoners, locked in separate rooms and unable to communicate, must makes choices that try to maximize their self-interest. The basic dilemma is that a greater long-term benefit can be achieved if each prisoner cooperates with the other—but each prisoner also has powerful incentives to cheat. This highly abstract model purports to show that cooperation is usually irrational and unlikely to solve collective-action problems.[15]

A third paradigm that offers a similarly pessimistic outlook on the ability of human beings to collaborate is "the logic of collective action," a term coined by economist Mancur Olson in his famous book of the same title.[16] Olson explicitly argued that "rational, self-interested individuals will not act to achieve their common or group interests" (even though he qualified this brash argument elsewhere in his book). The chief reason for this outcome, he claimed, is that an individual has little incentive to contribute to the creation or maintenance of a public good if he can gain access to it for free or if he cannot be excluded from it (the "free rider" syndrome).

All three metaphors—the tragedy of the commons, the prisoner's dilemma, and the logic of collective action—encourage commentators, writes Ostrom, "to invoke an image of helpless individuals caught in an inexorable process of destroying their own resources," as if this dynamic were self-evident and beyond argument.[17] These metaphors have given rise to a vast literature that attempts to explain why people often will not work together for the common good.

But they also exclude from consideration a wide range of human actions that the metaphors simply do not sanction.[18] The idea that people might volunteer their time to work on community gardens, or that scientists might openly share their research results with trusted colleagues, or that people might post worthwhile information on the Internet for free, is irrational by the terms of conventional economics. There is no financial payback or reward. Such types of cooperation do not adhere to the general rule of self-interested utility maximization, and so are alleged to be aberrational or at least marginal.

This pessimism persists, in part, because the commons is frequently confused with an *open-access* regime, in which a resource is essentially open to everyone without restriction. In an open-access regime, there is no identifiable authority. No one has recognized property rights, and the output of the commons is intended for sale on external markets, not for personal use by members of the commons. For all these reasons, no one worries about long-term sustainability. Without the "social infrastructure" that defines a commons—the cultural institutions, norms, and traditions—the only real social value in open-access regimes is private profit for the most aggressive appropriators.[19] Hardin's essay might more appropriately have been titled, "the tragedy of open access."

Many commons are regarded by economists as "public goods." These are resources from which it is difficult or costly to exclude people ("nonrival" and "nonexcludable" resources, as economists put it). A public good is typically an open-access regime, such as a lighthouse, city park, or the global atmosphere—resources whose benefits are accessible to everyone without any given individual having to pay for them. This is why government often steps in to pay for public goods, provided there is sufficient political pressure from influential constituencies. While a public goods analysis is certainly useful, it may not necessarily grapple with social management methods for governing the commons.[20]

A primary task of this book is to reclaim the narrative of the commons—

the stories that we tell about our capacity to work together toward shared goals. While the tragedy of the commons and the existence of free riders on public goods certainly do exist, they do not represent the final word, or even the general rule, on whether individuals can come together to pursue common goals. The democratic tradition in American life, in fact, is based on a type of collective "utility-maximizing behavior"—call it a patriotic commitment to the American experiment—that market economics simply does not recognize. And the ability of social negotiation and cooperation to manage the commons can be seen in dozens of instances.

Conventional market theorists prefer to focus on the individual, not the collective, and so tend to overlook the power of "exogenous" variables such as moral and social norms. We do not see the "thirty leaves" needed to make the apple, which consists of such resources as:

- *Government-owned property*, such as public lands, government research and development, and information resources;
- *Natural systems* such as the atmosphere, water, local ecosystems, and genetic structures of life;
- *User-managed regimes* for conserving land, managing community gardens, developing software, and controlling access to fisheries and other natural resources;
- *Gift economies*, or social networks based on gift exchange, which exist within, for example, academia, Internet communities, and local communities;
- *Shared, inherited knowledge* such as scientific research, historical knowledge, and folk wisdom, all of which comprise the public domain; and
- *Cultural traditions and norms*, which serve as a set of common moral presumptions and expectations for managing daily life.

Economic theory and public policy take scant notice of these neglected species of wealth, let alone mobilize aggressively to protect them. In many cases, these resources are not officially defined as anything of value, let alone as deserving of the same kinds of legal definition and protection enjoyed by private property. This is partly because these resources often cannot be "seen" through formal, quantifiable criteria. Marketeers prefer numbers—financial statements, computer modeling, and so on—to understand and manage a resource. Commoners realize that social factors matter a great deal. That is why the informal, idiosyncratic, and subjective factors that animate a commons cannot be represented on a computer spreadsheet.

What Should Be Commodified? What Should Remain a Commons?

The parable of the community gardens of New York City raises complicated questions about which resources and aspects of our daily lives should be commodified and which should somehow be protected from unfettered market forces. Should we cheer Giuliani's move to eke the maximum market value out of once-vacant lots in Manhattan, or should we preserve important segments of the urban landscape for satisfactions that are more collective than individual, more social than utilitarian, and more spiritual than economic?

This is a golden thread that runs through many of the commons examined in the following pages. It is not always self-evident whether public forests, for example, should be open to market exploitation, or whether they ought to be set apart from the market in order to generate their own kind of wealth as a commons. But to the extent that we barely understand the importance of the commons, market enclosure is rarely a thoughtful, informed choice about such consequences. It is typically a coercive *fait accompli*. Any thoughtful reckoning needs to understand what values and actual economic wealth are generated by the commons and what is therefore lost by enclosing the commons.

A good place to start is by a brief consideration of what it means to commodify something. In her book, *Contested Commodities*, Margaret Jane Radin explores the reasons that we consider it unacceptable to sell sex, babies, body organs, legal rights and votes (among other activities, rights, and things).[21] The idea that something should not be commodified, transferred, or sold to others is generally known as *inalienability*—a concept most famously expressed by Thomas Jefferson in the Declaration of Independence: all men are "endowed by the Creator with certain inalienable rights." Without offering a grand theory, Radin argues that something should not be alienated—converted into saleable property—if it conflicts with our shared visions of "human flourishing."

In our times, the rhetoric of the market presumes that everything should be and can appropriately be bought, sold, and owned. Market rhetoric advances a particular conception of human flourishing and promises that efficient market exchanges will maximize personal wealth and utility—which, practically speaking, are considered the same as satisfaction and happiness. Monetizing portions of our life and the natural environment has become so normative in our society that the genetic information of a patient is regarded as something that can be "owned" by university researchers,[22] and the airspace over Manhattan skyscrapers is something that is routinely commodified and sold.[23] Our society's penchant for alienating things is so reflexive and pervasive that *The Baffler* magazine came up with a wry title, *Commodify Your Dissent,* for its anthology of essays about the "business of culture in the new gilded age."[24]

In free-market theory, any intervention to stop propertization is considered "paternalistic" because it inhibits a purportedly free choice of the contracting parties. Third parties are seen as having little standing to intervene in the "private" contractual agreements of others. Such arguments verge on sophistry and political posturing, because the "free market" can be as coercive as any collective-choice or government policies, which at least have the virtue of being subject to an open democratic process and judicial review.[25]

In the real world, we all know that child-rearing, family life, education, socialization, sexuality, political life, and many other basic human activities require insulation from market forces. In fact, paying for many of these things can actually ruin them. We may pay for child care but worry that it is not the same as a parent's loving personal care. We may pay for college tuition, but real learning requires a voluntary personal commitment. A father cannot buy his son's affections, our votes should not be sold to the highest bidder, and paid sex is not the same thing as intimacy with a loved one.[26]

Such activities require personal participation in a gift economy, where the coin of exchange is not money but freely given gifts (personal attention, acts of kindness, sacrifices of time). Markets and money are impersonal. Gift exchange is the only real way to achieve the satisfactions of family life or sexuality.

The psychic and emotional values that are vital to human flourishing and community are generally regarded as incommensurable with the market.[27] We regard market alienation of certain things—our sexuality, our bodies, natural beauty, and democratic traditions—as degrading. That is why there was such an uproar over Fox TV's notorious special, *Who Wants to Marry a Millionaire?* and an eBay online auction of the ova of fashion models. It is why there was ethical outrage when it was learned that Ford Motor Company declined to replace the potentially explosive gas tanks in the Pinto compact, based on a cost-benefit analysis that concluded that it was not worth paying $11 per vehicle to avoid an estimated 180 burn deaths at $200,000 per death. This impeccable market logic so enraged the jury hearing a Pinto product liability case that it ordered $100 million in punitive damages.[28] In fighting proposed taxes on cigarettes in the Czech Republic, Philip Morris sponsored a study that argued that the Czech government actually saved $147.1 million from smokers' dying prematurely.[29] The study provoked public outrage. The simple truth is that market norms are highly offensive when applied to some of our deeper, more cherished values.[30]

Many of these ideas have animated the legal doctrines that historically have established limits to the market and carved out protected zones of inalienability. The environmental and conservation movements have sought to insulate the ecology from market despoliation. The consumer movement has sought to make "crashworthy cars" an inalienable universal right, not a market-bought privilege for Volvo owners alone. The labor movement has sought to make job safety an inalienable value that trumps any absolute property rights claimed by factory owners. The medical profession has historically insisted that organ donation be a voluntary act between donors, not a market transaction that reduces "sellers" to dehumanized "bags of spare parts" and strips the medical profession of its moral authority.[31]

It is a sign of our market culture that many of these "inalienable zones" are now under siege. Attempts to stave off commercial norms are criticized as meddlesome interventions in the "natural" order of the market, which "requires" deregulation, unchecked technological change, unfettered capital flows, and free trade.

The engine of market enclosure is fueled by its presumptuous claim to alienate whatever may be in the commons and then blindly to characterize this as "progress." It may in fact be progress, or at least benign, to commodify certain things in limited ways. The commodification of pollution rights may be such an example. But a progress based on the indiscriminate alienation of anything that can be packaged and sold is precisely what leads to the heedless exploitation of old-growth forests, predatory marketing to children, attacks on the public domain of creative works, and patents on slivers of the human genome. The rhetoric of the market is designed to assure continued private access to the commons by requiring that *everything* be for sale.

Much of the debate about the globalization of commerce revolves around this very issue of what can legitimately be commodified. Free traders consider it unalloyed progress to privilege economic values (i.e., investment returns) over environmental protection, labor rights, safety and health standards, or the democratic process itself. Critics of globalization argue that the World Trade Organization simply serves to empower the transnational corporation at the expense of the nation-state's ability to protect the commons. Government is shorn of many key powers to protect the noneconomic values that its citizens have chosen.[32]

The language of commodification affects a timeless objectivity. In fact, such language, especially as embodied in property laws, is a peculiarly modern worldview. As sociologist Clifford Geertz has put it, the law is not so much "a set of norms, rules, principles, values or whatever ... but part of a distinctive manner of imagining the real."[33] Legal scholar Theodore

Steinberg, studying how property law has been applied to land, concludes that "property law has, in effect, helped us to re-imagine and reinvent what we understand to be the real world."[34] So it is with the process of conceiving the world through a language of commodification. It can change our everyday perceptions, alter our social and political relationships, and contort our very sense of the possible.

Under the circumstances, it can be a significant challenge simply to imagine the world of the commons. The next chapter, therefore, attempts to convey the look and feel of some contemporary American commons, as embodied in gift economies. It turns out that personal, social, and moral forces are quite a bit more powerful in organizing value-exchanges than are generally imagined.

2.

The Stubborn Vitality
of the Gift Economy

The universe is the communion of subjects,
not a collection of objects.

—Thomas Berry, historian of cultures,
The Dream of the Earth

In the early days of computing, a great deal of software was developed through a gift economy in university settings. Hackers shared. That was the sacred ethic. As fanatics who followed their passions to create the best, most ingenious software, hackers saw themselves as members of an elite underground community. They took pleasure in creating cool things for one another's delight. Naturally, the programs that everyone helped invent, debug, and extend were seen as a shared product of the community.

The social and ethical norms of the hacker community at this early stage of the computer revolution were strikingly similar to those of the scientific method or Jeffersonian democracy. All procedures and outcomes were subject to the scrutiny of all. Openness allowed error to be rapidly identified and corrected. Openness built accountability into the process of change and allowed innovation and improvement to be readily embraced. Making money from the collective contributions of other hackers was seen as antisocial because it interfered with the sharing that produced great software.[1]

The commercialization of computing in the 1970s and 1980s introduced a very different dynamic to software development. As software programming moved from universities to the marketplace, a closed, proprietary process arose to mobilize expertise that could develop software, bring it to market, and reward private investors. It is fitting that Bill Gates epitomized this shift. His entrepreneurial passion was so great that he was nearly expelled from Harvard for using publicly funded labs to create commercial software—a violation of federal rules at the time and of the hacker ethic as well. After Gates was required to put his code in the public domain as free software, he quit Harvard and eventually went on to found Microsoft.[2] Over the past two decades, a vast industry of proprietary software companies has emerged to redefine the software development process.

Yet lurking in the shadow of this mighty new industry, the free software movement has quietly persisted and grown, exemplifying the stubborn vitality of the gift economy. Empowered by the Internet, a global corps of computer aficionados arose to develop, improve, and freely share software. This process has generated hundreds of top-quality software programs, many of which have become critical operating components of the Internet. Sendmail routes over 80 percent of all e-mail on the Internet; PERL allows dynamic features on Web sites; Apache is the most popular Web server software; and BIND is the *de facto* DNS (domain name system) server for the Internet. While computer techies are the most common users of these programs, millions of ordinary folks download free software from Web sites.

What most distinguishes free software from off-the-shelf proprietary software is the openness of the source code—and thus the user's freedom to use and distribute the software in whatever ways desired. Anyone with the expertise can "look under the hood" of the software and modify the engine, change the carburetor, or install turbochargers. Inelegant designs can be changed, and bugs can be fixed. Sellers cannot coerce users into buying "bloatware" (overblown, inefficient packages with gratuitous features), Windows-compatible applications, or gratuitous upgrades made necessary by planned obsolescence. Free software also allows users to avoid constant upgrades in computer hardware (such as the latest high-speed Intel chips).

This is where Richard Stallman, a Massachusetts Institute of Technology (MIT) programming legend, entered the scene as a hard-nosed visionary. Stallman realized that anyone could make minor changes in a free software program and then copyright it, converting it into a proprietary product. Without some new legal vehicle, the benefits of free software could be privatized and withheld from the community of users. The commons would collapse. Stallman's brilliant innovation was the General Public License—or GPL, sometimes known as "copyleft"—which is essentially a form of copyright protection achieved through contract law. "To copyleft a program," writes Stallman, "first we copyright it; then we add distribution terms, which are a legal instrument that gives everyone the rights to use, modify and redistribute the program's code *or any program derived from it*, but only if the distribution terms are unchanged."[3]

This contract language prevents any user from claiming the program (or any modified version of it) as his own property. The GPL creates a commons in software development "to which anyone may add, but from which no one may subtract."[4] The GPL, in short, prevents enclosure of the free software commons and creates a legally protected space in which it can flourish. This accounts for the "viral properties" of the GPL license. Because no one can seize the surplus value created within the commons, programmers are willing to contribute their time and energy to improving it. "Because defection is impossible, free riders are welcome, which resolves one of the central puzzles of collective action in a proprietarian social system," writes Columbia law professor Eben Moglen.[5] The commons is protected and stays protected.

The GPL has been a vital part of Stallman's larger vision, to help build a new universe of free UNIX-based software that could not be commandeered by any company. Through a new organization he founded, the Free Software Foundation, Stallman and his collaborators have written some widely used free programs such as the Emacs text editor, the GCC compiler and the GDB debugger. Known as the GNU Project, a recursive pun that stands for "GNU's Not UNIX," the programs are all protected by the GPL.

The success of free software programs has raised an important question: Should the software commons remain utterly segregated from the commercial market, or can a healthy combination of the two be orchestrated? In the 1990s, the "open source code movement" arose in pursuit of the latter. Its programmers started issuing various licenses for programs that *allow* users to redistribute them under copyleft, but do not *require* it. This means that open source software can be combined with free software and made proprietary—a choice that Stallman considers a betrayal of the commons and that open source champions regard as a merely utilitarian way to produce better software. However one stands on this complex issue, the GPL remains the best legal assurance that a program's source code will remain free and available to everyone in perpetuity, and that no company will be able to appropriate the code for itself.

The crowning achievement of the GPL may be the success of the Linux operating system. The program was begun as a kernel by a Finn graduate student, Linus Torvalds, and within months a community of programmers began to improve and extend the UNIX-based operating system, incorporating many of the GNU programs written by Stallman and friends. Despite having no bureaucratic organization, corporate structure, or market incentives—only cheap and easy communication via the Internet—tens of thousands of computer programmers around the globe volunteered their time throughout the 1990s to develop a remarkably stable and robust operating system, Linux.[6] The program, which many consider superior to Microsoft's NT server system, now commands a phenomenal 27 percent of the server market. The GPL is the chief reason that Linux and scores of other programs have been able to flourish without being privatized.[7]

The remarkable success of Linux and other open source software exemplifies the power of a larger gift economy, the Internet. Its open, accessible infrastructure facilitates social networking in unprecedented ways, which accounts for its phenomenal growth in such a short span of years. The unwritten ethic of Internet users, writes Howard Rheingold, "requires one to give something, and enables one to receive something.... I find that the help I receive far outweighs the energy I expend helping others; a marriage of altruism and self-interest." Web sites devoted to genealogical research, for example, are both socially satisfying and tremendously efficient in facilitating the exchange of desired information. It is precisely the effectiveness and speed of gift economies in facilitating certain kinds of value-exchange that have so alarmed entrenched industries.[8] Unable to compete with the power of online information sharing, defenders of the market are resorting to coercive laws and technologies to prop up a proprietarian system based on Old Economy business models.[9]

The Subtle Powers of the Gift Economy

The power of a gift economy remains difficult for the empiricists of our market culture to understand. We are accustomed to assigning value to things we can measure—corporate bottom lines, Nielsen ratings, cost-benefit analyses. We have trouble valuing intangibles that are not traded in the market and which therefore have no price. It is a truism that "you get what you pay for." How, then, should we regard something given to us for free, as a gift? How is something of value created by *giving away* one's time, commitment, or property? Traditional economic theory and property law cannot really explain how a social matrix as intangible and seemingly evanescent as that embodied in gift economies can be so powerful.

Yet the effects are hard to deny. Gift economies are potent systems for eliciting and developing behaviors that the market cannot—sharing, collaboration, honor, trust, sociability, loyalty. In this capacity, gift economies are an important force in creating wealth—both the material kind prized by the market as well as the social and spiritual kind needed by any happy, integrated human being.

What's remarkable about gift economies is that they can flourish in the most unlikely places—in run-down neighborhoods, on the Internet, in scientific communities, in blood donation systems, among members of Alcoholics Anonymous. Even though they may use the resources of the market economy, members of a gift economy do not come together through any cash exchange or economic transaction. What matters most is the ability to create and sustain caring, robust relationships within a group of people who share common commitments. Put another way:

> A gift economy is a web of enduring moral and social commitments within a defined community sustained through the giving of gifts (of goods, services, and courtesies) without any assurance of personal return.

New York City's community gardens thrive precisely because they are not governed by either the market or government. What distinguishes many commons, according to Jonathan Rowe, is the absence of two things that are otherwise pervasive in our society: *advertising* and *lawyers.* "The market is always pushing its 'goods' and 'services' in our faces, which might raise doubts as to whether these are really good or really serve. A commons, by contrast, is just there waiting to be used. Often it is discovered. If a swimming hole exists, people will find it. Social commons arise spontaneously—the city street that becomes a jump rope arena and vending bazaar, the old sofa in the vacant lot that becomes a ghetto equivalent of the village tree. That there's no need for advertising says something about the utility of the commons compared to the products of the modern market."10

Unlike the market, which revolves around trade and money, or government, which is based on law and police powers, the gift economy is driven by people voluntarily coming together to give of themselves in order to maximize their self-interests in a nonmarket way. Eventually that process can create a commons.

No one paid or forced thousands of New Yorkers—not a notoriously altruistic group—to clean up the abandoned lots and create lively, attractive urban gardens. They chose to do so. It was in their "self-interest," but not in the rational, calculating sense meant by most market theorists. The community gardeners transcended the prisoner's dilemma. They developed enough trust in each other and commitment to a common vision that they actually wanted to pitch in without calculation or a guaranteed payback, actualizing another sort of self-interest. The ongoing collaboration gave rise to a robust circulation of gifts that was able to redeem the trash-filled lots.

While the outcome had economic value, as Mayor Giuliani so keenly recognized, that was not the primary *meaning* of the resource to its creators. For members of a gift economy, value is based on personal, nonmonetary principles. They prize *particular* individuals, places, and shared experiences, such as the after-school gardening program for junior

[handwritten margin note: A × gypsy woman in spain / silver coins & bartering / no credit cards]

high school children that Janus Barton started at the Bushwick garden, across the street from a brothel and crackhouse.

If the gift economy requires personal commitment and authenticity, market transactions emphatically do not. Relationships in a market are impersonal, episodic, and based on monetary gain. In pure market theory, at least, the general presumption is that there is no community, just individuals. Unpleasant market results are justified with the disclaimer, "Nothing personal, it's just business," and economists take a peculiar pride in validating "hard realities" (objective and tangible) over "soft" ethical concerns (subjective and vague).

By economic metrics, the market *transaction* is paramount. Contextual factors such as community norms and moral values are largely extraneous. But in a gift economy, community norms and moral values are central concerns. That is why selling a piece of "community property" to outsiders is seen as a gross violation. It privatizes a shared resource. It asserts the supremacy of market values over the personal relationships and community values that built the resource. Hence the resentment that members of a scientific community may feel if one of its members "steals" jointly developed knowledge by patenting it for private gain in the marketplace. Hence Richard Stallman's hostility toward open source code software.

It is tempting to dismiss the gift economy as a relic of premodern societies, something of little relevance to today. This is not the case, however. Marcel Mauss, an anthropologist who wrote a famous 1925 essay on gift exchange in archaic societies, found that complex systems of gift-giving are universal in societies from ancient Rome to Melanesia and beyond.[11] If we sometimes take for granted the freedoms that a market society confers, we also tend to overlook some of the basic human needs—for identity, moral development, and community—that gift economies can satisfy.[12] Steeped as we are in a market culture, we sometimes have trouble understanding that a system based on noneconomic forces can be powerful in its own right.

Indeed, the gift economy is sometimes more effective in meeting economic and social needs than the market is. We have already seen this in the community gardens of New York City. But consider also the flourishing systems of "service barter" exchange that are used by networks of senior citizens and by poor people in some inner-city neighborhoods. The system uses a currency of "time dollars"—one "dollar" (credit) earned for every hour of service given, whether it be lawn mowing or baby-sitting. In areas where people do not have enough money and so cannot sustain a functioning market, this alternative currency allows people both to satisfy each other's everyday needs and deepen a sense of community in one fell swoop.[13]

The Gift Economy of Blood Donation

One of the most vivid case studies comparing the performance of market and gift economies is Richard Titmuss's examination of British and American blood banks in the 1960s. Is it better for hospitals and patients to acquire blood through a market system using paid donors or through a gift economy using volunteers? Titmuss's highly influential study is not only a critique of blood supply systems but a sobering study of the hidden costs of marketization.

Drawing upon extensive empirical data, Titmuss concluded that commercial blood systems generally produce blood supplies of *lower* safety, purity, and potency than volunteer systems. Commercial systems are also more hazardous to the health of donors and, over the long run, result in greater shortages of blood.[14] The risk of posttransfusion hepatitis, for example, was greater in countries where commercial acquisition of blood is the rule (Japan and Germany had infection rates of 10 to 25 percent versus less than 1 percent in Great Britain).[15] About 30 percent of the blood collected in the United States' commercially dominated system was wasted, compared to 2 percent in Britain. Commercial blood banks also produced greater (hidden) externalities: higher mortality rates and, when blood recipients became ill, higher lost earnings and additional medical care. Finally, prices of commercial blood (to patients and hospitals) were between five and fifteen times greater in the United States than in Britain.[16]

What can possibly account for these counterintuitive deviations from market theory, which holds that the price system produces the most efficient outcomes and highest quality product? The short answer: the overreaching premises of economic theory and our ignorance of the gift economy.

Donating blood in a safe, efficient manner requires an acute degree of truthfulness on the part of donors (who need to reveal any drug abuse, alcoholism, and disease history) and doctors (who must not take blood too frequently from the same donor or from donors in poor health). It turns out that the introduction of money into the blood transaction encourages doctors to skirt prescribed safety rules, leading to lower-quality, less safe blood. The lure of money has a paradoxical effect on donors as well: payment itself tends to attract more drug addicts, alcoholics, prisoners, and disease-ridden poor people than altruistic appeals do.

For Titmuss, these facts call into question the supposed efficacy of the market in mobilizing needed resources. For patients and hospitals who must buy blood, the facts also call into question the "consumer sovereignty" that is a central premise of market theory. It turns out that patients cannot truly exercise meaningful choice in the safety or price of blood supplies. Nor can they realistically identify the potential risks of a given supply of blood. The "freedom" that is supposed to result from the atomistic private market can be terribly coercive and harmful to patient health.

The gift economy of blood donation systems enables a different sort of freedom. It asks millions of people to give blood without any payment of money, and succeeds in eliciting sufficient high-quality supplies. The gift economy for blood mobilizes an aspect of human nature that, by the lights of Thomas Hobbes and Milton Friedman, does not exist: the public-spirited donor willing to sacrifice for the anonymous stranger. According to Titmuss, Britain's National Blood Transfusion Service "has allowed and encouraged sentiments of altruism, reciprocity and societal duty to express themselves; to be made explicit and identifiable in measurable patterns of behavior by all social groups and classes."[17] In this context, the gift economy regime is not simply "nice." It is actually more efficient, cheaper, and safer than the market.

The appearance of AIDS in the 1980s and the rise of an international trade in blood products have complicated the "commercial/bad, voluntary/good" dichotomy that once described the British blood supply.[18] But the larger policy lesson identified by Titmuss still holds:

> The ways in which society organizes and structures its social institutions . . . can encourage or discourage the altruistic in man; such systems can foster integration or alienation; they can allow the "theme of the gift"—of generosity towards strangers—to spread among and between social groups and generations. This, we further suggest, is an aspect of freedom in the twentieth century which, compared with the emphasis on consumer choice in material acquisitiveness, is insufficiently recognized.[19]

The Gift Economy in Scientific Communities

It is not widely appreciated that much of the power and creativity of scientific inquiry stems from a gift economy. While researchers are dependent upon grants and other sources of money, historically their work has not been shaped by market pressures. The organizing principle of scientific research has been gift-giving relationships with other members of the scholarly community. A scientist's achievements are measured by recognition in academic societies and journals and the naming of discoveries—Halley's

Comet, Tourette's Syndrome—not by salaries, stock holdings, or market share. Papers submitted to scientific journals are considered "contributions." There is a presumption that work will be openly shared and scrutinized and that everyone will be free to build on a communal body of scientific work.

Such a gift economy seems out of step with the contemporary faith in market norms. After all, is it not more efficient and rational for scientists to respond to price signals in the market and orient their work accordingly? Warren O. Hagstrom, a sociologist of science, has explored this apparent anomaly: "Why should gift-giving be important in science when it is essentially obsolete as a form of exchange in most other areas of modern life, especially the most distinctly 'civilized' areas? Gift-giving, because it tends to create particularistic obligations, usually reduces the rationality of economic action.... Why, then, does this frequently inefficient and irrational form of control [gift-giving] persist in science?"[20]

The answer, Hagstrom argues, is that a gift economy is a superior system for maintaining a group's commitment to certain (extramarket) values. In science, it is considered indispensable that researchers be objective and open-minded in assessing evidence. They must be willing to publish their results and subject them to open scrutiny. They must respect the collective body of research upon which everyone depends—by crediting noteworthy predecessors, for example, and not "polluting" the common knowledge with phony or skewed research. The long-term integrity and creative power of scientific inquiry depends upon these shared values.[21]

Market forces are ill suited to sustaining these values, however, because monetary punishment and reward are a problematic tool for nurturing moral commitment. If someone's ethics, loyalty to the community, or moral judgment can be "bought" by money, then those inner values are not really very deep or secure. An *inner commitment*, and not just external appearances, must be secured. Hagstrom notes that "whenever strong commitments to values are expected, the rational calculation of punishments and rewards is considered an improper basis for making decisions."[22]

By contrast, a gift economy is particularly effective in cultivating deep and unswerving values. "The prolonged and intensive socialization scientists experience is reinforced and complemented by their practice of the exchange of information for recognition," writes Hagstrom. "The socialization experience produces scientists who are strongly committed to the values of science and who need the esteem and approval of their peers."[23]

The Symbiosis of Gift and Market Economies

A growing movement within American business seeks to harness the gift economy in the workplace in order to improve a company's market performance. Instead of treating workers as automatons who respond chiefly to money or management fiat, the trend over the past decade has been for managers to do away with hierarchy and unilateral decision-making. The accent is on developing a more people-friendly environment that empowers workers and fosters cooperation. Reforms include greater shopfloor autonomy for individual workers, "flatter" management hierarchies, profit-sharing and employee stock ownership plans. The idea is to foster a more open, generous-spirited work environment, not one based on strict management control.

One of the more dramatic examples is "open-book management," developed by Jack Stack of Springfield ReManufacturing Corporation.[24] Stack taught everyone in a factory, from lathe operators to secretaries to middle managers, how to read the company's financial statements and understand how their jobs contributed to key performance metrics. Then each person was encouraged to apply his or her own creativity to improve those metrics and cooperate across departmental boundaries. Everyone received quarterly bonuses if the entire company met agreed-upon goals. Not only did this radical restructuring of an ailing International Harvester factory save it from bankruptcy, it created a happier, more productive, better paid workforce.

In a broad study of such collaborative corporate cultures, investor/analyst Roger Alcaly found that companies that foster workplace collaboration and offer profit-sharing plans are measurably more productive over the long term than their counterparts.[25] Even a market system depends upon a gift economy to function well.

Several proprietary computer and software companies are starting to realize that gift economies provide an excellent "social platform" for developing superior software. Increasingly, Silicon Valley companies are recognizing that the proprietary model of building software (hire the best talent as employees in the same company) is expensive and may result in inferior software compared to the cheap and efficient modes of collaboration made possible by the Internet.[26] This is one reason why IBM, Hewlett-Packard, Oracle, and others have embraced the Linux operating system and some types of open-source code software.

One of the more difficult things to comprehend is that the gift economies that sustain free and open source software can coexist with the market. This seems counterintuitive. But that is precisely what spurred Netscape to publish the source code for its proprietary browser. It hoped to nurture a gift economy of programmers who could improve the browser, while retaining some prerogatives to privatize the source code. Sun Microsystems has adopted open-source licenses for some of its products, and Red Hat has built a business around selling Linux along with technical support. One commentator has argued that "anarcho-communism is now sponsored by corporate capital."[27] It may be more accurate to say that the gift economy and market economy are finding new modes of invigorating each other.[28]

The Cornucopia of the Commons

A tragedy of the commons is more likely to occur if the resources of a commons are depletable, such as forests or minerals. But when the resources of a commons are not depletable and can be easily replicated and shared—as most digital information on the Internet can be—then a very different dynamic prevails. Software developer Dan Bricklin has called it the *cornucopia of the commons*—the almost magical multiplication of value as the commons is used more intensively. Programmer Eric Raymond calls it an "inverse commons," in which "the grass grows taller when it's grazed on."[29]

The basic concept is "the more the merrier." Yale law professor Carol Rose developed this concept in a brilliant essay that examines the legal and economic circumstances in which "increasing participation *enhances* the value of the activity [or property] rather than diminishing it."[30] Traditional economics often overlooks how "an expansive, open-ended public use might enhance, rather than detract from, the value of certain kinds of property," writes Rose. For example, the greater the number of people subscribing to telephone service, the more valuable telephone service becomes.[31] The more people that use a common standard, such as the QWERTY typewriter layout or Windows operating system, the more valuable that property or practice becomes.[32] And the more people participating in a free software development community, the higher the quality of software program that is likely to result.

This dynamic, sometimes known as "scale returns," has become particularly timely since the advent of the Internet. Often referred to nowadays as "network effects," it is one of the key factors driving the phenomenal growth of electronic commerce. Using the Internet's flexible, open, and inexpensive communications infrastructure, remarkable efficiencies can be had from consolidating markets on a much larger scale than was previously feasible. The more people who can interconnect and share information, the greater the value that is created: a key reason why the Internet has become so valuable to both commercial and noncommercial users. The meteoric popularity of the electronic flea market, eBay, exemplifies the cornucopia of the commons.

The deeper principle may be that knowledge itself is highly susceptible to the cornucopia of the commons, particularly because of the Internet. The "peculiar power" of an idea, Thomas Jefferson once wrote as the nation's patent commissioner, is "that no one possesses the less, because every other possesses the whole of it. He who receives an idea from me, receives instruction himself without lessening mine; as he who lites his taper at mine receives light without darkening me."[33] The more that information is shared (and then modified, corrected, and used as a platform for still further knowledge-creation), the more that knowledge grows and improves: a cornucopia of the commons.

The Internet is fabulously promiscuous about creating surplus value in knowledge. Commercial entities understand this, and many are seeking to privatize the gains that result. But can they? Can they successfully carve out proprietary franchises in the Internet commons—through copyright, proprietary technologies, "walled gardens" such as AOL, and so on—on a technical system designed to maximize the dissemination of information?[34] Or will they instead try to restrain their natural impulses to proprietize and come to see the wisdom of gift economies? As we will see in chapters 7 and 8, the current trends are not encouraging.

Why Gift Economies Work

Perhaps the indispensable condition for a successful gift economy is the robust circulation of gifts within a community. The essential rule is that "the gift must always move."[35] Constant movement of gifts—be it software code, blood, scientific research, personal services, or company profits—is how the vitality of the community is maintained. But once a gift is treated as "property"—once it can be exclusively owned and withheld from the community—its power as a gift begins to wane. That is because hoarding a gift or using it as capital takes it out of circulation. It breaks the spell, as it were.[36]

When anthropologist Bronislaw Malinowski studied the Trobriand Islanders in the western Pacific, he was stunned to discover that ritual gifts such as shell necklaces made a steady progression around an archipelago of islands over the course of ten years. People "owned" the cherished gift object for a year or two, but were socially obliged to pass it on. That constant circulation of gifts helped sustain the islanders' sense of connection and obligation to each other.[37] This is the same sentiment that an apprentice feels towards his master: an obligation to honor the gift of training freely given to him, by passing it along to a deserving successor.

A number of fairy tales—as well as the biblical parable of the man with the talents—warn that if a gift is hoarded, it loses its generative powers and becomes useless.

The vitality of gift exchange, writes Lewis Hyde, one of the most eloquent students of the subject, comes from the passage of a gift *through* one person to another and yet another. As a circle of gift exchange increases in size, an increase in *value* materializes. Economists might be tempted to characterize this increase as a function of "scale returns" or "network effects," as noted earlier. But the gift economy is not just about the scale of interaction. It has to do with an increase in *social* and *emotional* value that gift exchange generates in a community. It is an intersubjective force. Social and emotional forces have rich powers of their own, in many ways surpassing those of money. Alcoholics Anonymous is so effective in helping people stay sober for precisely this reason. It cultivates a strong personal ethic of gift-giving (unconditional support for fellow alcoholics) and a keen sense of obligation to repay the gift. This powerful ethic for recovery cannot be mobilized through fee-for-service medical care, which tends to have a less personal and spiritual approach to healing.[38]

The idea of the gift economy raises important questions about the deeper meanings of "value" and "wealth." Lewis Hyde astutely notes that "scarcity and abundance have as much to do with the *form* of exchange as with how much material wealth is at hand. Scarcity appears when wealth cannot flow ... [and] wealth ceases to move freely when all things are counted and priced. It may accumulate in great heaps, but fewer and fewer people can afford to enjoy it...." Thus the paradox that wealth can become scarce even as it increases."[39] Modern capitalist economies are famous for generating great material wealth that cannot or does not flow to those in need. It is a related paradox that great wealth can coexist with social alienation, what Paul Wachtel calls the "poverty of affluence."[40]

Markets and gift economies both produce surplus wealth. But that wealth differs in kind and in the "vector" in which it accrues. "In gift exchange, the increase stays in motion and follows the object," writes Hyde, "while in commodity exchange, it stays behind as profit."[41]

The Linux software development community does not commodify and privatize its "increase" as material profit; it keeps the increase in motion as a collectively "owned" form of (social and economic) wealth. By contrast, many people in scientific communities are starting to commodify the "increase" in scientific knowledge—new data, research tools, conceptual breakthroughs—that was previously accessible to the entire scientific community. This practice is eroding the ethic of openness and sharing that has historically made scientific research so productive. The privatization of knowledge about the human genome and embryonic stem cells is a timely example; many scientists fear that overly broad patents will seriously impede future scientific progress.[42]

The point is not that property is "better" if shared by a broader number of people, although most Americans would subscribe to that ideal. Nor is it an argument of "communism" versus "capitalism." Communism is as likely to turn surplus wealth into capital as capitalism is.[43] Rather, the point is that the market regards surplus property as material "profit" to be privatized, whereas the gift economy sees surplus wealth as a social gift to be freely and continuously used by all members of a commons.

Why should we care about our society's relentless propensity to "capitalize" and commodify gains—and its aversion to shared wealth sustained through gift economies? Because the market economy, through its enclosures, is increasingly disrupting the "hydraulics" of our social ecology.

Market exchange governs the flow of material wealth by seeking to establish a "moral equilibrium" between parties to the transaction. Payment for a good or service establishes an "even-steven" symmetry. But note how this also results in a kind of social entropy: market transactions require no enduring interpersonal connections, moral commitments, or community connections. Theoretically, at least, they are considered "private," the boundaries of ownership are clearly defined, and everyone remains a disconnected individual. This is a preferred mode of transaction in many if not most cases. We do not necessarily want to become friends with everyone with whom we do business, and efficient, productive markets need clear property boundaries to function well.

But when property boundaries and market norms become so pervasive and intrusive, the gift economies that our society needs are disrupted. A kind of social deterioration ensues. Unlike market exchange, the circulation of property in the form of gifts creates a social *momentum* that flows outward—and then back again. "An affluence of satisfaction, even without numerical abundance" becomes possible, in Hyde's words.[44] A gift economy helps sustain a social liveliness and satisfaction.

▪ ▪ ▪

Much more must be learned about the role of gift economies in the marketplace, especially on the Internet. But as these stories show, gift exchange is a powerful force in creating and sustaining the commons. It offers a surprisingly effective means of preserving certain values from the imperialism of the market. It may be tempting to patronize the gift economy as archaic or "soft," but the evidence is too strong to ignore: gift exchange can create a more civilized sense of community and more ethical, stable markets. More generally, the cooperation that animates gift economies has been a far more influential force in the evolution of life than social Darwinists would have us believe.[45]

It is a mistake, also, to regard the gift economy simply as a high-minded preserve for altruism. It is, rather, a different way of pursuing one's self-interest. In a gift economy, one's "self-interest" has a much broader, more humanistic feel than the utilitarian rationalism of economic theory. Furthermore, the positive externalities of gift exchanges can feed on each other and expand, creating a cornucopia of the commons.

This points to the folly of talking about "social capital," as so many sociologists and political scientists do. Capital is something that is depleted as it is used. But a gift economy has an inherently expansionary dynamic, *growing* the more that it is used. While it needs material goods to function, the gift economy's real wealth-generating capacity derives from a social commerce of the human spirit.

3.

When Markets Enclose
the Commons

The true friend of property, the true conservative, is he who insists that property shall be the servant and not the master of the common-wealth. The citizens of the United States must effectively control the mighty commercial forces which they themselves called into being.

—Theodore Roosevelt, 1908

In the wide-open prairies of the American West, cowboys and Indians alike once navigated the vast landscape using invisible boundaries and markers—the subtle rise in the terrain here, the faint smell of sage there, the sense of distance traveled as gauged by the sun's arc in the sky. Denizens of this landscape had an intuitive sense of their location even if the uninitiated were clueless.

The introduction of barbed wire in the 1870s began to profoundly alter this notional universe. The new property boundaries literally disoriented the former "line riders." In New Mexico, according to one account, "it was said that Standing Deer, the chief of the Taos Pueblo, could no longer find his way back home from the Oklahoma Territories in 1886 because barbed wire fences had appeared. The wire did not physically prevent his passage, but it changed the lines of the landscape. It was as if he was in a completely different world. And he was. In the barbed-wire world, a line that could not be touched did not exist."[1]

The images of this story suggest how the market can remake a landscape: it erects artificial fences that redesign the commons. Property rights and markets have an undeniable utility in exploiting resources, building an economy, and settling a region. We have become accustomed to them; they provide us with useful (and gratuitous) goods. Our society needs markets for their tremendous efficiency in producing and distributing goods. But commodification and market exchange also tend to impose cultural grids on preexisting "landscapes"—ecosystems, social communities, democratic traditions. The categories of market language—that all values can be reduced to money, that property is essentially fungible, that most things can be monetized and sold—superimpose an alien logic on nonmarket realms.

This chapter clarifies the basic questions raised by the intersection of markets and commons. What are the effects of enclosure on the commons? How do proponents of enclosure seek to redefine our ideas of the public good? And how has the American tradition of civic republicanism responded?

Champions of the market insist, with a kind of fundamentalist fervor, that only market forces can address our many social and economic problems. Defenders of the commons counter that certain human values cannot be advanced or respected by markets; only new (or revamped) public institutions and cultural traditions can preserve them. At issue is what kind of rapprochement the market and the commons can negotiate. How shall certain common values and resources be preserved in the face of market enclosure? For insight into this fundamental political question, it is useful to consider the history of the original enclosure movement in England.

The Enclosure Movement in England

The metaphor of enclosure derives from the enclosure movement in England, which occurred at various times from the late 1400s through the 1800s, but particularly during the Industrial Revolution in the 1800s. Throughout the Middle Ages, the traditional use of land was the so-called open-field system, in which arable lands were unfenced and communally managed. Peasants collectively owned rights to large portions of meadow, heath, moorland, and forests, which they used to grow crops; feed geese, sheep, and cows; gather firewood and cut peat; collect honey from beehives; and raise fruit trees.[2]

Environmentalist and poet Gary Snyder explains how common lands simultaneously served a number of important economic, community, and environmental needs:

> [The commons] is necessary for the health of the wilderness because it adds big habitat, overflow territory, and room for wildlife to fly and run. It is essential even to an agricultural village economy because its natural diversity provides the many necessities and amenities that the privately held plots cannot. It enriches the agrarian diet with game and fish. The shared land supplies firewood, poles and stone for building, clay for the kiln,

herbs, dye plants, and much else, just as in a foraging economy. It is especially important as seasonal or full-time open range for cattle, horses, goats, pigs, and sheep.[3]

As a way of managing lands in stable, premodern communities, the common lands did not lend themselves to new, more productive methods of agriculture. With the lands being used for subsistence, not market purposes, the incentives were not there. Nonetheless, the lands were an important collective resource for meeting daily needs in many villages—and a supplementary resource in other villages. The lands also had an emotional importance for villagers because they were community resources over which they had some direct measure of control.

As the landed classes of England began to realize that new riches could be had by developing common lands, they began to press Parliament to allow the seizure of the lands, justified by the need for "improving" them. Enclosure was attractive to these protocapitalists because new breeding methods for sheep were making wool production more profitable; the export market for wool was booming; and crop rotation of specialized crops and other agricultural methods could boost the productivity of arable land.

What ensued in the 1700s and early 1800s was a series of 4,000 acts of Parliament authorizing a small number of budding capitalists to seize some seven million acres of common lands. About two thirds of the lands were open fields that belonged to cottagers; another one third was woodland and heath commons. Village-held lands were fenced off and given to private interests. According to one account, "ambitious landlords found that by enclosing and amalgamating several farms and applying [new agricultural methods] they could raise the rents of their lands by phenomenal amounts. The government was happy to sanction this process, since it could derive increased taxes from these higher rents. . . ."[4]

The enclosure movement and other changes of the Industrial Revolution ushered in a host of technologies that were miraculously productive, and promoted the emancipations of liberal democracy and individual rights. But they also swept aside a stable and secure agrarian society and unleashed brutal social exploitation, neglect, and inequality, as chronicled with such acuity by Charles Dickens. The laborer, craftsman, and unpropertied poor were left to fend for themselves in a wage-based economy that had no place for them, even as the moral economy of the village was being swept aside.

"Valuable ancient meadows were ploughed up to take short-term advantage of artificially high corn prices," writes *The Ecologist*, "and then, when prices dropped, allowed to relapse to degraded pasture, and large amounts of heathland and forest were destroyed."[5] In the meantime, the new profits that the merchant class reaped from trade, colonialism, and more efficient production gave rise to the sumptuous rural mansions that still incongruously dominate rustic landscapes and village communities: grand monuments to the inequality associated with enclosure.

The gross inequality that stemmed from enclosure was also reflected in a greater concentration of land ownership. By 1876, it was estimated, 2,250 people owned half the agricultural land in England and Wales, and 0.6 percent of the population owned 98.5 percent of it.[6] The prodigious wealth-creation of enclosure, which made perfect sense in conventional economic terms, had the tragic side effect of destroying communities and eliminating the independence of tens of thousands of common people. In essence, Parliament had legislated into being a new social system, built in significant measure on the privatization and consolidation of resources previously used in common.

The Imperialism of Market Values

The English enclosures aggressively introduced a new social creature: the market-based society. This brought with it dilemmas which persist to this day. "Instead of economy being embedded in social relations," wrote economic historian Karl Polanyi, "social relations are embedded in the economic system."[7] This meant that the market would increasingly dictate the terms of the social order, not vice versa. For the first time in history, the market would no longer be embedded within the matrix of community, kinship, moral codes, or religion. Henceforth, these noneconomic institutions would instead be embedded in the market.[8] Polanyi dubbed this "The Great Transformation."

The ascendance of the market inaugurated an entirely new ordering principle for society. "The market ... through its extensive presence and its capacity to structure choices, creates a situation in which *pleonexia*, the ancient malaise of the acquisitive soul, becomes a systematic property driving out goods other than its own," writes political scientist William James Booth. "From that vantage point, the moral economic history of modernity can be read as a reaction to these perverse effects, as a struggle between the market and society's efforts to regain governance, to assert goods other than those of the self-regulating market."[9]

Instead of the sovereign community controlling the terms of the economy, the ideal of an autonomous, self-regulating market has become the dominant ideal of social governance. With this there emerged a new emphasis on competitive individualism, material acquisitiveness, and rational calculation. But it also brought a marginalizing of cooperation, community, and the collective good—traits that are equally a part of the human condition but which soon bore the stigma of being "irrational."

With the norms of the commons shunted to the periphery, anyone who would challenge the "natural" outcomes of market activity is forced to displace a large polemical burden: By what right or rationale should the "natural" verdict of a market be struck down? This task is made all the harder because theorists of the Chicago School of Economics, the Law and Economics movement in legal scholarship, and the Public Choice school of political science, have interpreted a huge expanse of social reality through a narrow economistic lens. Commonsensical human values and emotions are sometimes warped to fit into highly abstract theories.

A sometimes farcical brand of thinking can be seen, for example, in Law and Economics treatises that declare monogamy to be "the most efficient marital form,"[10] children to be commodities who are "presumed to have modest price elasticities because they do not have close substitutes,"[11] and rape as an unfair bypassing of "the market in sexual relations (marital or otherwise).... [which] therefore should be forbidden."[12] Analyses such as these, so deeply alienated from a basic sense of humanity, are not the ravings of fringe theorists, but the work of such prominent scholars as Judge Richard Posner and Gary Becker.

Viewing the family, sex, and rape in stark economic terms would strike most Americans as extreme, or at least not very empirical. Yet it is evidence of how far the efficiency-minded, wealth-maximizing catechism has penetrated in respectable circles, crowding out more humanistic perspectives. This parallels the actual workings of markets in its relentless commodification and privatization of land, labor, ecosystems, biological organisms, culture, and even consciousness. It is reflected as well in the retreat of civil society, which has fewer and fewer protected social niches in which to nourish itself.

The triumph of the market as a new and improved substitute for democracy is savagely portrayed by Thomas Frank in his book, *One Market Under God*. The plutocrats and cheerleaders of the New Economy—Bill Gates, George Gilder, Tom Peters, *Fast Company* magazine, *Wired* magazine—scoff at the idea that the market creates economic elites and social inequality. Today's business leaders see themselves as populist revolutionaries, liberating the world from labor unions, environmentalists, antiglobalists, and other malcontent "elites" who dare to challenge the "democratic" verdicts of the market.[13]

Varieties of Market Enclosure

The patterns first seen in the English enclosures find similar expression today. The economic calculus of the market replaces the shared norms of the commons. Private interests are increasingly committing "boundary violations"[14] as they erect barbed-wire fences on resources that are publicly owned and on terrain where no private fences should exist. Global water supplies and genetic structures are being marketized (see Chapter 5), and the public domain of knowledge is being fenced off into private holdings through new intellectual property rights (see Chapter 8). Areas of life that have historically had their own measure of autonomy, public orientation, or noncommercial value are being colonized by the market.

In the process, the character of these realms is changing. Dubious ethical conflicts seem to surface more frequently. Tensions between community norms and private gain become more acute. Conviviality and collaboration give way to calculation and moneymaking. Metrics that are considered hard and objective are given a higher standing than "soft" values involving community, morality, subjective feelings, or aesthetics. We see these trends as marketization washes over scientific inquiry, public education, government policy-making, Internet culture, mainstream journalism, and sporting events, among other areas. Today, proprietary interests are restlessly exploring new frontiers—the human genome, agricultural seedlines, the habitat of endangered species, the global atmosphere—seeking to commodify resources that have historically been regarded as the common heritage of mankind.

There are three primary harms associated with market enclosures:

1. Common assets and revenues that belong to the American people (and in some instances, all of humanity) are being siphoned into the hands of private interests.
2. This is producing an unjust redistribution of wealth and greater inequality, compromising the government's ability to address public purposes, and eroding democratic accountability over common assets.
3. The robust gift economies that sustain so many commons are being dismantled and revamped as market regimes. Resources, activities and values long regarded as inalienable are being marketized. This dramatically transforms the ways in which property changes hands and the character of social interactions.

"Market enclosure" is a useful term, first of all, because it helps identify publicly owned assets and gift economies that are otherwise taken for granted and used as hidden subsidies by private enterprises. Market enclosure describes the drug makers who use their political muscle to extend their patent protection and so extend their ability to charge monopoly prices. Market enclosure describes the landowner who wants to build subdivisions in wetlands and destroy species habitat, asserting market uses over the elemental needs of an ecosystem.

It is important to speak of market enclosure because it reframes the economic narrative of the market. What the market considers incidental externalities (toxic waste, species extinction, safety hazards), the narrative of the commons regards as an assault on the community. Marketeers presume an entitlement to privatize clean air and water, public spaces, and even shared images and words. Cultural traditions that belong to the commons are drained of meaning. George Washington's birthday is now more renowned as a big sales weekend than as a patriotic celebration, Nike has insinuated its logo into every nook and cranny of sports, and the Walt Disney Company, which once touted itself as "the people who taught you how to laugh," has appropriated classics such as Br'er Rabbit, Pinocchio, and Aladdin, and converted them into slick properties for mass-merchandising.[15]

The central role of market forces in American life is not as distressing as their *ubiquity* and *reach*. It is not market activity itself which is objectionable; it is the intrusion of market activity into the commons on terms that expropriate public wealth and/or violate important shared values.

Contemporary market enclosures take two primary forms, and possibly a third:

1. Appropriation. These are enclosures in which the public holds clear property rights in a resource, but the government, acting as a trustee for the public, cedes the asset (or use rights) to private interests at below-market prices or for free. This is a recurrent pattern in the government's stewardship of public lands and in the giveaway of federal R&D and information databases. The public pays twice: through its taxes to develop assets that companies then appropriate, and through monopoly pricing of the resulting commercial product.

Appropriation has different implications insofar as it involves depletable assets (minerals, oil, etc.), nondepletable resources (electromagnetic spectrum, satellite orbital sites), or renewable resources (timber, fisheries). The damage that occurs from the appropriation of depletable assets tends to be more severe and irreversible financially and environmentally. By contrast, the appropriation of nondepletable resources such as the airwaves used by broadcasters is chiefly an allocation issue that can be reversed; there is no lasting harm to the asset. Similarly, the appropriation of renewable resources need not have permanent effects (even though overexploitation is a serious risk).

2. Marketizing the Inalienable. This is the most intrusive sort of enclosure: when commercial interests seize a common resource which embodies deeply held values and so is "not for sale." This is the objection that many people have to the patenting of the human genetic code or to selling captive audiences of schoolchildren to national advertisers. Allowing the market to exploit these "resources" is seen as degrading to our sense of personhood, our sense of community, and shared civic and public values. It is a boundary that is frequently violated and for which there are few easy remedies.

3. Incomplete Commodification. A third form of commodification may or may not represent a market enclosure. This is the category of "incomplete commodification," which lies between the two poles of outright appropriation and the marketizing of inalienable resources. This term is used by legal scholar Margaret Jane Radin to refer to property or interactions in which the social meanings of marketization are mixed.[16]

The regulation of workplace safety, for example, places limits on how private property may be deployed. Rules to protect wetlands affect the "bundle of rights" that property owners can enjoy. In essence, a balancing of community and private interests is achieved, as mediated by politics and government. Incomplete commodification either reflects a pragmatism in reconciling certain values we wish to be inalienable (breathable air, clear water) with a market order, or it may simply reflect an inconclusive political struggle over the degree to which commodification will occur or inalienability be preserved: *there is neither complete commodification nor complete noncommodification, but a coexistence of the two in some form.* Some employers truly treat people as cogs in a machine—as objectified commodities—while other employers treat them with great respect and dignity. Yet both the "high road" and the "low road" approaches to business management exist within a market order.

The Dynamics of Enclosure

Enclosure is not just a shift in ownership and control. It is a conversion in the *management* and *character* of the resource. An excellent case study is the enclosure of organic agriculture by the "organic-industrial complex." As described by journalist Michael Pollan, organic farmers have traditionally grown "natural foods" as part of a larger commitment to pesticide-free nutrition, a more local, energy-efficient food-distribution chain, humane animal husbandry, and preservation of family farms and the local landscape. Historically, the values inherent in organic food production, distribution, consumption, and lifestyle were . . . *organic*, so to speak. Over the past generation these values have been embodied in a diverse network of farms, cooperatives, and community-based organizations dedicated to healthy, chemical-free foods.[17]

As the popularity of organic food grew, especially after the Alar pesticide scare in 1990, large food corporations saw the great profits to be had from enclosing this commons. By acquiring and consolidating small farms serving local customers, and integrating them into national markets bolstered by "branding" and advertising, food conglomerates have begun to remake the character and meaning of "organic food."

Pollan writes:

> In the eyes of General Mills, an organically grown fruit or vegetable is not part of a revolution, but part of a marketing niche, and health is a matter of consumer perception. You did not have to buy into the organic "belief system" to sell it. . . . The broccoli is trucked to Alberta, Canada, there to meet up with pieces of organic chicken that have already made a stop at a processing plant in Salem, Oregon, where they were defrosted, injected with marinade, cubed, cooked, and refrozen.

National food processors were eager to appropriate the name and credibility earned by organic farmers, but worked hard to water down the organic food standards eventually issued by the U.S. Department of Agriculture (USDA).

For the food company executive, lunch is "just lunch"—a commodity that you buy. His commitment to organic food is not personal or moral, but legalistic: it extends no further than the USDA's organic standards. But to Pollan, organic food is tightly related to a stable local community, ecological sustainability, and a personal connection to the food production system. "Farms produce more than food," he writes. "They also produce a kind of landscape, and if I buy my organic milk from halfway across the country, the farms I like to drive by every day will eventually grow nothing but raised ranch houses." Through enclosure, certain inalienable personal values are overrun by the impersonal, amoral norms of the market system.

One of the most common types of enclosure is the conversion of social communities and movements into markets. As the women's movement grew in popularity, for example, corporate marketers were not far behind in trying to channel the movement's powerful social energies into consumerism: "You've come a long way, baby!" as one cigarette maker famously crowed. So, too, with the gay pride movement. Years ago gays and lesbians started community parades to proclaim their personal liberation: "Out and Proud!" Now corporate sponsorships at gay pride parades and festivals have become so pervasive that the social meaning of the events is being eclipsed by commercialism. Founders of the movement sometimes find they cannot afford booth rentals at gay pride festivals because corporate marketers have bid up fees. In response, a renegade Gay Shame group denounces the loss of the gay community's sovereignty with the slogan, "It's a movement, not a market."[18]

Enclosure can also consist of the conversion of robust, diversified markets into homogeneous, consolidated markets. This is evident in the many attempts by proprietary pharmaceutical companies to undermine generic drugs, to the extent of paying off the competition.[19] Enclosure can be seen in the rise of major book chains in shopping malls, superstores, discount warehouses, and online—and the decline of independent booksellers to 15 percent of the market by 2000. Enclosure is now occurring in broadcast television as the major networks, thanks to deregulation, acquire even more broadcast stations, resulting in less diversity and localism in programming.[20] The franchising of America is a form of enclosure, as fastfood chains such as Subway and Pizza Hut squeeze out quirky local restaurants and convenience stores, "trading the spark of creativity for the safety of numbers," by one account.[21]

Enclosure may be epitomized by the global expansion of McDonald's, which has not just homogenized its own restaurants in thousands of locations around the world, but remade large sectors of the American economy, including the meat and potato industries, in order to deliver predictable, standardized burgers and French fries.[22] Enclosure is now sweeping across the European hotel business as major hotel chains convert distinctive local inns with claw-foot bathtubs and antiques into standard-issue rooms with plastic furniture, minibars, and corporate advertising in the hallways.[23]

Enclosure has it benefits, to be sure: efficiency, predictability, and profitability. What is lost is the unexpected, the local, and the creative. Enclosure tends to engulf the charming and distinctive as well as the unpleasant and troubling, and collapse them all into the familiar bland aesthetic of modern life. Some call it "Americanization." Others call it a loss of authenticity.

Enclosure has reached such far-reaching dimensions that we have trouble imagining how to preserve values and resources that we do not want to see commodified. How shall the commons be preserved in the face of the market's great potency in enclosing them? What regimes of partial commodification might be feasible (through regulation, for example) as an acceptable middle ground? Or is the unfettered market destined to swallow up everything we hold dear?

Civic Republicanism and the Market

In American history, the traditional response to such questions has come from the proponents of civic republicanism. The *commonwealth* is seen as an instrument of the people for containing the abuses associated with property and the market. This strand of legal scholarship and political activism is described by Gregory S. Alexander in his magisterial history, *Commodity and Propriety*, about competing visions of property in American life. The "proprietarian" tradition, Alexander writes, regards property not just as a commodity to sell in the market but as an important tool for sustaining the American commonwealth: "According to this view, property is the material foundation for creating and maintaining the proper social order, the private basis for the public good."[24]

This tradition's roots can be traced back to Aristotle, who notes in his *Nichomachean Ethics* that the friendship of community helps promote virtuousness. Civic republicanism understands human beings as inherently social and inevitably dependent on others not only to thrive but to survive. This irreducible interdependency means that individuals owe one another obligations not by virtue of consent alone but as an inherent incident of the human condition. To proprietarians, the state is fully justified in forcing individuals to act for the good of the entire community when they fail to meet their basic obligations to other humans.

This is the vision of commonwealth, the idea of a civic republic, which was given great elaboration by Thomas Jefferson and the Anti-Federalists. A core concept of republicanism, explains Alexander, "was the idea that private 'interests' could and should be subordinated to the common welfare of the polity."[25] The people of the populist commonwealth, not surprisingly, are a different human archetype from the selfish utility-maximizers of economic theory. The civic republican sees production as a vehicle for family and community well-being, not just for oneself. People are not just producers and consumers but citizens who have an active interest in community decisions and the common good. Civic republicans seek to cultivate self-restraint and personal responsibility. They disdain the hedonistic self-interest rewarded by the market. A rough equality and diffusion of property ownership is also considered desirable because it helps thwart any tyrannies of concentrated economic wealth. A society with no extremes of wealth and poverty is more likely to sustain a virtuous citizenry.[26]

This "civic meaning" of property favored by Jefferson and other civic republicans, however, was soon transmuted into a similar but distinctly different brand of *commercial* republicanism. To Alexander Hamilton and Noah Webster, it became important for property to be *alienable*, or transferable to others through markets, so that the vestiges of feudal privilege, based on inalienable land and property, could be swept aside. Thus alienability of property was seen as a way to promote individual freedom and democratic equality. Bringing resources into the market would liberate them from the feudal order and unleash the dynamic energies of a free market. In this context, direct restraints on the alienability of property were seen as improper because, according to the *American Law of Property*, "resources would be more likely to be wasted because they would be taken out of the stream of commerce, improvements would be discouraged, wealth might become more concentrated, and creditors potentially could be misled."[27]

In this way, the idea of civic republicanism was transmuted into an ideal of commercial republicanism. Republican virtue no longer focused on the community or the ability of citizens to participate in public life. It focused on the ability of individuals to pursue wealth and social prestige through commerce.

The common good was not forgotten, however. It was artfully redefined as the Invisible Hand. Adam Smith's famous metaphor of how individual self-interest expressed through markets yields the common good may have made sense when moral law and political tradition actually stood above the market economy.[28] But circumstances have obviously changed, transforming the Invisible Hand from an explanatory metaphor into an ideological shibboleth. Morality and politics have only irregular influence these days in controlling the amoral behavior of markets, whose excesses are generally curbed only when a visible public backlash can be mobilized to punish irresponsible sellers.

Note how the concept of alienability of property, which once had been so important in sweeping aside the old aristocratic order, now takes on a new importance in justifying an open-ended expansion of the market. Alienability now legitimates the idea that nearly everything *ought* to be available for commodification, privatization, and market exchange and that these principles will assure the common good. This presumption generally holds sway today, of course, and is now applied not just to American society but to the nations of the world. The Market is King.

But can the market take care of social and personal needs to which the commons once ministered? The answer is problematic. As economic commentator Robert Kuttner explained in his probing 1997 book, *Everything for Sale*: "As society becomes more marketized, it is producing stagnation of living standards for most people, and a fraying of the social fabric that society's best-off are all too able to evade. One thing market society does well is to allow its biggest winners to buy their way out of its pathologies."[29] Despite an unprecedented bull market in the 1990s, more children are growing up poor in America than in any other industrial nation, and millions of workers are actually earning less money today in real dollars than they did twenty years ago. The number of millionaires has skyrocketed, and so has the number of people who cannot afford health insurance—some 43 million Americans.

There are obviously complex reasons for each of these phenomenon, but clearly the surging marketization of American life—the leitmotif of the 1990s—has not solved our social problems. In fact, in a great many instances the market's erosion of our extramarket values and norms has aggravated, not alleviated, our nation's savage inequalities and unmet social needs. This is a theme to which humanistic-minded economists and sociologists have returned to again and again: the tendencies of markets to undermine public institutions and democratic values. These economists and sociologist include John Kenneth Galbraith in *The Affluent Society* (1958), Daniel Bell in *The Cultural Contradictions of Capitalism* (1976), Robert Kuttner in *Everything for Sale* (1997), and George Soros in *The Crisis of Global Capitalism* (1998), among others.

Market exchange has been around for centuries, of course, and few quarrel with the civilizing effects it has had in numerous arenas. But never before have markets been so powerful and ubiquitous. The *market system*, as political scientist Charles Lindblom points out, is not just a transaction between a buyer and seller but a societywide apparatus for organizing and coordinating human activity on an unprecedented scale.[30]

There is a growing sense that a useful tool in promoting material progress may have become a sorcerer's apprentice, at least in the United States. Do we really want market forces deciding what sorts of radically new species shall be unleashed into the ecosystem? Do we really regard the market as an adequate vehicle for expressing our democratic aspirations, as today's "market populists" urge us? When even our democratic process is seen as controlled by the highest bidders and our cultural values as the modeling clay for a colossal Overmind of media, film, and computer game conglomerates, it should not be surprising that people may have trouble conceiving of shared values and intertwined fates. What then is to become of the commons, this necessary incubator of creativity, this safe harbor for individualism and localism, this crucible for democratic culture?

There may be an even more elemental question: Can the planet's natural systems survive a gauntlet of intensifying market enclosures?

Part II.

Varieties

of Market

Enclosure

4.

Enclosing the Commons
of Nature

The first person who, having fenced off a plot of ground, took it into his head to say *this is mine* and found people simple enough to believe him, was the true founder of civil society.

—Jean-Jacques Rousseau,
Discourse on the Origin of Inequality, 1755

In 1805 a certain Lodowick Post and his dog did "upon a certain wild and uninhabited, unpossessed and waste land, called the beach, find and start one of those noxious beasts called a fox." As Post gave chase, another hunter, Jesse Pierson, suddenly appeared, shot the fox, and claimed it as his own. An enraged Post argued that the fox really belonged to him, and filed a lawsuit in a New York State court. Thanks to this obscure hunting dispute, every law student today is introduced to the moral and philosophical complexities of "owning" nature through *Pierson v. Post*. By what rationale should Pierson or Post (or neither) be considered the "owner" of the fox?

The case illustrates some deep ambiguities and tensions between nature and property law. Nature, after all, is a vast, constantly moving web of interdependent creatures, plants, and processes. It is sovereign and unpredictable. Nature transcends our systems of economics, law, politics, and culture. It transcends *us*, the human species.

But our modern ideas about "property" presume that nature is amenable to strict individual control, use, and sale. Property law attempts to fence nature into ownable parcels. It artificially severs each parcel from the ecological whole so that the "bundles" of property rights can be freely traded in the marketplace for whatever purposes are seen as useful or lucrative. A fundamental question of our times is whether the natural world can be routinely subdivided, commodified, and alienated from its context without inflicting lasting ecological damage.

In his trenchant and entertaining *Slide Mountain, or the Folly of Owning Nature*, Theodore Steinberg explores the dilemmas of living in a culture "in which the natural world has been everywhere, relentlessly, transformed into property." The book explores the absurd, destructive results that occur when people try to claim ownership of groundwater reservoirs in Arizona and land at a river bend that is constantly eroding and accumulating elsewhere. Steinberg explores the daffy logic of property rights applied to the weather (do farmers have a legal claim against a company that purports to make rain?) and airspace over Manhattan buildings (why is the empty air above Grand Central Station worth tens of millions of dollars?).

These may be unusual instances of property claims on nature, but they also show how deeply rooted our legal categories really are. We allow the estates of dead celebrities to own and license their images, and the rock band U2 to sue rival claimants to that letter and numeral. Many landowners consider their property rights to be so absolute that they are waging pitched legal fights against the Endangered Species Act and other environmental laws as unconstitutional government "takings" of their real property.

We forget that property law is not an immutable, self-evident set of principles but a contrived artifact of our politics and culture. Steinberg notes that "the impulse to turn everything into property has not just confused but impoverished our relationship with the natural world by reducing that world in all its complexity a giant legal abstraction. The natural world's continual resistance to human meddling suggests the weakness of a system of thought that centers so thoroughly on possession. Moreover, this impulse to transform nature into property may continue to limit our ability to adapt successfully to the physical environment."[1]

We know at some level that nature cannot really be owned. But because the doctrines of property law generally "work"—at least on an individual level—and are widely accepted cultural norms, we easily forget that nature has its own ideas about "control." We are too invested in the specious accounting of conventional economics which regards the resources of nature as free and inexhaustible, not finite and fragile. And why not? The system has returned handsome profits for decades. It brings to mind Woody Allen's closing joke in *Annie Hall* about a guy with a crazy brother, who thought he was a chicken: "The doctor says, 'Why don't you turn him in?' The guy says, 'I would but I need the eggs.'" Common sense tells us that wildlife, genes, and the atmosphere cannot really be owned and that finite natural resources cannot be consumed indefinitely. But who are we to question the limits of our cultural fictions when they seem so functional and (for some) so lucrative? We need the eggs.

The tensions between nature as a sovereign force and property law as an instrument of human control—so obvious upon reflection—is the primary theme of the next three chapters. For millennia, nature has served as a commons for the human species. It has been a remarkably resilient, enduring system of diversity and self-replenishment, a source of both material plenty and spiritual renewal. Now nature's sustainability is being challenged by unprecedented human encroachments.

Armed with technologies, traditional property law, and faith in the "progress" of market expansion, human beings are reengineering the genetic blueprints of life and clear-cutting tropical rain forests for quick gains. We are expanding human habitations further into the wild and disrupting regional ecosystems from coral reefs to Arctic tundra. We are releasing countless toxicants that become ubiquitous in the food chain, and emitting chemicals that are warming the global atmosphere and depleting its ozone layer. Clearly some new rapprochement between our market-based culture and the sovereign needs of nature must be reached.

Any renegotiation must acknowledge that a significant change occurs when an economic and technological calculus of control is superimposed over something that is wild, free, and common. The closed, entropic system of the market interrupts and often supplants the open "gift economy" of nature, masking the actual costs of the externalities it generates. This chapter examines what happens when markets enclose nature. It is followed by a look at enclosures of "frontier commons" such as wildlife, icebergs, and genetic structures (Chapter 5) and natural resources on publicly owned lands (Chapter 6).

Enclosing the Commons of Nature

"Without doubt, the single most damaging aspect of the present economic system," writes Paul Hawken, the eco-minded business analyst, "is that the expense of destroying the earth is largely absent from the prices set in the marketplace. A vital and key piece of information is therefore missing in all levels of the economy."[2] Many markets routinely fail to take full account of the actual externalities they impose upon nature. Commercial perturbations once thought to be trivial—chemical waste at the parts-per-trillion levels, the draining of wetlands, the use of logging roads in forests—are later discovered to have serious consequences. Markets tend to impose a homogeneity, predictability, and uniformity on natural systems that, in their pristine state, are extravagantly fertile, diverse, complex, self-replenishing, and unpredictable.

The replacement of prairie landscapes with monocultures of corn may be exceedingly shrewd and efficient in the eyes of the marketeer. But from an ecological perspective, "the result is a 'leakier' system that lets more energy, nutrients and topsoil slip away and shows less resistance to pests and other natural shocks," as one scientist has put it.[3] It may be more "efficient" over the short term for mining companies to rip off the tops of mountains in West Virginia to extract coal. But the enduring damage to streams and wildlife, not to mention to the natural beauty of the landscape, makes the practice grotesquely destabilizing.

Contemporary market regimes tend to interfere with biological diversity, species interdependence, and closed-loop cycles that generate no waste. They introduce a shift in basic priorities—from natural sustainability to market logic, from a self-correcting and stable natural system to a brittle, jerry-rigged human system requiring constant intervention, from a commons managed to benefit all to a private property regime managed to generate profit for a few. Enclosures of nature not only disrupt the normal functioning of the earth's life-support systems, they aggravate social and economic inequities in the fashion of English land enclosures.

These acts are of a piece with a culture that treats nature as an inert object, not as a living essence. From what we know about the fierce autonomy of nature, many market enclosures amount to "control fantasies"—a superimposition of rigid technologies and short-term market logic on a dynamic natural order that operates according to evolutionary time horizons.

Exploiting the profit potential of nature often means "taking it private" in some respect. This might entail the benign "branding" of some component of nature (e.g., Chiquita stickers on bananas, a Perrier label on spring water), but it can also involve insidious strategies such as patent claims for common plants. By way of genetically engineered "improvements," multinational drug, agricultural, and biotechnology firms are laying proprietary claim to common plants and crops, removing them from the folk commons. Paradigmatic examples are corporate patents on substances from the neem tree in India, and Rice-Tec Corporation's patent on basmati rice that has been grown in India for thousands of years (see Chapter 5).

Why is conventional economic activity so seemingly at loggerheads with the imperatives of nature? A legendary plant breeder put it well: "Our demand for immediate gratification and quick, carefree returns on all investments leaves no time to wait for intricate things to be worked out, no time to evaluate true worth, no willingness to listen to those who contend with natural complexity."[4] The invention of new technologies may help us better understand natural principles, but they also embolden us to substitute short-term business-driven priorities for long-term ecological principles.

The culprit is not economic activity *per se*, but the *kind* of economic activity that so often prevails. It is possible for market forces to be harnessed to achieve more environmentally benign outcomes, as a number of commentators have explained.[5] Recently Paul Hawkens, Amory Lovins, and L. Hunter Lovins have marshaled a wide array of practical examples in their important book, *Natural Capitalism*.[6] Rather than assume that the bounties of nature are free and inexhaustible, as our current economic thinking does, "natural capitalism" understands that nature itself is a form of capital—finite, valuable, and irreplaceable—which must be assiduously preserved and maintained. Under natural capitalism, it becomes strategically important for companies to recognize the scarcity value of ecosystem services and to strive to integrate them seamlessly into product design and manufacturing. Nature can be regarded as a *commons*, subject to individual and collective restraints, not as an open-access free-for-all.

Hawken and the Lovins set down four basic principles for reorienting the economy toward a more ecologically benign path: radical resource productivity to slow the depletion of natural resources; the redesign of industrial systems so that they can imitate the closed-loop efficiency and waste-free character of biological systems ("biomimicry"); a "service and flow economy" that measures affluence by quality and utility, not by the sheer acquisition and "throughput" of material; and new investment in natural capital so that the biosphere can be maintained properly and produce more abundant ecosystem services. Each of these principles, in different ways, seeks to minimize the impact of market externalities on the environment. Historically, of course, business actors have generally ignored such considerations because they are seen as "bad for business."

This gets to the nub of the problem. When the defining matrix for business activity is quantitative and economic—the "bottom line"—it becomes harder to see, let alone honor, moral, social, aesthetic, and ecological considerations. The lamentable consequences of narrow market thinking has been expressed in different ways over the past century by Aldo Leopold, Rachel Carson, John Muir, David Brower, Barry Lopez, Wendell Berry, Peter Matthiessen, among many other conservationists, ecologists, activists, scientists, and poets. Their common message, crudely put, might be: Nature must have the room to be nature. Human beings must have the humility to respect the mysteries of nature. Ways must be found to restrain the market or to reform the culture in which it functions.

In his prophetic call for a "land ethic" in *A Sand County Almanac*, Aldo Leopold argued in 1949 that:

the "key-log" which must be moved to release the evolutionary process [of cultivating a land ethic] is simply this: quit thinking about decent land-use as solely an economic problem. Examine each question in terms of what is ethically and esthetically right, as well as what is economically expedient. A thing is right when it tends to preserve the integrity, stability and beauty of the biotic community. It is wrong when it tends otherwise.[7]

The root problem is that economic categories of thought and commitment are now so pervasive and controlling. Culturally, we do not know how to integrate non-economic values into the operations of the marketplace in routine, efficient ways. Perhaps more accurately, the imperatives of business organizations and our political culture militate against it. Most attempts to "internalize" market externalities—to make polluters pay the real costs of their harm, to integrate long-term consequences into today's choices, to develop more accurate indices of sustainability—end up as pitched political struggles. We end up with double-entry accounting: in one column, an economic theory that discounts or ignores market externalities, and in the other column, the real-life economy and our political culture, which sanctions a reckless production of externalities and an inept process for forcing companies to internalize those costs.

The failure of our society to develop a robust environmental ethic in the half-century since Leopold's clarion call testifies to the tenacity of our market loyalties—and the great difficulty in effecting a cultural transformation. Our very consciousness is so steeped in the ethic of material "progress" that after two generations of environmental tragedies and tocsins we have trouble respecting ecological limits even when we know about them. Industry resistance to improved environmental performance remains the norm, even for goals that are plainly needed, such as improved auto fuel efficiency, greater waste recycling, reduced carbon emissions into the atmosphere, and safeguards for genetic engineering. Significant strides have been made in our scientific knowledge, legal and regulatory systems, technological practices, and public consciousness. Yet the enclosure of the commons of nature continues apace.

Given the deep and seemingly irreconcilable tensions between the market system as it now functions and the biosystems of nature, it is gratifying to see some new bridges being built between the two conceptual kingdoms. A new generation of ecologists is starting to demonstrate that "nature's services," if regarded in conventional economic terms, are actually a phenomenal bargain. The argument is made that businesses will suffer serious harm—in their own coin, lower profits and market share—

if they continue to take for granted the economic services that the commons of nature provide for free.

For example, as the number of honey bee colonies in the United States has declined by one half over the past fifty years (from 5.9 million in 1947 to 2.8 million in 1994), the "pollination services" performed by bees has also declined, and with it, the yields of pumpkins in New York, almonds in California, and of dozens of other fruits, vegetables, and oilseeds. One study found that the potential value of non-*Apis* (wild) pollinators in the U.S. agricultural economy is on the order of $4.1 to $6.7 billion a year.[8] If cultural prejudices can be overcome, this insight could provoke affected businesses to become environmental advocates in order to protect their economic self-interests.

Nature quietly provides countless other benefits to the economy. Biodiversity represents a "genetic library" that is increasingly used to develop new medicines and increase the productivity of wheat and corn crops.[9] The world's oceans are important in biologically filtering water, detoxifying some pollutants, providing food, and encouraging tourism.[10] Natural pests provide a highly valuable service to farmers in improving crop yields and lowering costs (a benefit that is most apparent when the ecosystem service has broken down).[11] All told, it has been crudely estimated that nature's services provide some $39 trillion of value to the economy—this in a global GDP estimated at $35 trillion.[12]

The analyses of "nature's services" are compelling within the framework of economic theory but are more problematic in the real-life arenas where it matters: corporate investment, government regulation, consumer demand. Documented evidence and button-down rationality simply do not carry the day. "If the payoff [from treating nature as finite capital] is so darn good," asks journalist William Greider, "why are major sectors of industry still fighting old wars, gutting environmental laws when they can, stalling on compliance, propagandizing with scare stories about how environmental values kill growth, jobs, profits?"[13] The answer, he concludes after a conversation with eco-theorist Paul Hawken, is that the financial boom of the 1990s, with its promise of quick returns, made it far less attractive for companies to make serious investments in long-term solutions even if they would be profitable. Such investments seem counterintuitive, after all—the culture does not affirm them—and so they receive little support from most institutional investors, government, and major companies.

If compelling facts and logic about "natural capitalism" can be so ineffectual in bringing about change, the real problem may lie at a deeper level: the cultural attitudes with which we interact with nature.)

The Gift Relationship with Nature

Because we are so accustomed to regarding nature's bounty as "capital" to be husbanded or "property" to be marketized, we easily forget that the economic value of nature is ultimately rooted in a gift economy. This was the lesson of the community gardens of New York City, which were capable of generating economic value only because the sites enjoyed an insulation from unfettered marketization. The availability of nonmarketized open space was a prerequisite to neighborhood residents' coming together to create their own gift-exchange network. It was this web of relationships that, over time, generated both social and economic wealth.

So too, it may be argued, with nature. Too much meddling will destroy the natural nonmarket exchanges that are vital to a robust ecology. An ecosystem must have its own relative autonomy in order to be free to generate nature's services—to carry out its incomprehensibly complex "gift exchange." An overregimentation of nature for human purposes (crop monocultures, overuse of antibiotics, overharvesting of a species, alien species introduced to an ecosystem) can inflict irreversible, long-term damage to an ecology. Markets draw much of their power from regimenting nature into paths that are more "productive" and useful to humans; but ecosystems are fantastically complex and fragile webs of life that have their own sovereign needs.[14] The paradox is that the subtle generative powers of nature are not appreciated by many marketeers, who famously know the price of everything and the value of nothing.

As the industrialization of agriculture has replaced family farms, for example, the universe of domesticated birds and animal species has narrowed. Selective breeding has been used to produce animals of desirable sizes and colors and able to produce maximum quantities of eggs, milk, and meat. This inbreeding, however, has resulted in a sharp reduction in genetic diversity both between breeds and within breeds. The nation's eight million Holstein cows have all descended from 37 individual animals, making them more susceptible to various neurological, autoimmune, and fertility problems. Meanwhile, hundreds of breeds of livestock are now at risk of extinction and many minor breeds have already disappeared. The enclosure of the genetic pool of domesticated animals is reaching dangerous limits.

The problem is not just the overregimentation or disruption of nature, however. The deeper problem may be our cultural propensity to treat nature as a machine, an Other upon which abusive demands can be made. A market-based culture accustomed to monetizing values is more likely to objectify natural systems and so push them to their limits and beyond. A society that respects nature as a living entity is more likely to respect nature's inherent limits and consume its income only. It is more likely to recognize that nature is ultimately a part of a gift economy in which the human species is intimately involved.

Why does a gift relationship with nature help assure sustainability? Because, as we saw in Chapter 2, gift-exchange nurtures personal commitments and respect and fosters its own increase. Furthermore, the gains associated within the gift community are not commodified, privatized, and exported outside the community as "profit." They are collectively shared—and preserved in their noncommodified forms—as long as the gift stays in circulation. The market relationship turns nature into a commodity-object and encourages an impersonal relationship between seller and buyer. But the gift-relationship fosters affection, empathy, and respect.

This stance toward nature is seen in most premarket societies. Each winter the Indian tribes of the North Pacific once performed "first salmon" rituals to enact their gift relationship with nature. When the first salmon of the season was spotted, the tribal priest would make a formal welcoming speech, everyone would consume a bite, and the intact bones would be ceremonially returned to the sea as a gesture of supplication, expressing the hope that the salmon would return next year. While such rituals strike the modern mind as rank superstition, they have some highly practical results, writes Lewis Hyde. They help a people express and establish among themselves a gift relationship with nature: "a formal give-and-take that acknowledges our participation in, and dependence upon, natural increase," Hyde explains. He continues:

> Where we have established such a relationship we tend to respond to nature as part of ourselves, not as a stranger or alien available for exploitation. Gift exchange brings with it, therefore, a built-in check upon the destruction of its objects; with it we will not destroy nature's renewable wealth except where we also consciously destroy ourselves. Where we wish to preserve natural increase, therefore, gift exchange is the commerce of choice, for it is a commerce that harmonizes with, or participates in, the process of that increase.[15]

Cynics might call it tree-hugging. Ecologists would call it respect for the earth. The difference lies in whether an individual is allowed to develop a respectful attitude toward nature, with identifiable limits on market appropriation, or whether nature shall be regarded through a scrim of economic abstractions. The point is not to engage in rituals that seem silly, but to honor the fruits of nature as singular and finite and to acknowledge that there are other animate forces on earth besides human beings.[16] The language of traditional economics cannot help but treat natural resources as essentially fungible and scarcities (of oil, timber, or open space) as remediable through higher prices. Market language sees exchange value, not the thing-in-itself. This tendency can be put to good use in limiting our appetite for natural resources or our willingness to pollute (through pollution rights auctions, for example).

But this tendency can also be dangerous, essayist Wendell Berry points out, because "we know enough of our own history by now to be aware that people *exploit* what they have merely concluded to be of value, but they *defend* what they love. To defend what we love we need a particularizing language, for we love what we particularly know."[17] The "objective" abstractions of the market are frankly intended to alienate nature for market use. Such categories of thought cannot help us love the natural environment in its particularity or impel us to defend it more passionately.

Nurturing gift relationships with nature, however, opens the door to such possibilities. It offers a promising strategy for getting beyond the compulsive instinct of market culture to alienate nature and for honoring deeper humanistic and ecological values. Curiously, this desire may sometimes express itself *through the market*. A good example is the land trust movement, which uses the institutions of the market (property law, market exchange) to acquire land in order to retire it from market acquisition in perpetuity. Another example is cooperatives, which have market relationships with outsiders while allowing more democratic, equitable relationships internally. This paradigm—described earlier as "property on the outside, commons on the inside"[18]—is a model that may help us inscribe functioning commons within a market society.

On the other hand, the passion needed to champion new models for protecting the commons is not likely to emerge from market culture alone. It will arise from people who relate to human and ecological needs as sovereign forces in their own right, and not as commodified objects subject to market control. The sophistication with which we can blend the personal and inalienable with the monetized and marketable is becoming a more urgent matter. With each passing day, market forces are colonizing territories of nature that were previously inaccessible to humankind— wildlife habitat, global water flows, the planet's atmosphere, and other realms, big and microscopic. The rapid enclosure of these "frontier commons" is a worrisome development indeed.

5.

The Colonization
of Frontier Commons

You can do better than nature.

—James Young, executive vice president,
MedImmune, a biotechnology firm[1]

In 1896, a major shift in the nation's cultural consciousness was occurring, as famously noted by historian Frederick Jackson Turner in an essay announcing "the closing of the American frontier." For the first time in the country's history, there were no longer any unknown territories to explore, said Turner, just the mundane task of colonizing the remaining spaces. For an entrepreneurial nation weaned on the idea of a vast, endless frontier, this was a startling realization: the existence of limits.

Today, more than a century later, the classic American quest for social regeneration through frontier exploration persists. But now it is focused on a rather different kind of frontier: the basic processes of nature. Today's entrepreneurs are not rushing to claim geographic spaces; they are seizing the habitat of wild creatures, the flow of global water supplies, and the genetic structures of plants, animals and humans. Minerals on the bottom of oceans, the orbital zones of outer space, the global atmosphere—all are objects of competitive acquisition.[2] Realms of the natural world that we have always regarded as shared and infinite are being rapidly depleted and privatized.

This is a radical new step in humankind's history. Until recently, humans did not have the knowledge or tools to consider a reengineering of nature at its smallest and largest scale. The idea of remaking the planet's life-support systems was comic-book fare. Creating clones of living creatures or inventing new species was the stuff of science fiction.

It is our peculiar modern superstition that more knowledge, in and of itself, is beneficial or at least benign, and that what can be done should be done. Yet as the history of nuclear weapons and nuclear power suggest, there are limits that humankind ought to respect, or at least not give over to high-tech hucksters. There is a disturbing banality to the *New York Times* story announcing that scientists experimenting with "directed evolution" in the laboratory are trying to achieve in weeks what previously took millennia. The headline, "Selling Evolution in Ways Darwin Never Imagined," suggests just how far market forces are penetrating into nature.[3]

This chapter looks at three frontier domains now besieged by commercial forces that aim to convert basic elements of nature into lucrative feedstock for the market. They are global water supplies; wildlife and ecological areas threatened by the "takings movement"; and the genetic structures of life itself.

The Market Enclosure of Global Water Supplies

The ready availability of fresh water for drinking, agriculture, and industry is generally taken for granted. Aren't the world's supplies of water vast and virtually limitless? In fact, they are not. Most of the world's water is seawater or frozen water in ice caps. Less than one half of one percent of the world's water is available as freshwater. As the world's population swells, global industry expands, and clean water sources become depleted, water supplies are actually becoming extremely scarce, particularly in developing nations and in equatorial regions. Demand for freshwater is intensifying so rapidly that a top World Bank official predicts that "the wars of the next century will be about water."[4]

Sensing a keen market opportunity, a handful of multinational corporations are maneuvering to commodify and privatize whatever water supplies can be had, and then transport millions of cubic meters of water to nations around the globe. Two French multinationals, Vivendi SA and Suez Lyonnaise des Eaux, are the dominant leaders in privatized water, owning water companies in approximately 120 countries on five continents and distributing water to nearly 100 million people. But many other water transport enterprises are trying to capitalize on water shortages by buying up rights to water—in Alaska, Canada, Scotland, and elsewhere—and assembling the distribution technologies and partnerships to make some serious money.

The envisioned global market for water would divert massive supplies of freshwater and send them by tanker, pipeline, and even floating plastic bags to thirsty regions of the world: Spain, Morocco, the Middle East, Southeast Asia, the Southwestern United States. Just as oil and coal are treated as basic commodities, so water would become just another natural resource for exploitation, trade, and speculation. While Americans may take for granted public-sector management of water supplies, the new water-supply businesses hope to privatize the world's public water utilities and integrate them into the global market.

The sweeping ambition of these companies is set forth in a remarkable 1999 report by Maude Barlow, *Blue Gold: The Global Water Crisis and the Commodification of the World's Water Supply*.[5] The report describes the coming global marketization of water and its alarming consequences for the environment and poor people. (Much of this section relies upon Barlow's report.)

The idea of a global market for water might seem benign, ingenious, or even humanitarian were it not for the fact that it is likely to usher in devastating ecological consequences and gross social inequities. Commodifying water means that it is no longer regarded as having a local context. If there is a market—a seller of water in Canada, say, and a buyer in Saudi Arabia—then according to market logic, there is no reason why that transaction should not occur. Canada contains nearly one quarter of the world's freshwater. Why not sell it around the world and let Canada become the future OPEC of water?

This market logic blithely ignores the imperatives of nature. Canada's lakes and river systems flow northward. "To move large volumes of this water would massively tamper with the country's natural ecosystems," writes Barlow. In areas where the water is diverted, the vitality of plant and animal life, not to mention human communities and local economies, would suffer. As hydroelectric dams have shown, water diversions can cause local climate change, reduced biodiversity, mercury poisoning, loss of forest, and the destruction of fisheries habitat and wetlands.[6] The environmental fallout of privatizing control of water may soon materialize in California, as a large farming company, Cardiz, Inc., prepares to sell vast quantities of water from an aquifer under the Mojave Desert. Environmentalists contend that overpumping of the water will occur, which in turn will result in major air pollution as winds blow away dried-up soil. This has already occurred in the nearby Owens Valley.[7]

Champions of the new global market for water claim it would improve efficiencies and lower prices. It would supposedly help cash-strapped nations to improve their water-supply infrastructures. Opposing commodified water amounts to irrational "religious fervor," say marketers.[8] But like most other markets, the global water market would depend upon all sorts of hidden government subsidies. For example, many cities already give industrial water users reduced water rates or special tax subsidies. This practice artificially lowers costs to businesses and discourages conservation—at the expense of everyone else, especially taxpayers and low-income water users.

The marketization of water means that equity issues take a backseat to the needs of the wealthy. When water was privatized in the Sacramento Valley in the early 1990s, large buyers hoarded vast quantities of water, waiting to sell it on the open market when prices were higher. "A small handful of sellers walked away with huge profits, while other farmers found their wells run dry for the first time in their lives," writes Barlow. "[T]he results were disastrous; the water table dropped and the land sank in some places."

When water becomes a commodity, affluent businesses, cities, and nations will be able to buy what they want. But the rest of the world, especially the poor, are likely to go thirsty. In the "free trade" zone of Calexico, California, for example, water is so scarce and expensive that nearly all of it goes to manufacturers for the U.S. market. Infants and children reportedly drink Coca-Cola instead of water. In Bolivia, the World Bank engineered a private takeover of the water supplies in 1998, allowing a subsidiary of the Bechtel conglomerate to sell permits for access to water. Prices rose from 35 to 300 percent, forcing many people to spend nearly half their monthly budgets for water. After a general strike, civil violence, and martial law, protesters forced the government to rescind its water privatization deal.[10]

Such scenarios will become more common if a global water market materializes. After all, the private purchasing power of cities like Phoenix and Los Angeles will more likely prevail against the economic and political power of farmers, small towns, and indigenous peoples living thousands of miles away. One can easily guess who would win such bidding wars.

"Human lives depend on the equitable distribution of water resources," declared the South African Municipal Workers' Union in its fight against the privatization of water supplies in that nation. "The public should be given a voice in deciding whether an overseas-based transnational corporation whose primary interest is profit maximization, should control those critical resources. Water is a life-giving scarce resource which therefore must remain in the hands of the community through public sector delivery. Water must not be provided for profit, but to meet needs."[11]

There is another cost incurred when public-sector control of water supplies is transferred to private corporations: traditional standards of public disclosure and accountability are lost. A private company is more directly answerable to shareholders, after all, and not the general public. A private company can more easily resist demands for better water quality, safety, and information disclosure than a publicly owned or regulated utility.

Because the imminent enclosure of the global water supplies could wreak far-reaching ecological, social, and political havoc, groups such as the International Forum on Globalization are seeking to persuade international bodies to declare water a human right.[12] Water should be left to its natural flows whenever possible, and should be conserved and treated as a public trust. Establishing the principle that water is a common, inalienable good that should be protected from market enclosure will be one of the most formidable global challenges of the next few decades. Considering that one billion people on earth already lack access to fresh drinking water, and that demand for freshwater is expected to rise by 56 percent in the next quarter century, the private commodification of public water supplies is a distressing trend.

The "Takings" Movement

As the environmental movement has succeeded in enacting new laws and regulatory systems to protect wetlands, wildlife, rivers, coastal areas, and other ecological commons, a countermovement dedicated to "property rights" has arisen to claim that these protections are unconstitutional. This movement of developers, private landowners, and conservative ideologues bases its claims on the Just Compensation Clause of the Fifth Amendment, or the Takings Clause, which states, "[N]or shall private property be taken for public use, without just compensation."

Historically, this clause has been used to assure that government does not abuse its powers and physically seize private property without paying just compensation. The clause was inspired by abuses during the Revolutionary War in which armies arbitrarily seized private property to support the war effort. But the takings movement, or so-called Wise Use movement, ignores the plain language of the clause and any pretense to a strict construction of the Constitution. It audaciously asserts a broader, more tendentious meaning: that any government regulation that diminishes the value of private property, especially real estate, constitute an unconstitutional "seizure" of property. For example, if federal law prevents a landowner from building on wetlands, or if the Endangered Species Act prohibits development on a fragile breeding ground for migratory birds, such laws are said to violate the Takings Clause.[13]

Notwithstanding the slender historical and legal evidence for such a reading of the Takings Clause, the Wise Use movement has used it as the centerpiece of an aggressive political and litigation campaign. In virtually every session of Congress for more than a decade, the movement has introduced legislation seeking to make it easier for landowners to bring "takings" claims against federal, state, and local governments. The goal is to sanction nearly absolute property rights for landowners and to cripple the government's ability to protect the environment. It is an ideologically driven effort that willfully misrepresents the original intent of the Constitution's framers and falsely recruits such thinkers as John Locke and James Madison as champions of *laissez faire*.[14]

The essence of the Wise Use movement is to recast government as an instrument for converting natural resources into private property, and then to strictly protect that property against any other claims.[15] The movement is largely financed by large agribusinesses, mining interests, and land developers who invoke the western myths of self-reliant, independent farmers as a *faux*-grassroots public face.

As much as they respected individual rights, the Founders were not absolutists. They believed in the importance of *commonwealth* and saw property rights as a means for serving the common good and not as an end in itself. The Takings Clause was intended as a straightforward prohibition against seizures of property and was not meant to undermine the very premises of republican government—its ability to protect and defend the "common welfare."[16]

Despite these arguments, the Wise Use movement has sought to apply the Takings Clause to dozens of environmental battlefronts. One of the latest and most radical campaigns asserts private ownership in wildlife. The Wise Use movement is challenging the government's right to restrict development and tree harvesting as means to protect threatened and endangered species. Individual landowners argue that wildlife essentially belongs to them and that the government must therefore pay for what they regard as public infringements of their property rights. The position is patently extreme. Since the Romans and early English law, wild animals have been considered inherently public property, *res publica*, that governments have the right to manage.[17]

The Wise Use movement refuses to recognize the value of government actions that *enhance* the value of private property either through regulation (by maintaining or improving the quality of land) or through infrastructure investments such as canals, railroads, and highways (which create new commercial opportunities). These sorts of government actions amount to a windfall for private property owners. Predictably, the Wise Use movement sees no need to balance alleged "takings" with such "givings." The environmental movement, particularly the Environmental Policy Project at Georgetown University Law Center, has mounted a stalwart legal response to the Wise Use movement. But this has barely checked, and certainly not reversed, the well-funded and relentless campaigns to expand private property rights at the expense of the commons of nature.

Commodifying the Genetic Structures of Life

Few enclosures of the commons threaten to usher in as many profound changes as the commodification and privatizing of genetic structures. In disruptive, unpredictable ways, humans are asserting the prerogative to engineer the genetic boundaries that separate species to introduce entirely new organisms that threaten the stability of regional ecosystems, and to tinker with the genetic codes that shape our personalities, bodies, and health. Biotechnology holds a huge if unknowable potential for conquering ancient scourges—and for unleashing worldwide contagions and environmental catastrophes.

There are many complicated dimensions to biotechnology, but one worrisome trend is the conversion of our shared genetic heritage into a privately owned inventory managed for commercial gain. The genetic structures of life, which have "belonged" to everyone from time immemorial, are being propertized in order to move them from the public commons to private markets, with all the shifts in power, accountability, and moral norms that that conversion entails.

Substituting Market Monocultures for Agricultural Diversity

Since the dawn of agriculture some 11,000 years ago, farmers have worked within the gift-exchange system known as the ecology. Nature has provided an integrated, interdependent system of soil, plants, insects, microorganisms, and weather within which food could be grown. While farmers have learned many agricultural techniques for increasing crop yields, none has permanently disrupted the basic functioning of the ecosystem.

That began to change in the postwar years with the introduction of massive quantities of synthetic agricultural chemicals, which saw a 33-fold growth of pesticide usage from 1945, peaking at 1.1 billion pounds in 1995. The fantastic improvements in crop yields made possible by chemicals and farm machinery have been celebrated as the "green revolution." But they have also poisoned the environment, depleted vast quantities of topsoil, and caused insects to become pesticide-resistant.

Implicitly acknowledging that contemporary practices are not ecologically sustainable, companies such as Monsanto are pioneering a new generation of agricultural technologies, especially genetically engineered crops. The idea is to produce even more productive yields and novel traits by altering the genetic blueprints of crops. Already Monsanto has marketed NewLeaf potatoes, which are resistant to some insects; Bollgard cotton and YieldGard corn, which can survive droughts; and Roundup Ready seeds, which allow farmers to spray plentiful amounts of Monsanto's herbicide, Roundup, without harming the plant.[18] Other companies are exploring exotic possibilities such as implanting mouse genes in tobacco leaf, bacteria in cucumbers and tomatoes, and chicken genes in potatoes. Some biotechnologists hope to develop crops that will contain high doses of vitamins and vaccines.

The shift to genetically modified (GM) crops has happened quietly and rapidly. In 1995, virtually no genetically modified food was being grown in the United States. Three years later, farmers planted some 28 million hectares of it. By 2000, 36 percent of the U.S. corn crop was coming from GM seeds, along with 55 percent of soybeans and 43 percent of cotton. The USDA has approved some 50 GM crops for unlimited use.[19] While many GM innovations may ultimately prove valuable and benign, they often entail a perilous enclosure of the agricultural commons. This is seen in a reduction in genetic diversity, proprietary control of seeds at the expense of farmers, new corporate controls over research and information exchange, and greater industry consolidation.

Perhaps the most serious impact of this market enclosure is the "genetic erosion" fostered by the consolidation of the life sciences industries. "We're down to about ten companies that control in excess of one-third of the global commercial seed market," said Pat Mooney of the Rural Advancement Foundation International (RAFI), a leading advocate for socially responsible agriculture and conservation. "Twenty years ago not even one company occupied a significant percentage of the global seed market."[20] Among leading seed companies, 68 acquisitions occurred between 1995 and 1998, furthering industry concentration and reducing the diversity of seedlines available to farmers.[21]

Industrial agriculture prizes uniformity of product and monocultures over the rich biodiversity of nature. This familiar tendency can be seen in overbred apples, tomatoes, strawberries, and asparagus. Agribusiness researchers have sacrificed the natural taste and juiciness of these fruits and vegetables for hard, uniform, and bland substitutes that are seen as more compatible with the huge scale of industrial farming and distribution. The payoffs from a consolidated mass market with uniform product are seen as a better investment risk than a diversified, decentralized marketplace. Yet as consumers turn away from a narrow offering of bland-tasting apples, some apple growers are having second thoughts about having homogenized a once-diverse, robust marketplace for apples.[22]

But such trends are not easily reversed. Industry consolidation is accelerating a decline in agricultural biodiversity by making fewer seed varieties available to the market. As less natural cross-fertilization of seedlines occurs, the genetic diversity of crops shrinks. The result: a still-narrower, less resilient genetic base that is more vulnerable to serious crop failures like the Irish potato famine and the U.S. corn failures of the 1970s.

The enclosure of the agricultural commons has other manifestations. In trying to "improve upon" nature with a more market-friendly product, genetic engineers introduce transgenic novelties that nature would never produce on its own. This can be very dangerous because plants with bizarre traits may reproduce and fan out into the wider environment, causing unpredictable disruptions. If GM plants reproduce with other species, it is entirely possible that farmers could inadvertently create new "superpests" and "superweeds" that could not be controlled with conventional pesticides and herbicides.[23]

One genetic innovation that has been roundly criticized is Monsanto's gene-splicing of the natural insecticide Bt (*Bacillus thuringiensis*) into potatoes and corn. The idea is to repulse pests such as the corn borer without having to use chemicals. But over time, the Monsanto-engineered potato and corn could result in widespread insect resistance to Bt while hurting other species in the bargain. (Cornell researchers found that corn pollen with GM Bt can kill monarch butterflies.)[24] "For private gain, Monsanto will have destroyed a public good—the natural pesticidal properties of Bt," one farmer complained. "They are hoping to make a mint selling Bt-laced potatoes and, in the process, deprive their competitors (organic farmers) of an essential time-honored tool. The strategy is brilliant, and utterly ruthless."[25]

Going beyond most other technologies, genetic engineering externalizes unknown costs to future generations and the workings of nature itself. By traversing the species barrier that nature has erected, for example, biotechnology threatens to undermine nature's way of isolating pathogens. "Transgenics may let pathogens vault the species barrier and enter new realms where they have no idea how to behave," write Amory and L. Hunter Lovins. "It's so hard to eradicate an unwanted wild gene that we've intentionally done it only once—with the smallpox virus."[26] Unlike many industrial accidents, the "genetic pollution" that could result from slipshod genetic engineering could be irreversible and calamitous. "You cannot recall a new form of life," said Dr. Erwin Chargoff, the eminent biochemist who is often called the father of molecular biology. "It will survive you and your children and your children's children."

The agricultural commons is diminished in yet another way by corporate enclosure: new intellectual property rights thwart the open sharing and sale of seeds with others, as in a commons. To assure its proprietary control of genes that were once accessible and shared by all, Monsanto, through patents and contracts with farmers, has sought jealously to control who can have access to the seeds. Farmers who buy GM seeds are required to sign a contract that allows the company to dictate how the seeds are planted and to police the farmers' lands to assure compliance. Farmers are also charged an extra "technology fee" for GM seeds, over and above the normal cost of the seeds.

[margin note: Arendt's idea — uncontrollable effects of creation]

The ultimate attempt to secure proprietary control of seeds can be seen in the so-called Terminator seeds. The goal of these seeds, genetically modified to be sterile, was to prevent farmers from saving their own seeds for later use. If plants with sterile seeds could be made the norm, farmers would have to buy seeds every year from biotech firms such as Monsanto and AstraZeneca. Even better, sterile seeds were seen as a way to displace nonhybrid crops such as wheat, rice, soybeans, and cotton, whose seeds can be used each year. (Hybrid seeds cannot be used without a degradation in quality and consistency in the crop.)

Not surprisingly, the world's subsistence farmers are alarmed at the prospects of sterile seeds becoming more common. The UN African delegation has warned that sterile seeds will "destroy an age-old practice of local seed saving that forms the basis of food security in our countries" and "undermine our capacity to feed ourselves."[27]

Essentially, sterile seeds were part of the biotech industry's attempt to supplant nature's common pool of seeds with a private inventory of proprietary seed. (The strategy resembles Microsoft's notorious attempts to subvert open software programs and standards by substituting its own proprietary programs and protocols.) In defense of its property rights, Monsanto argued that sterile seeds are a way to protect a company's R&D costs in developing more productive, pest-resistant, and drought-tolerant crops. Growers who save and replant patented seeds "jeopardize the future availability of innovative biotechnology for all growers," said a Monsanto ad. "And that's not fair to anyone."[28]

But critics correctly realize that the enclosure of the agricultural commons would be worse. Seed companies would dominate the market with expensive seeds that have dubious long-term benefits. Farmers were especially outraged at the idea of abrogating the gift-exchange ethic that has sustained farming for centuries. "It is really a vicious, anti-farmer technology," said Kent Whealy, director of a seed exchange organization in Iowa. "Using genetic engineering to break that chain of seed that has always fed us just for a corporation's profit is wrong. If this technology were to become widespread, it would essentially end anything except what genetic engineering gives us."[29] Farmers would be turned into junkies, say other critics, because farmers who converted to GM plants would become utterly dependent upon the biotech suppliers.[30]

After a mounting wave of protest from consumers as well as food processors such as Heinz, Gerber, and Frito-Lay, in October 1999 Monsanto announced that it would not seek to commercialize sterile seeds. Some biotech companies are now promoting GM seeds that have genetically engineered traits that can be turned on and off by spraying certain chemical activators on them. Critics have dubbed these Traitor seeds, and point out that the GM seed toxins and activation sprays could change the mesofauna of the soil and harm birds and insects.

Genetically modified seeds have become controversial because, in their largest perspective, they represent an enclosure of the commons—a seizure of power and prerogatives once shared by farmers working in concert with nature. GM seeds are only one part of an ominous new regime of centralized factory farming, recently sketched by journalist William Greider.[31] Corporate agriculture is increasingly coming to resemble a coercive oligopoly that "organizes a complex, floating network of affiliated producers and subcontractors who adhere to its brand standards—think of Nike," he writes. No longer able to participate in truly open, competitive markets, farmers are being reduced to the status of contract producers working under fixed-price contracts with distant corporations. Removing seeds from the commons and making them proprietary is simply one of the strategies by which the new agglomerations of seed, chemical, and agribusiness corporations are seeking to control the food chain "from seed to feed to food."

Bioprospecting in Developing Countries

Does the shared knowledge and wealth of a local community have affirmative value in its own right? Or is the market the most reliable measure for what is valuable? Is the Western system of intellectual property rights the most effective and sustainable way to promote innovation, or do the cooperative regimes of indigenous cultures have some lessons to teach the market-driven First World?

These questions are becoming more urgent as multinational companies prowl the world seeking to convert the cultural knowledge and biological resources of indigenous peoples into marketable properties. The enterprise is often known as "bioprospecting," or to critics, "biopiracy." The life sciences industries—pharmaceutical, agricultural and biotechnology fields—have realized that the biodiversity of nature in the developing world represents a rich raw resource for new medicines, genetically engineered plants, and other products.[32] More than two-thirds of the world's plant species—at least 35,000 of which have medicinal value—come from developing countries, according to RAFI, a leading defender of indigenous knowledge.[33]

Costa Rica, for example, is estimated to contain 5 percent of the world's biodiversity. The Merck pharmaceutical company is now rummaging through some 10,000 genetic samples of this treasure trove for only $1.3 million, the fee it negotiated with the Costa Rican government. Madagascar, which has been described as "the biological equivalent of an Arab oil sheikdom," is another cornucopia of genetic wealth.[34] Compounds found in the rosy periwinkle of Madagascar have already been used to create a drug cure for Hodgkin's disease that earns $100 million a year, little of which has benefited the people of Madagascar. RAFI estimates that the value of germ plasm in developing countries taken in the early 1990s by pharmaceutical companies was worth about $32 billion a year; only a minuscule fraction of that sum has accrued to developing countries.

There are dozens of examples of Northern, developed countries reaping huge economic and social benefits from using the germ plasm and local knowledge of developing countries. Mildew-resistant barley varieties from North Africa have prevented hundreds of millions of dollars of crop losses in Europe and the United States. A tomato from the Philippine uplands has been used to breed cold tolerance into U.S. tomatoes. Bacteria collected from Costa Rican soil is being patented by the University of Massachusetts for a product that will kill nematodes and fungus on crops.[35] Dozens of companies have filed patents for products and processes that use seeds or other parts of the neem tree of India.[36] Companies have obtained patents on genes from nutmeg and camphor, and for certain varieties of basmati rice.[37] Universities and government agencies have sought to patent the wound-healing properties of turmeric and the leukemia-resistant genes of a Guyami Indian living in the Panama forests (both patents were either rejected or abandoned after protests).[38] An Australian biotechnology firm has contracted with the Polynesian kingdom of Tonga to build a private genetic database from the 108,000 people there.[39] Westerners are also commercializing the sacred artworks of Australian Aborigines and the folklore of native cultures without their permission.[40]

And so on.

The key question, writes journalist Seth Shulman in his important book *Owning the Future*, is, "Who, if anyone, should be able to claim ownership rights to the globe's genetic and cultural inheritance?"[41]

For the moment, the answer is largely dictated by intellectual property laws that favor Western multinational corporations. The scope of intellectual property has radically expanded over the past twenty years to allow individuals and companies to own life forms, genetically engineered life-forms, and basic research, not to mention business methods, software functions, and mathematical logarithms. Champions of global trade are pushing hard to make these laws the singular global norm. Under the GATT trade negotiations of the 1990s, especially the treaty known as the Trade Related Aspects of Intellectual Property (TRIPs), signatory countries must adopt certain standards calling for the private ownership of plants and microorganisms. Countries that fail to do so may face trade sanctions.

Critics such as RAFI, Global Trade Watch, and the *Multinational Monitor* argue that multinational companies are simply crafting international law to legalize the theft of commonly owned cultural and biological property. They say it is patently unfair to regard cultural knowledge painstakingly generated by distinct communities over the course of centuries as "free" and give exclusive economic rewards (through patents) to companies that may make derivative improvements to the common property.[42] That amounts to a privatization of the commons. It disrupts a highly effective, community-rooted system for creating value. It also transforms a public resource that is freely used and shared—genetic resources—into a tradable commodity. Communities that once maintained control over their cultural norms are being coerced to accept a market regime and its alien cultural assumptions. Or sometimes a Western entrepreneur simply asserts ownership of knowledge or genetic structures that have been used in common for time immemorial.

North American entrepreneur Larry Proctor presumed to patent a bean having "a particular color yellow," claiming ownership of a product of nature that Mexicans say has been used in common for generations.[43] Biotech concerns presume to "buy" exclusive rights to the gene pool of isolated populations—the islands of Tonga and Iceland are two examples— so that the genetic discoveries can then be privately owned and sold or withheld at will.[44] The propertization and privatization of genetic information have become so intense that, as a defensive maneuver to protect their interests, a family with a rare congenital illness has patented its own genes in order to become a power broker over their unique "intellectual property."[45] Many other patients with special genetic traits are starting to demand some equity stake or payment from researchers who use their body tissue to obtain lucrative patents.[46] Current trends in the ownership of genes have alarmed some researchers who fear that future biotech research will not be open and robust but dominated by the largest, richest companies. "We can't afford the equivalent of a biological Microsoft," warned a research fellow at the Molecular Sciences Institute in Berkeley.[47]

The Western world generally perceives the agricultural and medical knowledge developed by indigenous peoples over the centuries as a happy accident—naturally occurring wealth that is free for the taking. But this knowledge is not akin to moss naturally accumulating on stones, as RAFI puts it—something that "just happens." Rather, indigenous knowledge is the fruit of a "cooperative innovation system" that is deeply rooted in native cultures and their relationships to local ecosystems. The knowledge is the bounty of a gift economy.

This is why most of the world's 15,000 culturally distinct ethnic communities consider the idea of owning life a sacrilege. They regard the land and its life as communal resources to be used for the good of every member of the community. It is an integrated whole whose integrity must be maintained, not ripped asunder. To commodify portions of the local ecosystem—and then privatize and export those portions for sale outside the community—is to violate the integrity of the commons. It is to undercut the gift economy that over generations has generated rich reservoirs of knowledge and natural wealth. To neoclassical economists who focus on individual entrepreneurs, however, the sociocultural basis of this cooperative system of innovation is invisible.[48]

One reason that the gift relationships of indigenous communities remain so inscrutable to the Western mind is the West's mythologies about individual authorship and genius. In his pioneering work, *Shamans, Software, and Spleens,* Duke Law professor James Boyle traces the history of the Western idea of individual "authorship," as embodied in copyright and patent law.[49] Indigenous peoples are keenly aware that "the author" is a Western social construct, and that no individual is the sole or necessarily even the most important source of "originality" and value-creation.[50]

Upon reflection, this should be obvious. Elvis Presley could never have become the King of Rock 'n Roll had he not liberally used the rhythm-and-blues tradition. Presley did not invent this music; it came into existence and was sustained by a rich community of African-American performers who freely shared and built upon each other's talents through a musical commons.[51]

The Western legal tradition prefers to ignore the reality of the commons and its gift economies. It customarily severs a work from its community sources, canonizes a particular version, and then propertizes and sells it as the work of an individual. The economic rewards go to the "original author," not to any sponsoring community. The same dynamic propels "biopiracy." Boyle writes: "The farmers [in developing nations] are everything authors should not be—their contribution comes from a community rather than an individual, from tradition rather than innovation, from evolution rather than transformation. Guess who gets the intellectual property right?"[52]

This is richly ironic, because the gift economies of indigenous cultures are "a major source of innovation in both agriculture and pharmaceuticals in developed countries," notes RAFI, "and their role in other forms of industrial production can be expected to increase substantially in the decades ahead."[53] Protecting indigenous knowledge is important for its own sake. Most of the people of the world rely on indigenous knowledge and resources to survive. They save and exchange seeds, share knowledge about productive farming techniques, share access to medicinal plant remedies, and cooperate to prevent overexploitation of finite resources. When their shared resources are enclosed by market forces, excluding them from the commons, they are often forced to cut down the rain forests through slash-and-burn farming to survive. Thus can a market regime engender poverty.

To gain some perspective on bioprospecting, it is worth recalling a controversy that faced the British Parliament in the 1870s. At the time hundreds of prehistoric artifacts and ruins such as Stonehenge were privately owned; many were being casually destroyed by landowners with no interest in their scientific, historic, or cultural value. Were these property owners committing heinous acts of cultural vandalism or were they merely exercising their basic legal rights as property owners?[54] The question facing Parliament was whether there is such a thing as community property. Could a public right of historic preservation be asserted against individual property rights?

A heated legislative debate gave rise to the legal idea of "national heirlooms," which recognized that property has two distinctive elements: its economic value, which belongs to its owners, and its collective cultural value, which belongs to a larger community of people as well as to future generations. National heirlooms, or property that has deep importance and meaning to a community, should be owned by some public entity or, if privately owned, managed as a public trust with strict fiduciary duties to the community. Any patriotic American would consider it wrong for a private party to own or profit from the Statue of Liberty. The owners of the great artworks of civilization are thought to have an implicit moral obligation to share them with the public. "Artistic and historic treasures are not just ordinary property but artifacts whose fate define the nation's commitment to 'civilized' values," wrote Frenchman Abbé Grégoire in 1793. "In this sense are they 'common property.'"[55]

The challenge faced by Parliament in the 1870s is similar to the one that bioprospecting poses for us today: to forge new principles and legal institutions to protect common property (this time on an international basis). The perils of owning life have a long and sordid history in slavery. Our enthusiasm to sanction private ownership of the genetic structures of life has all sorts of practical, cultural, and moral consequences that we barely comprehend. But the inequities and disruptions of bioprospecting are clear enough in the meantime. Before it is too late, it is important to develop new legal regimes for the protection of plant species and animal breeds, so that the "cooperative innovation systems" of indigenous peoples can survive and continue to invigorate the innovation fostered by the conventional intellectual property system.[56]

Conclusion

Legal scholar Theodore Steinberg points out that we are:

> a society that organizes its relations with the world, the natural world in particular, around the concept of ownership. Such a culture is so dedicated to control, so obsessed with possession, that it is willing to deny the complexities of nature to satisfy its craving to own. It is a culture lost in a fantasy world, a society that has long dealt with nature through the American dream of property ownership.[57]

The commons of nature ultimately cannot be owned or fully understood, and attempts to colonize and propertize its very essence are likely to come to a bad end—a genetic catastrophe, the erosion of nature's biodiversity, a blight on nature's glory. Bill Joy, the software legend and cofounder of Sun Microsystems, has warned that genetic engineering is too powerful for us to manage prudently within the fields of our cultural prejudices and time horizons. Which is why he counsels the "precautionary principle" that Europeans have embraced—study thoroughly before taking serious risks—and why sometimes the only safe, realistic choice may be *relinquishment*—the limit of our pursuit of certain kinds of knowledge.[58] Or as Wes Jackson, an ecological philosopher, puts it, with reference to nuclear power and genetic engineering, "We ought to stay out of the nuclei."[59]

One way that we might relinquish our obsession with ownership and begin to reintegrate ourselves with nature is by rebuilding the commons. "The commons is a curious and elegant social institution within which human beings once lived free political lives while weaving through natural systems," writes Gary Snyder, the poet and ecologist. "The commons is a level of organization of human society that includes the nonhuman. The level above the local commons is the bioregion. Understanding the commons and its role within the larger regional culture is one more step toward integrating ecology with economy."[60]

There are limits to our abilities to regiment nature, to make it adhere to the contrived orderliness of the market. Market enclosures of nature can trigger long-term consequences that we do not and cannot anticipate. Unfortunate "externalities" occur precisely because the field of vision sanctioned by markets is so parochial. That is why we must at a certain point respect the integrity of the commons, which insists upon a more holistic perspective on nature, humanity, and economic activity. We must begin to appreciate how the gift economy subtly undergirds the work of the market. It is not just a matter of aesthetics or culture that we respect the commons, but a foremost practical imperative as well.

6.

The Abuse of the
Public's Natural Resources

We have to remain constantly vigilant to prevent raids by those who would selfishly exploit our common heritage for their private gain. Such raids on our natural resources are not examples of enterprise and initiative. They are attempts to take from all the people for the benefit of a few.

—President Harry S. Truman, December 1948,
at the inauguration of Everglades National Park

Not many Americans realize that they collectively own one third of the surface area of the country and billions of acres of the outer continental shelf. The resources are extensive and valuable: huge supplies of oil, coal, natural gas, uranium, copper, gold, silver, timber, grasslands, water, and geothermal energy. The nation's public lands also consist of vast tracts of wilderness forests, unspoiled coastline, sweeping prairies, the awe-inspiring Rocky Mountains, and dozens of beautiful rivers and lakes. Public lands represent an unparalleled commons for the American people, held in trust by the U.S. government.

As the steward of these public resources, the government's job is to manage these lands responsibly for the long term. The sad truth is that government stewardship of this natural wealth represents one of the great scandals of the twentieth century. While the details vary from one resource domain to another, the general history is one of antiquated laws, poor enforcement, slipshod administration, environmental indifference, and capitulation to industry's most aggressive demands. Through sweetheart deals pushed through Congress and federal agencies, corporations have obtained discount access to huge quantities of publicly owned oil, coal, minerals, timber, and grasslands while wreaking serious environmental havoc. As we will see below, the dimensions of the fiscal malfeasance and scope of ecological harm are truly staggering. Mine tailings have destroyed rivers and contaminated groundwater. Overgrazed grasslands have eroded topsoil. Timber clear-cutting has destroyed valuable species habitat.

Every few years, another unsavory episode of public lands abuse finds its way into the mainstream press. Almost invariably, however, reform efforts are slowed down or stopped as politicians "owned" by the affected industries flex their muscle in quiet, backroom ways. Time after time, a compliant Congress and captive federal agencies agree to throw open public lands to commercial exploitation on some of the cheapest terms imaginable. If the Reagan or Bush I administrations had fulfilled their pledge to run the U.S. government like a business, and the Democratic administrations before and since had shown greater political resolve to end corporate welfare, the American people would have reaped untold billions in new revenues. Instead, not only has the government too often failed to perform its fiduciary duties to the American people, but its slack management of public lands has often resulted in new environmental abuses, intensified pressures on endangered species, aggravated public health problems, and worsened concentrations of corporate power.

The sorry history of public lands management is not just about venal political leaders, inept bureaucracies, and a cultural compulsion to exploit natural resources (although it is that). At a more fundamental level, it is about the rise of a "corporate capitalism" in the late 1800s, supplanting Adam Smith's free market capitalism—which in turn has neutralized the accountability mechanisms otherwise exercised by citizens and consumers. As described by forestry scholar Richard W. Behan in his book *Plundered Promise*, in such a political economy it is only natural that public lands would be managed for maximum short-term private gain. The resulting overdevelopment—overcut forests, overdammed rivers, overgrazed rangelands, overused parks—is an institutional symptom of excessively powerful corporations and a predatory political system.[1]

This chapter examines corporate appropriations and U.S. government mismanagement of four major types of natural resources: minerals, oil, timber, and grasslands. While the details vary in each area, the general themes are similar, which is why any policy agenda to reclaim the commons must pay special attention to public lands.

Minerals for the Taking

The granddaddy of all corporate welfare giveaways may be the Mining Act of 1872, a relic of the Old West that allows mining companies to extract $2 to $3 billion of gold, silver, copper, and other minerals every year without paying a cent to the federal government. The Mining Act allows anyone to enter any public lands not specifically stipulated as off-limits and explore for minerals there. If minerals are found, they can be removed without the claimant needing to pay any royalties. If a discovery is made, as defined by the act, the claimant can apply for a "patent"—full title to the land—and receive it for either $2.50 or $5 an acre, depending upon the type of minerals discovered.[2]

In its original vision, the Mining Act was meant to encourage the development of the West. Like the Homestead Act of 1862, it was portrayed as a populist vehicle to help the independent miner make a living while settling the West. In practice, the Mining Act, passed during the notoriously corrupt presidency of Ulysses S. Grant, has served as a nearly impregnable fortress of corporate welfare for the nation's leading mining companies.

Astonishingly, this giveaway scheme for minerals on public lands has prevailed for the past 130 years with little modification. Under its auspices, a mass of land the size of Connecticut—3.5 million acres—has been acquired for $5 or less an acre, and billions of dollars of minerals have been carted away for free. In 1999, there were 3.1 active mining claims on federal lands comprising more than 20 million acres.[3] Total revenues from mining leases in 1999 were a paltry $8.8 million. Since 1872, the federal government has given away more than $245 billion of mineral reserves through patenting or royalty-free mining. According to the U.S. Public Interest Research Group (USPIRG), the government could reap $1 billion over five years by charging modest royalties of only 8 percent on gross revenues.[4]

Over the decades, politicians have found it convenient to rail against "welfare queens" bilking the public treasury, while giving a wink and a nudge to a rogue's gallery of mining companies that have found a quiet, lucrative subsidy in the form of the Mining Act of 1872. The Canadian-controlled company American Barrick Resources has mined the largest single known gold deposit in the United States—the Goldstrike mine in Nevada, worth an estimated $7 billion in 1990—without paying any royalty fees. Under the Mining Act, the company later acquired the land for $5 an acre. Phelps Dodge has mined billions of dollars of copper from the Morenci mine in Arizona. The company bought the land atop the mines, and thus the mining rights, for $5 an acre—"federal land for the price of a cheeseburger," as one critic put it. Fifty years after exploiting the deposit, Phelps Dodge estimated that the copper reserves remaining in the mine were worth $10 billion.[5]

Sometimes mining patents are used to acquire land for development or other purposes at a huge discount, with no mining even contemplated. One of the more infamous cases was a speculator's purchase of land in Keystone, Colorado, for $2.50 an acre, which he promptly resold to a developer for $11,000 an acre. Other mining claims have been used for hunting cabins, ski slopes, and growing marijuana. Challenging such abuses of Mining Act claims in court can be difficult, however, because of the legal burden of proof that the government must meet.

Apart from the huge revenue loss, the Mining Act is an environmental disaster. It explicitly designates mining as the highest priority for public lands on which minerals are found. This makes it difficult, and often impossible, for government agencies to balance competing uses of the land, including uses that would be more environmentally benign or economically sustainable. For example, a company mining pumice above the Jemez River in New Mexico, a congressionally designated wild and scenic river, could not be stopped from siting its mine above the river.

The water pollution associated with abandoned mines and mine tailings is another cost that mining companies simply pass on to taxpayers and nearby residents. Acids, cyanide, other toxic runoff from mines routinely kill vegetation, wildlife, and streams—an estimated 12,000 miles of streams nationwide. There are more than half a million abandoned and polluting mines in the country, with 70 of them officially designated as Superfund sites. The people who live near mines suffer much greater risks from unsafe drinking water, soil contamination, and lead poisoning.[6]

Even after the Environmental Protection Agency spent $200 million cleaning up after the Bunker Hill lead smelter in Silver Valley, Idaho, sediment contaminated with cadmium, arsenic, and zinc was found across 1,500 miles of the Coeur d'Alene River basin. Approximately 26 percent of two-year-olds in the area have been found with dangerous levels of lead in their blood. Cleaning up abandoned mine sites could cost as much as $32 to $72 billion, according to the Environmental Protection Agency (EPA).

That a law so flagrantly irresponsible in its fiscal, environmental, and public health impacts can remain in force is a testament to the political power of the mining industry and key Western senators under its sway. Efforts to revamp the 1872 Mining Act have repeatedly been defeated over the past 130 years. It is no coincidence that the National Mining Association and other mining-related political action committees gave nearly $40 million in congressional campaign and soft money contributions from 1993 to 1998: merely the most recent installments of industry "incentives" to politicians. "Considering that the mining industry received $1.2 billion during that period," writes USPIRG, "mining industry contributors received a 30:1 return on their investment."[7]

With a straight face, the industry argues that it needs incentives to continue mining. But the need for it to pay royalty fees to owners of *private* lands does not seem to discourage its mining there. In any case, mining companies already enjoy so many tax write-offs—for exploration, reclamation, and normal business expenses—that the tax benefits can actually exceed the costs of digging a mine. The industry even enjoys a percentage depletion allowance for the diminishing value of their initial "investment" in mineral reserves—reserves for which they paid nothing! The tax revenues foregone do not begin to take account of royalty-free access to public lands or the massive environmental cleanup costs. The scenario is particularly outrageous considering the very high profits of mining companies and large foreign ownership within the industry.

Oil from Public Lands

At least since the 1960s, the nation's leading oil companies administered a running accounting scam, only recently stopped, that allowed them to evade billions of dollars in royalty payments for the 600 million gallons of oil they were extracting each year from public lands. Even when the underpayments were brought to the attention of the Interior Department's Minerals Management Service, the agency charged with collecting oil royalties, the deception was allowed to continue and fiercely defended by key oil industry-backed senators and representatives. "Not since the Teapot Dome scandal of the 1920s has the stench of oil money reeked as strongly in Washington as it is in this case," wrote the *Los Angeles Times*.[8]

The oil industry enjoys an array of special tax breaks that significantly lower its companies' operating expenses.[9] While the wisdom of these tax subsidies may be debated, the terms on which the U.S. government was granting access to public lands to drill oil amount to a politically sanctioned fraud. The public was not the only victim. State governments, too, lost a large percentage of oil royalties to which they were entitled— revenues earmarked for public education, environmental projects, parks, historic preservation, and recreational lands. All of these programs have been shortchanged billions of dollars over the past several decades.

Here's how the scheme worked. Customarily, oil companies pay rental fees, or royalties, for the right to extract crude oil from public lands. The royalties are usually 12.5 percent for federal onshore production and 16 to 33 percent for federal offshore production. But through the revelations of oil industry whistle-blowers and the Project on Government Oversight, a public interest watchdog, it was learned that the nation's largest oil companies had used a variety of accounting subterfuges to lower the "posted price" for oil upon which the royalties are based, often by as much as $4 a barrel.[10]

The posted price is the publicly stated price at which oil refinery companies will buy crude oil from independent producers on the open market. But because the various stages of oil production—drilling, transport, refining, distribution, and so on—are so integrated and controlled by the leading oil companies, there is no meaningful "open market" at any given stage of production. For decades, oil companies artificially depressed the price of crude oil, choosing to recover their profits "downstream" at the refinery level. This had the double advantage of allowing integrated oil companies to "squeeze out competition from the smaller independent producers and refiners, and pay the government less in royalties, as royalties are based on the price of the crude oil."[11]

The scam of "posted prices" eventually became something of an open secret, because few in the industry or stock exchanges regarded the posted price as a meaningful market price. Posted prices were widely regarded as artificial sums whose chief purpose was to calculate (and reduce) royalties. The posted price was sometimes used as the price at which independent producers with no transportation options could sell their crude to refineries. But by the late 1980s, even independent producers began to be paid more than the posted price.

For years, the Department of Interior played along with the game, unwilling to admit that the posted price was a fiction that was allowing 18 oil companies to avoid paying royalties of about $66 million a year. The State of California was a leading force in challenging the royalty under-payments via pressure on the federal government and litigation pursued with other states against the oil companies. One lawsuit resulted in a settlement that will give $5 billion to seven states; other cases are pending.

Even though the Interior Department in 1997 proposed a new system for collecting royalties, powerful oil-state senators repeatedly blocked its implementation. Finally, in September 1999, the issue burst into the national press when Texas Senator Kay Bailey Hutchison attempted, for the fourth time, to postpone the new Interior rules. It was only because the issue was forced onto the Senate floor and into the klieg lights of C-SPAN that a firestorm of national outrage materialized. The searing public scrutiny may have proved politically fatal to the royalty charade. Hutchison squirmed as it was revealed that oil and gas interests had given her $1.2 million in campaign contributions between 1994 and 1998; other oil-state senators were similarly discomfited. All told, oil and gas interests spent $93 million on lobbyists in 1997 and gave $14 million in contributions to political candidates in the 1997 to 1998 election cycle.[12]

The Clinton administration used these revelations to press its advantage, and by March 2000, the GOP had capitulated. The Interior Department was finally able to begin collecting royalties based on actual market prices, not bogus "posted prices." Whether the new, more equitable royalty plan can survive the oil industry's entrenched political clout and legal subterfuges is another question.

Clear-Cutting the Public's Forests

After decades of rapacious exploitation of forests in the West during the 1800s, the U.S. Congress in 1891 created the U.S. Forest Service, a novel enterprise to manage 21 million acres of Western forest reserves in the public interest.[13] Concerned about the concentration of corporate power and environmentally destructive logging, land-use reformers sought to shift federal policy from the simple disposal of public forests to a more intelligent, conservation-minded management of the land. The size of national forests has since swelled to more than 191 million acres, or about one tenth of the surface area of the United States.

Despite this goal, the U.S. Forest Service's primary goal for most of the twentieth century was to promote commercial logging—the more, the better. To the Forest Service, the national forests were seen primarily as an economic resource: a rich repository of cheap timber to meet growing demand at a time when private timber reserves were dwindling. "Industrial forestry" was especially emphasized in the postwar years, when "intensive management" (i.e., maximum production) became the byword of the U.S. Forest Service. This focus meant, among other things, the use of aggressive new tree harvesting methods such as clear-cutting and the construction of a 360,000-mile system of logging roads—some eight times longer than the interstate highway system.

Predictably enough, timber harvests soared. Forest Service officials who considered 200 million board-feet to be a "sustainable yield" in 1949 consistently raised that threshold, so that by 1968 a harvest of 560 million board feet was (erroneously) considered sustainable. Tree harvesting in federal forests continued at the 450-to-500-million-board-feet level for the next two decades until, by the end of the 1980s, old-growth forests (trees older than 200 years) constituted less than 14 percent of federal forests. Of the old-growth trees that remain, all but 30,000 acres, or 2 percent, were "ecologically 'fragmented' into small, isolated, vulnerable blocks."[14]

Paul Hirt, a leading historian of the national forests, calls the drive by timber companies, the Forest Service, and political leaders to extract maximum output from the forests "a conspiracy of optimism."[15] Initially propelled by the postwar faith in material progress and technology, high-yield logging was sustained in the 1970s and 1980s only by denying the growing environmental fallout: massive soil erosion, degradation of streams and rivers, the loss of valuable wildlife habitat. Despite its ostensible commitment to "multiple use" forestry and "sustainable yields," the U.S. Forest Service presided over "an orgy of unsustainable logging of the public's forests," according to Hirt.[16]

Throughout this time, the prevailing ethos was set by professional

foresters, who regarded the public lands as a commodity-input for production. Only over the past forty years has the ecological importance of forest
lands has been given due recognition. Some two thirds of the big game in
the West and hundreds of endangered plant and animal species occupy
national forests. Half of the West's rain and snowfall courses through the
national forests en route to serving farmers and communities throughout
the Western U.S. In the Pacific Northwest, the Rocky Mountains, and
dozens of other areas, the Forest Service sought to meet high production
quotas by allowing huge swathes of forest to be clear-cut, often resulting
in irreversible harm to all of these ecological concerns.

The agency's failure to protect the ecological integrity of the public's
forests has been matched by its notorious failure to get fair-market
payment for timber sales. It has been pointed out that if the U.S. Forest
Service were a Fortune 500 firm, its assets would put it among the top five
corporations and its revenues among the top fifty. Yet the stock in this
massive company would likely be zero because it routinely *loses* between
$1 and $2 billion a year. These losses represent huge, hidden subsidies for
companies such as Boise-Cascade and Louisiana-Pacific.

Below-cost timber sales were first exposed by a series of journalistic and
government reports in the 1980s and extending into the 1990s.[17] The
U.S. General Accounting Office pointed out that 96 percent of the Forest
Service's timber sales in the Rocky Mountain Region in 1981 and 1982
lost money, while 60 percent and 93 percent of sales in other Western
regions also lost money. Perri Knize, writing in *The Atlantic*, documented
decades of environmental destruction and pork-barrel politics that were
disguised by bogus claims of "sustainable forestry," "multiple use" forestry,
and creative accounting.[18]

For example, the annual cost of building and maintaining logging roads
in the national forests is about $95 million. The U.S. Forest Service also
spends more than $500 million a year on overhead expenses, the costs of
reforestation and improvements, and payments to states in lieu of taxes.
The Forest Service has also amortized some expenses for reforestation and
roads over the course of hundreds of years or ignored amortization costs
entirely. Other costs of logging were disguised by assigning them to separate accounting categories such as pest control and environmental
protection.

In the 1990s, there were signs of change within the U.S. Forest Service.
The logging binge of the Reagan/Bush years and the willful neglect of its
ecological consequences began to discredit the agency, exposing it as a
stultifying, ingrown bureaucracy more attentive to industry than to the
public. In recent years, the Forest Service has begun to grapple with its
larger, more complicated public responsibilities beyond logging: environ-

mental protection, recreation, and pest and fire management. In the words of Paul Hirt, a "sobering climate of greater resource scarcity, fiscal conservatism, management humility and awareness of ecosystem degradation is driving the Forest Service into unfamiliar new territory."[19] Real reforms in Forest Service management are being made.

It remains to be seen how durable this new attitude will be, but the Clinton administration did take one of the most important land conservation initiatives in generations by declaring a ban on road-building and logging in as many as 60 million acres of national forest. After the huge ecological damage wrought by the "Great Barbeque" of timber harvests over the past century, other initiatives, such as an outright ban on commercial logging, are gaining new momentum. But that kind of conscientious stewardship of the public forests will occur only if strong public vigilance and political action continue.

Subsidizing the Abuse of Public Rangelands

It is the conceit of Western cattle ranchers that they are hardy mavericks living an independent, self-sufficient life. In truth, many of the West's cattle ranchers are highly dependent upon Washington for cheap leases of public lands, for government programs to kill predators of cattle, and for political fixers to squelch vital environmental reforms.

Contrary to the public image cultivated by corporate cattle ranchers, ma-and-pa operations account for only a small fraction of total grazing on public lands. According to a major series of articles on cattle grazing published by the *San Jose Mercury News* in 1999, the bottom half of grazing-permit holders on national forests (based on amount of grazing) control only 3 percent of all livestock, while the top 10 percent control nearly half of livestock. On lands managed by the U.S. Interior Department's Bureau of Land Management (BLM), the bottom half of permit holders control only 7 percent of all livestock, while the top ten percent control 65 percent.

While hundreds of family ranchers cling to cattle ranching as an economically marginal if treasured way of life, cattle ranching on public lands is in fact dominated by a corps of wealthy hobby ranchers and large corporations that rely heavily upon taxpayer subsidies. As the *San Jose Mercury News'* reporters conclude, "When it comes to grazing at the federal trough, no one sits taller in the saddle than corporate cowboys."[20] Among the top recipients of below-market grazing fees on nearly 270 million acres of public rangeland are Idaho billionarie J.R. Simplot, hotel magnate Barron Hilton, Anheuser-Busch Inc., Sinclair Oil Corp., and Hunt Oil.

For decades, corporate cattle ranchers have paid federal grazing fees that were far below those charged by state governments and private ranches. In 1999, the government's fee of $1.35 per head of cattle per month was *one eighth* the average fee of $11.10 charged by private landowners in the eleven westernmost states.[21] Federal fees are based on a complicated formula that takes into account beef prices, operating costs, and other factors. But the complexity amounts to a charade of fairness, because the ultimate fees charged by the federal government have always ended up being far lower than actual market rates for comparable grazing lands.

In 1999, the federal government received $94 million for its grazing leases on federal lands. If these leases are in fact worth eight times more, as the *San Jose Mercury News'* analysis of 26,000 billing records suggests, then the federal treasury should have pocketed something in the neighborhood of $750 million. The shortfall represents a massive taxpayer subsidy that chiefly benefits large corporations and affluent ranchers. With ranching-related political action committees giving nearly $1.3 million to congressional and party campaigns from 1993 to 1998 to help preserve the $350 million in acknowledged ranching subsidies over the course of that period, the 270-to-1 "investment" in friendly legislators has yielded rich returns.[22]

Below-market grazing fees are not the only subsidies that cattle ranchers enjoy. Half of the grazing fees collected by the federal government are earmarked for "range betterment" purposes such as fences and water tanks, which ranchers might otherwise have to pay for themselves. Ranchers are also beneficiaries of drought relief assistance to help feed and water livestock herds when necessary. Finally, the Agriculture Department's Wildlife Services bureau spends $14 million a year killing coyote, wolf, foxes, grizzly bears, and other livestock predators on more than 9,000 ranches.

These kinds of subsidies might be understandable if there were a vital economic or social purpose being served. But for the most part, this is not the case. Only 3.8 percent of the beef sold in the United States comes from cattle that graze on public lands, according to the Agriculture Department, and cattle ranchers who use public lands account for only 2 percent of the nation's 1.1 million cattle operations. Thomas Powers, a Montana economist and author of *Lost Landscapes and Failed Economies*, calculated that only 0.06 percent of total employment in eleven Western states is dependent on federal grazing.[23]

Federal subsidies for livestock grazing are particularly odious in light of the horrendous ecological impact.[24] While it is possible to graze cattle in an environmentally sensitive way, this has not been customary in the history of cattle ranching in the West, and the effectiveness of recent reform efforts is not impressive. Livestock are native to Europe, not the American West, and so grasslands in much of the West are inherently ill-suited for constant grazing and trampling by large herds of livestock.

When thousands of half-ton cattle tramp across the fragile, arid landscape and overgraze native grasses, it hastens soil erosion and alters the mix of both plants and animals that can survive in the ecosystem. Cattle like to linger by rivers and streams, which means that they destroy sensitive stream banks and deposit large quantities of wastes in the water. "Runoff from hillsides stripped of vegetation by too many cattle pollutes streams with silt and sediment, clogs waterways and contributes to water quality degradation in Western rivers and streams and a decline in salmon populations," notes the National Wildlife Federation, one of the leading opponents of abusive grazing on public lands.[25] Critic George Wuerthner points out that "species as varied as the Bruneau Hot Springs Snail to the willow flycatcher to the Bonneville cutthroat trout are all endangered as a consequence of habitat loss or degradation due to livestock production."[26] The *Mercury News* report found that large cattle ranchers tend to inflict greater damage on public rangelands than smaller operators do.

While cattle ranchers put forward many brave arguments to depict grazing as environmentally benign, a comprehensive review of 143 government reports and peer-reviewed scientific studies on livestock grazing in the West shows otherwise.[27] The review concludes that if livestock grazing is not severely restricted within the next thirty to fifty years, restoration of the landscape will become impossible. Already 60 percent of BLM rangelands are missing at least half of their native plants and grasses.[28] Some 80 percent of streams and riparian ecosystems in arid regions of the West have been damaged by livestock grazing, according to the Interior Department in 1994.[29] A 1990 EPA report found that riparian areas throughout much of the West were in "their worst condition in history." And so on.

The irrationality of federal management of rangelands can only be explained by politics. For decades, a few powerful Western senators, acting on behalf of wealthy ranchers, have stymied attempts to raise grazing fees and introduce grazing reforms to protect the environment. Interior Secretary Bruce Babbitt sought to enact "Rangeland Reforms '94," but Senators Peter Dominici (New Mexico) and Larry Craig (Idaho) rallied other Republicans to defeat the reforms on numerous occasions over the next five years. Because banks consider grazing permits a form of collateral on ranchers, many banking lobbyists also weighed in against reform. And so, despite the grim ecological prospects and outright waste of taxpayer monies, the cattlemen's lobby has been able to prevail politically.

"Rolex ranchers" addicted to the federal giveaway continue to fancy themselves rugged individualists, and the subsidized ecological abuse of the public's rangelands continues.

Conclusion

The exploration in this chapter of enclosures of public lands is hardly comprehensive. Private interests have long exploited coal, oil shale, and the outer continental shelf belonging to the public without full compensation or appropriate environmental safeguards. The Department of Interior is allowing biotechnology firms to conduct "bioprospecting" for genetically interesting microbes in Yellowstone Park—a "microbial gold rush" that is being challenged by a number of environmental groups.[30] For twenty-five years a Japanese biotech company has been harvesting the blood of horseshoe crabs in the environmentally sensitive Cape Cod National Seashore in order to make a substance that detects dangerous bacteria in injectible drugs.[31]

There is little question that the federal government has the legal and moral authority to manage public lands in a more responsible manner. Why, then, has it failed to do so in one instance after another? The answer, crudely put, is because oil corporations, mining companies, lumber companies, big cattle ranchers, and other market interests are able to use the political process to thwart the public's interests. Especially with our corrupt campaign financing system, organized commercial interests wield much greater political clout than public interests that are largely unorganized and noncommercial.

This familiar pattern of powerful private interests subverting conscientious management of the public's own assets is replicated in many spheres. Fisheries, water resources, and satellite orbital sites are three additional examples. (The broadcast industry's free or cheap use of the public's electromagnetic spectrum for broadcasting, wireless services, and other uses is examined in detail in Chapter 10.)

Fortunately, the fight to reclaim control of public lands has many advantages over the long term. First, it is difficult for subsidized industries to make persuasive defenses of their subsidies. In addition, the ecological harm is usually well documented, and the moral inequities of the "corporate welfare" are fairly obvious. What has been missing, historically, has been a focused public exposure of abuses in a politically consequential arena. When this happens—as it did in the Clinton administration fight against below-cost oil leasing in 1999—congressional apologists for an industry are highly vulnerable, and reforms can be achieved. Another effective strategy has been the annual "Green Scissors" campaign by environmental groups, which compiles a compendium of "polluter pork programs."[32]

To break through the moral torpor and news clutter of Washington, D.C., an aggressive citizens' lobby is needed to marshal the facts and publicize them, and a few committed legislative leaders must mobilize political support and provoke a political fight. Despite the daunting difficulties of such a scenario, few battles offer greater opportunities to curb environmental abuses, shut down egregious instances of "corporate welfare," and generate significant new revenues—all in one fell swoop.

7.

Can the Internet Commons Be Saved?

The value of a piece of scientific work only appears to the full with its further application by many minds and with its free communication to other minds.

—Norbert Weiner, computer scientist[1]

It is no exaggeration to say that there has never been a commons as big, robust, and socially creative as the Internet. Since its emergence as a popular communications medium in the mid-1990s, the Internet has unleashed a remarkable explosion of knowledge, commerce, and virtual community on a global scale.

Much of this growth has stemmed from the astonishing commercial development of the Internet platform since 1994, particularly since the rise of the World Wide Web, stimulated by the Netscape Navigator. But this unprecedented boom in public communications owes a critical primary debt to the system's open, end-to-end technical architecture. By allowing the "intelligence" of the network to be placed at the user level—in applications rather than in the network itself—the Internet has enabled individual creativity to emerge and flourish in unprecedented ways. Millions upon millions of decentralized users can interact in an open and stable public space, which itself has the structural capacity to grow and accommodate innovations that were once unimagined, such as the World Wide Web, streaming audio and video, and wireless appliances and applications.

With so much focus on electronic commerce, people often forget that the Internet developed as a government-sponsored project that grew and flourished through its gift-exchange ethos. Much as Silicon Valley may like to claim the Internet as the vision of Bill Gates, Larry Ellison, and other entrepreneurs, the Internet's success has at least as much to do with its structural architecture as a commons and its incubation in the (non-market) social milieu of academia. The commercialization of the Internet since the mid-1990s certainly helped to extend the infrastructure rapidly to millions of new users. But it also set in motion new commercial forces that may also threaten the Internet's vitality. Call it the dark side of the digital revolution: the growing attempts by businesses to enclose the cybercommons by erecting new proprietary barriers of control over information and users.

The next two chapters explore the multiple threats to the Internet as a commons. The first part of this inquiry focuses on the *infrastructure*—the technologies, shared protocols, and governance structures that allow the Internet to function seamlessly as a commons. As this chapter explains, various computer, media, and telecommunications companies—in defense of their parochial business models—very much want to transform the Internet into a more centralized, controlled system for selling access and use of content.

A companion strategy to this enclosure is the attempt to propertize the *information commons*. The information commons, as we will see in Chapter 8, consists of the new spaces for information exchange and cultural expression enabled by Internet technologies. If the Internet infrastructure enables these spaces to exist, various intellectual property laws and computer technologies control how different sorts of digital information can be acquired, shared, and transmitted. Chapter 8 looks at how Big Content—the major book publishers, film studios, record labels, and information vendors—is seeking unprecedented expansions of intellectual property law and erecting new technological "fences." Big Content desperately wants the exchange of "digital artifacts"—text, music, video, data—to be a marketplace, and a marketplace only, and wants to outlaw or discourage the free sharing of digital information through a commons. Over time, this agenda threatens to shut down the cultural commons that has historically fueled our nation's economic progress and sustained our open democratic traditions.[2]

Can the cybercommons be saved? A pivotal question for the future is whether the Internet-as-commons can survive or whether champions of new market regimes will radically transform it. The open architecture and collaborative cultures of the Internet are not sacrosanct, after all. They are highly vulnerable to future shifts in technology design, new market structures, and retrograde public policies. It is too early to guess the fate of the great Internet commons. But the current threats to its integrity do loom large and ominous.

Entrenched commercial interests now have the upper hand in molding the public policies and technologies that shape the Internet as a marketplace and cultural space. But some farsighted leaders of e-commerce also realize that the distributed intelligence made possible by the Internet has distinct advantages. It may prove shrewder over the long run to leverage the power of the commons and the gift economy than to try to force people to abide by highly restrictive regimes of proprietary control. The music industry's reactionary war to impose its stodgy business models and cultural norms on music consumers is a prime example.

It may well be that the Internet commons has more intrinsic resilience and inalienable power than we have imagined. Consider the phenomenal growth of free software and open source software, particularly in the past five years. Who would have guessed that the mainframe-oriented IBM would actually embrace the GNU/Linux operating system as the strategic centerpiece of its battles against Microsoft? Apache, PERL, and other free software and open source applications have become workhorses of the Internet, and hundreds of smart businesses now recognize that an open Internet is what enables them to reap huge gains from flexible, decentralized management practices.

Origins of the Internet Commons

To read *Wired* or techno-utopian George Gilder, one might think that rugged individualists out of an Ayn Rand novel are responsible for the Internet. In fact, the real history of the Internet reaches back to that terribly traditional, often-reviled institution of our collective aspirations: government. While business enterprises have played many important roles in shaping and expanding the Internet, it was government leadership, in an environment insulated from the famous "discipline of the market," that proved essential in imagining and implementing the Internet.

"Virtually all of the critical technologies in the Internet and Web revolution were developed between 1967 and 1993 by government research agencies and/or in universities," writes entrepreneur and policy consultant Charles Ferguson. "During the same period, there arose in parallel a private, free market solution—a $10 billion commercial online services industry.... The commercial industry's technology and structure were inferior to that of the nonprofit Internet in every conceivable way, which is the primary reason that they were so rapidly destroyed by the commercial Internet revolution."[3]

The government agency responsible for incubating the Internet was known as ARPA, the Advanced Research Projects Agency. This small, elite agency within the Department of Defense had a reputation for using broad discretion and a healthy budget to pioneer high-risk innovations in defense technologies. In the 1960s, as Cold War tensions inflamed

Washington policy-makers, ARPA sought to create a communications network that would be flexible and efficient enough to allow thousands of defense researchers and vendors to share information and access to each other's computers. ARPA also wanted a network hardy enough to survive a nuclear attack.

The eventual result, in 1970, was the ARPANET, a communications network that was designed to facilitate resource-sharing among users on a national scale. As historian Janet Abbate writes, project director Lawrence Roberts envisioned ARPANET as "a way to bring researchers together." He stressed early on that "a network would foster the 'community' use of computers," something he called "cooperative programming."[4] The early designers of the ARPANET were, in truth, building a commons: a diverse community dedicated to shared goals and self-governed through a cooperative social ethos and informal decision-making forums. Since a great many of the early ARPANET users were academics, where a gift culture generally prevailed, it was only natural that a similar social ethic would prevail in the new online world.

But what is also significant is that the very technical architecture of the Internet was critical in enabling this gift culture to develop on such a vast scale. The end-to-end architecture of the Internet is designed to be fairly simple, open, and stable at the network level while allowing users the freedom to develop innovative applications to run on top of it. Users remain the driving force in the system even as it scales to a size millions of time larger than its original size. The system allows enormous flexibility and extensibility without altering the basic technical protocols.

Another reason that a commons emerged as the Internet grew is because the core designers and users of the ARPANET were the same people. They were not sellers and buyers negotiating their distinctly different interests through a market transaction. They were co-users and codevelopers carrying on a social conversation. This can be seen in the famous series of documents called Requests for Comments, or RFCs, which were collections of tentative ideas and informal comments posted online by ARPANET users and edited by University of California at Los Angeles (UCLA) graduate student Jon Postel. "RFCs were specifically designed to promote informal communication and the sharing of ideas in the absence of technical certainty or recognized authority," writes Janet Abbate. Eventually, "a consensus would emerge on protocols and procedures, and this consensus was generally accepted by ARPA as official policy for the network."[5]

Robert Kahn, one of the key designers of the Internet's architecture, credits the success of the Internet to this process of participatory democracy in setting standards and developing norms:

The vitality of the current process derives from the broad involvement of the many communities that have a stake in the Internet. Unlike typical top-down standards-setting operations that implement decisions formed by consensus, the Internet process works essentially in reverse through a kind of grassroots mechanism. . . . A key to the success of the Internet is to ensure that the interested parties have a fair and equitable way of participating in its evolution. . . .[6]

The sense of shared purpose and decorum evolved over time into "netiquette," a set of ethical practices that Internet users expected each other to respect. This code of social norms has eroded but not disappeared as the Internet community has expanded beyond academia and become more diverse and commercially oriented.

The gift culture of the ARPANET proved to be a prolific incubator for so many innovations that now lie at the heart of the Internet and computing. One of the most important is the packet switching of data, which allows more efficient and flexible transmission of digital information over networks. Another innovation is an internetworking architecture that allows different computers and types of packet networks to interconnect and communicate more easily with each other. Known as TCP/IP (for the Transmission Control Protocol and Internet Protocol), this set of standards became a central design feature allowing the Internet to evolve flexibly and rapidly. ARPA-funded labs also gave rise to some of the most important computing innovations of the past generation: electronic mail and e-mail lists, word processing programs, the computer mouse, and the Windows computing environment.[7]

These technological innovations were forged through collaboration and the free sharing of new ideas. "When minds interact, new ideas emerge," is how the first director of ARPA's computer office, Joseph Licklider, put it in an influential 1960 paper, "Man-Computer Symbiosis."[8] The ethic that has come to be known as "free software" (free to share, not free in price) was critical in developing a range of vital software programs for the Internet—Sendmail, Apache, PERL, BIND.[9] The stability and technical superiority of these programs is widely attributed to the gift culture *process* that gave rise to them.[10]

The Catalytic Leadership of Government

While many inventors and companies have played critical roles in developing the Internet, the federal government has been the primary visionary and funder. Its leadership was indispensable in the creation of new technology, professional networks, and common technical standards. Massive defense spending in California during and after World War II helped build a large high-tech infrastructure in the Bay Area, especially around Stanford University. Two thirds of all computer-related R&D in the 1950s and over half in the 1960s came from the federal government. It is hard to imagine the emergence of Silicon Valley as we know it today without this government role.

There are reasons why only government could have incubated the Internet and many related computing innovations. Government has the wherewithal and longer-range vision to fund basic R&D, while commercial enterprises, especially in today's economy, are virtually forced by investors to act in more opportunistic, short-term ways, commercializing only what is known or nearly known.

There is another reason why government has been vital. "When you motivate people with money," writes Charles Ferguson, "you shouldn't be surprised if they behave selfishly. . . . But if people are doing something for intellectual greatness, for their principles or for posterity, they think differently. You wouldn't want most computer science professors running your company, but you wouldn't want the average high-technology executive deciding how the world should be wired, either."[11]

Looking back on the past thirty years, Ferguson writes, "Every brilliant, important, technically farsighted Internet development came either from government agencies or universities. In the meantime, decision making in the competitive marketplace was narrow, shortsighted, self-protective and technically far inferior to its Internet equivalents."[12] Visionaries such as Vincent Cerf, Robert Kahn, Lawrence Roberts, Jon Postel, Bill Joy, Tim Berners-Lee, Mark Andreesen, and Linus Torvalds, and other computing pioneers emerged out of work cultures that did not revolve around short-term market results.

While much is made in popular mythology about computer geniuses tinkering in their garages and going on to create giant corporations, less is made of the indispensable role of public investment in enabling this process. By insulating so many projects from market pressures and nurturing them in a broader matrix of resources and human aspiration, ARPA helped give birth to important new "spaces" for new kinds of technology, scientific inquiry, and social interaction.

Government intervention has had at least three types of catalytic impact: the sponsoring of basic R&D has led to innovative new principles in computing science; the establishment of common, open technical standards has fostered competitiveness, innovation, and consumer choice; and FCC regulatory policies have ensured network openness and interconnection. Each of these have been critical to developing the Internet commons.

Government Research as a Market Creator

In the late 1970s ARPA funded University of California at Berkeley researchers, led by Bill Joy, to write a new and improved version of UNIX, a versatile operating system popular among ARPANET programmers. The new "Berkeley distribution" of UNIX became a widely used open standard, especially within universities. A year later, when Stanford graduate Scott McNealy, Bill Joy, and others founded Sun to make high-performance computing workstations, they chose Berkeley UNIX as the operating system because it catered to the large, ARPA-seeded community of university users who were thrilled to buy a better Internet-friendly version of UNIX. And so a new market grew. Sun's franchise was bolstered in 1986 when the federal government declared that no company could bid for government computer contracts unless it offered UNIX as an option, which helped consolidate the market behind Sun's and AT&T's versions of UNIX.[13]

Cisco Systems, too, was born through a synergistic involvement with defense procurement. At a time when computer networking at universities was burgeoning, two Stanford academics, Leonard Borsach and Sandy Lerner, devised a router, a new hardware and software system that could cheaply transmit data packets from one computer to another. "What really made their business possible," writes Internet historian Nathan Newman:

> was the ARPANET, which allowed them to cheaply let other Net engineers know about their new product.... Technically in violation of ARPANET guidelines prohibiting commerce on the Net, Cisco was the first major company to build a market from scratch based on direct Internet marketing. Of course, it helped that Lerner and Borsach came out of the same milieu of the Internet as the university engineers doing the buying, and that the National Science Foundation and other federal agencies were supplying much of the cash during this rapid expansion of the Internet at universities.[14]

Cisco has since gone on to be valued at more than $128 billion (2001).

Open Standards as the Base for an Internet Commons

Technological standards are typically designed by companies to advance their strategic competitive interests. That is one reason why IBM so dominated computing in the 1960s and 1970s; its technical protocols were pervasive and proprietary. Other computer companies—Xerox, Digital

Equipment, Burroughs, Honeywell, and others—sought to promote their own standards to compete in the market, with varying degrees of success. As this suggests, technical standards are a form of politics and power. That is why they are generally designed to advance a company's market interests and not necessarily the public interest.

What made the advent of the Internet so significant was that it established a common base of technical protocols that belonged to everyone, as a commons. This prevented any single company or industry from "owning" the Internet or any of its key components. Equally important, the technical standards of the Internet did not vest the most power with either computer companies or telephone carriers, who were the chief disputants over technical standards, but with the end users themselves.

This was a radical innovation. It was not selfless; ARPA had its own military reasons for wanting Internet protocols to accommodate a diversity of computer networks, and for eschewing the design features preferred by carriers (such as embedding control of network operations *within* the system rather than at its periphery, with users). But ARPA's design standards had the result of creating a "constitutional architecture" for the Internet that would allow maximum adaptability, openness about standards and innovation, decentralized authority, and user participation: key ingredients for a functioning commons in any context.

Much of the credit must go to ARPA for hosting spirited debates about the Internet's architecture and especially the formulation of the TCP/IP networking protocols. "Perhaps the key to the Internet's later commercial success," writes Janet Abbate, "was that the project internalized the competitive forces of the market by bringing representatives of diverse interest groups together and allowing them to argue through design issues. Ironically, this unconventional approach produced a system that proved to have more appeal for potential 'customers'—people building networks—than did the overtly commercial alternatives that appeared soon after."[15]

Regulatory Policies to Insure an Open Commons

Ask any technolibertarian what's the best way is to assure the vitality of the Internet, and the common refrain is: keep government's hands off! But in truth, the only reason that the Internet commons developed was because government actively intervened with regulatory policies to assure openness, competition, and user choice. For more than twenty years, the Federal Communications Commission (FCC) has adopted a variety of policies designed to prevent telephone carriers from abusing their monopoly power in limiting access to their networks, charging excessive prices, or erecting barriers to interoperability among networks. "America's stunning success in promoting the Internet revolution," argue François Bar and colleagues, "owes a major debt to determined regulatory action that encouraged all aspects of network openness and interconnection."[16]

While telephone carriers would have preferred to charge distance-related fees for data transmission, the FCC's flat-fee policies allowed a new competitive market for open access to emerge via hundreds of local Internet Service Providers. Free to develop without the constraints of a metered usage system, the Internet's structure allowed users readily to assert their own needs and offer up their own innovations. Access to the network could not be prevented by monopolistic carriers; open, non-discriminatory access was mandated so dominant firms could not use their market power or technical standards to exclude new entrants to the market. Instead of an entrenched array of sellers offering services that suited their competitive purposes—the 500-channel TV environment envisioned by telephone companies and cable operators—a user-driven, bottom-up process of continuous innovation was made possible.

The open infrastructure policies mandated by the FCC meant that "the principal source of new ideas driving economic growth emerged from a long-term process of experimentation and learning, as business and consumer users iteratively adopted and shaped applications of information technology and e-commerce," write Bar and colleagues:

> Such user-centered innovation processes flourish when users are granted access to a wide range of facilities, services and network elements.... Diversity of experimentation and competition on an increasingly open network were key, since nobody could foresee what would eventually emerge as successful applications. Openness allowed many paths to be explored, not only those which phone companies, the infrastructure's monopoly owners, would have favored.[17]

As the foregoing suggests, creating a robust commons may require the same kind of infrastructure support as any market regime. In the case of the Internet, one of the most vibrant commons in history, one cannot discount the important role played by government-sponsored research, open technical standards, and pro-user regulatory policies.

Market Enclosures of the Internet

If there are many ways to enclose a commons, as previous chapters have shown, there are many more ways to enclose a virtual commons. As the public value of computer networking has grown, driven by the dynamics of "the more, the merrier" described in Chapter 2, it has become irresistible for commercial enterprises to try to claim some portion of the Internet commons as a proprietary franchise. The potential payoffs are just too juicy.

This section examines three major strategies through which the Internet commons is being enclosed or eroded piecemeal. These include: (1) the use of proprietary technical standards to sabotage common open standards, innovation, and the open sharing of information; (2) the use of concentrated market power to limit access to the Internet and corral users within proprietary "walled gardens"; and (3) the privatization of Internet governance to the detriment of ordinary users. A fourth enclosure of the Internet commons—the expansion of intellectual property rights at the expense of user freedoms, openness, and free speech—is examined in Chapter 8.

Using Proprietary Standards to Erode the Internet Commons

As mentioned earlier, one of the primary reasons for the Internet's robustness is its open architecture and standards. While stable and extensible, the system does not strictly regulate the behavior of its users. Indeed, users are affirmatively empowered by the system's architecture. They can share information in easy, fluid, virtually free ways with few external controls or gatekeepers.

There is nothing intrinsic to computer networking that requires it to function as a commons. The Internet's architecture is the result of deliberate ARPANET choices that are now embedded in the very design of networking hardware and software. The Internet could just as easily be designed to regulate and control individual behavior. It could be designed to facilitate the interception of e-mail or the monitoring of suspect citizens. It could be structured to allow anonymity or to require online identification. It could be structured to restrict access in selective ways (such as banning Nazi-related Web sites, as the French have done) or to entice users to stay within proprietary spaces (as Microsoft and AOL are seeking to do).

Stanford professor Lawrence Lessig has eloquently argued that the design and ownership of the Internet's architecture is a key factor in determining how control will be exercised over people and the flow of information.[18] That is why we should be concerned about preserving open standards on the Internet. They are an affirmative means by which ordinary people can assert their civic, cultural, and economic interests over and against those of government and business, which have their own distinct interests in how the Internet architecture should be designed.

Open standards for Internet software are useful, for example, in preventing any single company from seizing private control of the technology and designing it to restrict competition, thwart innovation, or censor speech. Intel designed its Pentium III computer chips with unique identification numbers that could be used by governments, retailers, and marketers to track the online computer habits of individuals. (The feature was later disabled after vigorous public protests.) Microsoft's proprietary control over the Windows operating system and its Office suite of programs has allowed it nearly to eliminate competing word-processing software.

Just as common open standards provide an unparalleled platform for competitive innovation—the story of the Internet—so they help generate greater surplus wealth for everyone to share within the commons. As we saw in Chapter 2, this is one of the basic principles of network economics: the more the participants in certain kinds of commons, the greater the value created.[19] To businesses competing in the marketplace, it is irresistible to try to privatize this surplus value, if a suitable means can be found.

It turns out that one of the most effective tools for doing this is for a company to substitute its own proprietary technical standards for open standards, if it can. This enables a company to export surplus value from the commons (e.g., a useful online product or an aggregated base of consumers) and divert it to company shareholders.

One of the earliest instances of this behavior was the Netscape Navigator browser, which had its origins at the National Center for Supercomputing Applications (NCSA) at the University of Illinois at Champaign-Urbana. For years the center had been pioneering software for high-performance information-sharing and collaboration. One of its innovations, Telnet, became a popular tool for PCs and Macintoshes, enabling users to connect to remote computers via the Internet. Another university computer center in Illinois developed the Eudora client for electronic mail, an innovation that greatly boosted e-mail usage. Then, in 1993, a forty-person team of programmers at the NCSA produced the popular Mosaic browser, whose graphical user interface made it much easier to navigate the recently created World Wide Web.

Despite this huge advance, Tim Berners-Lee, the inventor of the Web, recalled becoming "uneasy about the decidedly peremptory undertones behind the NCSA's promotion of Mosaic."[20] He worried that Mosaic might undermine the standardized HyperText Markup Language (HTML) protocols that were the basis for the Web and just beginning to catch on. Berners-Lee also worried about the fragility of the consensus-driven standard-setting process of the Internet Engineering Task Force, an open international forum for setting technical specifications in computing.[21]

By the mid-1990s, entrepreneurs were beginning to see rich profits in carving up the commons. As Nathan Newman tells the story, "Silicon Graphics CEO Jim Clark, a veteran of the workstation standards war, understood how much money could be won if a company could take control of the standards of this new Internet tool. So Clark left his company and set out to destroy Mosaic and replicate its government-backed standards."[22] He hired Mark Andreesen, a Mosaic team member, and five other programmers to become the nucleus of a new company, Mosaic Communications, that would develop a new version of Mosaic with faster graphics and a user-friendly interface. The new browser would also be deliberately incompatible with the original Mosaic, thus marginalizing the NCSA browser and subverting open standards. Ingeniously, the company gave away its new browser for free, helping to establish it as the industry standard, while earning money by charging for proprietary server software. The novel business plan and the product itself were so successful that Netscape Communications was soon worth $9 billion.

One happy result of the Netscape Navigator was to expand use of the Web dramatically and trigger a new era of Internet entrepreneurialism—significant achievements. But the Netscape browser also set a very bad precedent—that a company could, without penalty, take an open standard private and reap phenomenal profits. Netscape's bid to become a monopoly in the browser space by freely appropriating government-developed software did not result in any intellectual property lawsuits (Netscape claimed its new browser was significantly different). Perhaps cowed by the antigovernment rhetoric of Newt Gingrich's "Contract for America," the federal government did not condemn the privatization of its browser software or the damage to open standards. Nor did it alter its procurement practices to penalize products that jeopardized open standards.

In the end, Jim Clark agreed to NCSA's demand that he change the name of his company from Mosaic Communications to Netscape and pay $2.3 million to the University of Illinois.[23] Now that browser standards were to be a proprietary matter, Microsoft waded into the game with its Internet Explorer, which it integrated into Windows. By 2000, Microsoft controlled 85 percent of the market for browsers on personal computers.

The Netscape experience and the prospective splintering or monopolization of common software standards convinced Berners-Lee to form a new organization, the World Wide Web Consortium, to develop consensus technical standards that might preserve the commons. Without such a body, he realized, privatization and fragmentation of standards "would defeat the very purpose of the Web: to be a single, universal, accessible hypertext medium for sharing information."[24] The Web had become the fastest-growing communications medium in history precisely because it was based on common standards available to all for free, and not on closed, proprietary standards.[25] Berners-Lee's fears were well founded. Gopher, a popular early program for sharing plaintext documents, receded from view after the developer of Gopher, the University of Minnesota, tried to charge companies an annual fee for using Gopher server software. Commercial developers quickly abandoned it for fear of running afoul of patent or licensing provisions.

Netscape's commandeering of the Mosaic browser, of course, is small potatoes compared to the cunning strategies by which Microsoft has stifled competition and subverted open standards. One aspect of this behavior, documented by the Justice Department's antitrust lawsuit against Microsoft, was the company's notorious "embrace, extend, and extinguish" strategy of *embracing* a target software by integrating it into its Windows operating system; *extending* its functions with proprietary modifications; and then *extinguishing* the competition as consumers turned away from applications that were suddenly incompatible with Windows. According to Judge Penfield Jackson, Microsoft deliberately leveraged its monopoly control over the desktop operating system, Windows, used in 90 percent of all personal computers.

Using this embrace-extend-extinguish strategy, Microsoft has undermined open standard protocols for HTML (for Web pages), Java (the cross-platform software), RealAudio (the Internet audio software), and QuickTime (multimedia software) by trying to make its own proprietary modifications the *de facto* standards. It seems to be using similar tactics in its new Internet initiative known as .Net, which critics argue will prevent software programmers from writing programs independently of Microsoft.[26] Other critics fear that the new Windows XP program represents a brazen attempt to leverage Microsoft's virtual monopolies in operating systems and browsers into dominance of electronic commerce and online subscription services. The company's bold strategy to capture the Internet can be seen in its initial use of so-called Smart Tags, which would have allowed Microsoft to insert unauthorized links on other people's Web sites as a way to channel traffic to Microsoft-friendly sites.[27]

Scott McNealy offered a wry comment on Microsoft's crafty use of its Windows monopoly: "The only thing I'd rather own than Windows is English or Chinese or Spanish because then I could charge you a $249 right to speak English and I could charge you an upgrade fee when I add new letters like 'n' or 't'."[28]

An infamous set of leaked Microsoft documents, the "Halloween memos," advised the company to "de-commoditize protocols and applications" by "extending these protocols and developing new protocols."[29] This would undermine the core advantages of open source software—its ability to integrate diverse hardware and software through common commodity protocols. This is why Microsoft finds open-source-code software in general and the Linux operating system in particular so alarming. They threaten to subvert Microsoft's proprietary integration of systems—and thence its monopoly rents. This is one reason why Microsoft quietly changed its protocols to render Samba, an excellent open-source-code communications software, incompatible with Microsoft's NT and Windows 95/98 software. This also explains why Microsoft is hostile to the Internet Engineering Task Force, which has historically resisted the special pleadings of any single vendor in adopting technical standards for the Internet.

There is a richly paradoxical end point to any company's lust to impose its own proprietary standards. When everyone pursues this goal, it can end up creating a dysfunctional market or, in Michael Heller's words, "a tragedy of the anti-commons."[30] When *too much* of the raw input for an industry becomes propertized, innovation and growth are impeded. Now that patent claims in the semiconductor industry have become so profuse and complex, the industry finds it increasingly difficult to design new products without paying expensive cross-licensing fees (substituting expensive legal oversight for engineering innovation). A solution reportedly being explored by industry leaders is a patent pool—a commons—which would allow participants to share patent rights and so enable innovation to proceed more readily.[31]

One wonders whether a commons will also have to be invented for the wireless telephony industry. Its attempts to forge a common set of protocols—a prerequisite for more robust growth—always seem to fall apart because someone in the back of the negotiating room stands up to say, "But I hold the patent on that technology, so each of you is going to have to pay me x million dollars."

So it is that an enclosure of the commons can reach such extremes that it engenders a sterile, terminal *involution* of creativity.

The Use of Market Power to Enclose the Commons

When the giant media corporations enclose the information commons, one inevitable result is a loss of diversity. Media concentration tends to constrict *the range* of expression that is available to the public. Professor Yochai Benkler, a brilliant legal scholar of the information commons, explains that enclosure raises the cost of an essential input—information—and thereby makes information production more expensive to everyone else. The barriers to entry are raised.

In particular, writes Benkler:

enclosure is likely to have the most adverse effects on amateur and other noncommercial production. These strategies are the source of the greatest potential diversity because, unlike market-oriented strategies, they are undisciplined by the need to aggregate tastes. As among commercial information producers, enclosure tends to benefit organizations with large owned-information inventories ... and will lead to consolidation among organizations devoted to commercial information production.[32]

The truth of Benkler's analysis is vividly illustrated by the number of major media mergers that have occurred in recent years.[33] It is also seen in the decline of smaller, independent media venues and the rise of ratings-driven tabloid journalism in mainstream media venues. The over-propertization of information tends to reduce its diversity and foster greater concentration among information producers. This, in turn, gives the surviving media giants even greater market power and political clout.

The merger of AOL and Time Warner is a case in point. In the years ahead, the breadth of free expression available online—its diversity, liveliness, noncommercial content—is likely to shrink as a result of this merger. This is partly because the new company will try to make its content production more cost-efficient and reap new cross-promotional synergies. But it will also stem from the company's likely attempts to discriminate against competing Internet Service Providers seeking access to its network. It will also try to keep its subscribers within its "walled garden"—its proprietary online mall of services—rather than encourage them to venture out onto the open Internet.[34]

Historically, federal telecommunications law has required that the owners of the communications "conduits" be different from the owners of "content." The goal has been to prevent conduit owners from thwarting competition, charging discriminatory prices, or suppressing undesired speech. But this long-standing principle may change if the new media giants succeed in controlling high-speed Internet access and interactive TV. They could establish themselves as a small clique of gatekeepers that can decide what content will and will not be available to Americans. That is essentially what the May 2000 squabble between Time Warner and ABC was all about (which led to Time Warner's blackout of ABC), and why rigorous enforcement of an "open access" rule for cable broadband systems is needed.

Further industry consolidation could profoundly change the character of the Internet by sanctioning a new, discriminatory architecture.[35] Cable broadband companies will have strong incentives to offer different tiers of data transmission speeds, quality of service, and content packages. They may well use the latest router systems to identify all sorts of things about the "network traffic"—the types of software applications being used, specific brands, types of interfaces, and even individual users and site addresses—in order to enhance their competitive advantages.[36] "With a plethora of new tools and mechanisms to identify, control and discriminate the levels of quality for Internet content," writes James Love, a Nader-associated consumer advocate, "cable companies can do to Internet data traffic what they have done for years to video content—pick winners and losers, charge different content providers for different rates for access and exclude rivals."[37]

It is instructive to see how the existing architecture of AOL's "walled garden" has already eroded some basic principles of the Internet commons. AOL's system allows it to monitor users' every move and intervene to prevent a wide range of unacceptable online behaviors. Significantly, AOL also offers no "public space" where a subscriber can address all members of AOL (online "crowds" are limited to no more than 23 people). Since AOL subscribers represent 43 percent of domestic Internet users, the potential for a private company to redefine free speech and the character of public spaces is significant.[38] It resembles a company supplanting Main Street (open to all; mixed civic and commercial uses; free speech rights) with a shopping mall (strictly private and commercial with highly limited free speech guarantees).

The threat of enclosure facing the Internet was aptly put by a *Business Week* profile of high-tech companies seeking to gain control over critical components of the Internet: "Whose Net Is It, Anyway?"[39] Consumers and regulators are not just worried about open access to cable Internet services. They fear that corporate oligopolies will control Internet backbone services (and thereby exclude rivals who link to smaller networks) and dominate e-commerce business exchanges (such as a travel site owned by five major airlines that could refuse to share its fare data). The largest media companies could dominate wireless Internet services (by offering only bundled services rather than *à la carte* options) and use instant messaging system to fend off competition (by refusing to interconnect with rival messaging systems).

The consolidation of online media companies can be seen in how Internet users now spend their time. According to Jupiter Media Metrix in June 2001, the number of companies controlling 60 percent of all U.S. users' minutes online declined from 110 in March 1999 to only fourteen two years later—an 87 percent decrease. The number of companies controlling *half* of users' online minutes shrank from eleven to four during the same period.[40]

The Privatization of Internet Governance

Finally, the Internet commons is also threatened by a new regime of governance that aspires to privatize control over domain names. Although ostensibly a technical matter, control of domain names is a highly political issue that affects free expression, privacy, and national sovereignty.

For example, should companies be allowed to use trademark laws to shut down Web sites that criticize them? (Dozens of sites use "sucks" in their domain name, as in walmartsucks.com.) Should commercial enterprises have first claim to own domain names with common words or place names, as opposed to ordinary people? (A corporate consortium tried shut down a nonprofit site called "canada2.com"; the singer Madonna succeeded in shutting down a site using the name "madonna"; and an online retailer, Etoy.com, tried to shut down an online artists' forum, eToy.org.)[41] Should European nations be allowed to ban domain names with the word "nazi" in them, or should American free-speech norms prevail internationally? The answers to such questions are not self-evident but political by definition.

Yet in 1993, just as the Internet was beginning to experience significant growth, the U.S. government ceded this important authority. Through the National Science Foundation (NSF), which was then administering the Internet, the American people lost control of one of the most important equity assets of the Internet, the right to manage most domain name registrations. NSF relinquished this right, without even a competitive bidding process, by contracting it out to a private company, Network Solutions Inc. (NSI), which was given exclusive control over sales of domain names to the public.

It should not be surprising that NSI used its monopoly control to charge exorbitant registration fees for the .com suffix and other valuable domain names. Bought a few years later for $3.9 million by a company called SAIC, NSI's market capitalization later soared to $2.5 billion as Internet usage took off. Not only did the company reap a huge windfall from its control of a public asset, it used its monopoly power to lobby Congress and the executive branch to prevent the creation of any competing domain-name registration rivals. In the classic dynamics of enclosure, NSI also commodified the resource it had captured—millions of Web names and related data—by selling it to marketers, resulting in new privacy invasions and advertising intrusions.[42]

Today, selling Web domain names represents a revenue stream of up to $875 million a year, based on the 25 million addresses currently registered at a standard rental price of $35 per year.

Beyond this financial giveaway, however, is a larger issue of legitimacy and due process in governing the Internet commons. The Internet is a powerful communications platform created by the U.S. government, and as such there are some serious First Amendment and democratic implications to how Internet speech ought to be governed. In 1998, however, the government washed its hands of this issue by instigating the creation of a new private-sector, not-for-profit corporation to administer the Internet name and number system. The new organization, ICANN, for the Internet Corporation for Assigned Names and Numbers, was charged with managing the domain name system and encouraging competition in domain name registration.

The creation of this hybrid policymaking body, officially a nonprofit chartered in the State of California, was an attempt to develop a new private, flexible, bottom-up governance system. Unfortunately, ICANN's very constitutional design is seriously flawed and is likely to hasten the commercial enclosure of the Internet. First, the Commerce Department, which is responsible for the creation of ICANN, did not stipulate substantive limits to ICANN's authority. It is therefore unclear whether the organization can legitimately adopt policies that, while officially related to domain names alone, also affect privacy, free speech, and consumer rights in significant ways.

The vague delegation of authority to ICANN is especially worrisome because the group's private policy-making is not legally subject to the customary procedural protections of government policy-making. Unlike a federal agency, ICANN does not have to host open meetings, provide public access to documents, prohibit conflicts of interest, or insure fair administrative procedures. The rigorous legal protections that assure moral legitimacy and democratic accountability in government do not necessarily apply to ICANN. While ICANN has agreed, for political reasons, to have generally open meetings and public access to records, these customs are revocable, not mandatory. And ICANN's policy-making is not subject to traditional judicial remedies and accountability that govern federal agencies.

The dangers of ICANN's mutant legal charter was made clear when the organization chose to restate trademark law principles in a way that allows trademark owners to silence their critics. If a URL were seen as tarnishing the reputation of a trademark—particularly the "sucks.com" Web sites—ICANN would allow the trademark owner to force the deregistration of the offending domain name. This represents a reversal of existing law, in which First Amendment principles prevail over trademark law. But since ICANN is a "private" body and not a government agency, the First Amendment is not seen as controlling. Free speech in the most basic sense is diminished.

For an organization that elects fewer than half its board members from the general public and that will likely never have any meaningful consumer representation, such powers raise serious questions of legitimacy. With no clear legal limits to its authority, dubious democratic safeguards, and a board skewed to represent e-commerce interests, ICANN is a perfect governance vehicle for transforming the Internet commons into a privatized commercial infrastructure.

Some critics have properly raised questions about the constitutionality of ICANN's policy authority.[43] The Property Clause of the U.S. Constitution requires that Congress, and only Congress, can permit the sale or disposition of property belonging to the United States. And since the domain name addresses, root server, and other technical protocols that control the Internet were created by the U.S. government, and were once its property in a strict legal sense, a reasonable person could question the constitutionality of the Commerce Department's right to give away this property. (Use of these communications protocols by a global constituency does not alter this fact.)

ICANN's authority may be also be questioned as an unconstitutional delegation of congressional authority.[44] The Supreme Court has ruled that Congress may not delegate its power to make laws to private parties nor make overly broad delegations of authority to governmental bodies. But here we have a nonprofit organization registered by the State of California presuming to govern some of the core processes of the Internet.

Conclusion

It is not the premise of this chapter that commercialization of the Internet is harmful. Quite the contrary. The emergence of thousands of profit-making Internet companies has had incalculable value for the American economy, scientific inquiry, social connection, and cultural creativity. But the renaissance of innovation wrought by the Internet is not simply due to "market forces." The Internet revolution owes a primary debt to the open, end-to-end architecture of public communications, and there is no reason that commercial progress in cyberspace requires abandoning this architecture. In fact, any enclosures of the Internet commons are more likely to privilege existing companies and discourage innovation and competition by newcomers.

We have seen how the Internet infrastructure is seriously threatened with enclosure by the subversion of open standards, growing market concentration, and the privatization of Internet governance. But there is an equal threat looming: the blind expansion of property rights in digital information. As we see in Chapter 8, the *information commons* turns out to be a supremely important force in economic progress, technological innovation, and democratic culture. That is not stopping the Disneys, AOL Time Warners, and Random Houses of the world from trying to create a new pay-per-use vending machine that seeks to propertize virtually every vowel and grace note of our common culture.

8.

The Privatization
of Public Knowledge

One member of a self-appointed committee of copyright lawyers has boasted that they have developed restrictions on every means of transmission of thought except smell, taste and extrasensory perception.

—Charles F. Gosnell[1]

It is one of the egregious misconceptions of our time that the public domain amounts to little more than an intellectual junkyard, a place where out-of-print books and antiquarian art languish like so many rusty cars picked over by scavengers. The *real* locus of value, according to the mandarins of the market, lies in that art and knowledge that has been properly recognized as "intellectual property."

In fact, the public domain consists of a great, invaluable bounty of knowledge, art, and culture. Its value lies in the paradoxical fact that it is openly accessible to all. It is priceless, indeed, because the shared heritage that constitutes the public domain is indispensable to creativity. Without the ability to draw upon certain prior knowledge and art—to quote past creativity, to modify it as one wishes, to express it in new ways to new audiences—future innovation is doomed.[2]

Yet copyright law and patent law have never given full recognition to the scope and importance of the public domain. They have always taken for granted the commons of knowledge and culture, presuming it to be a vast, self-replenishing resource as unlimited as the Western frontiers once were. Thomas Jefferson expressed this faith when he said: "If nature has made any one thing less susceptible than all others of exclusive property, it is the action of the thinking power called an idea, which an individual may exclusively possess as long as he keeps it to himself; but the moment it is divulged, it forces itself into the possession of everyone, and the receiver cannot dispossess himself of it."[3] Justice Louis Brandeis expressed a similar belief in 1918 when he wrote that "the general rule of law" is that once information is communicated to others, it becomes "free as the air to common use."[4]

Clearly neither Jefferson nor Brandeis anticipated the power of electronic technologies or the cunning imaginations of the content industries and copyright bar. Increasingly, creative expression, knowledge, and art are not "free as the air" for all to enjoy, but tightly controlled units of "intellectual property" measured out in precise dollops based on one's ability to pay. Market forces and technology are rapidly converting great expanses of open public knowledge into closed private enclosures. And if, in the future, the senses of smell, taste, and extrasensory perception can be given suitable legal definition and hooked up to a meter, they too are likely to become lucrative new genres of intellectual property.

Reneging on the "Cultural Bargain" of Copyright Law

At the first Hackers' Conference, in 1984, Stewart Brand put his finger on a central paradox about digital information that is causing us so much trouble today. "On the one hand," Brand said, "information wants to be expensive, because it's so valuable. The right information in the right place just changes your life. On the other hand, information wants to be free, because the cost of getting it out is getting lower and lower all the time. So you have these two fighting against each other."[5]

The phenomenal growth of the Internet has greatly intensified the force of this paradox. Copyright owners want strictly to control their creative and informational works—in all markets, on all media platforms, and even in how people can use copyrighted products. This is propelling an unprecedented expansion in the scope and duration of intellectual property protection, as well as more intrusive kinds of enforcement and new technologies of control.

Enterprises ranging from Microsoft to the Scientologists to the *Washington Post* are trying to use copyright law to thwart criticism, parody, and other fair uses of creative work on the Internet. Content owners are inventing alarming new kinds of technological surveillance of people's Web-surfing and reading habits, and seeking to make Internet Service Providers act as copyright police. Film studios are trying to shut down Web sites that openly talk about DVD encryption technologies. Companies are trying to use trademark law to shut down critics who might use their name in any fashion. Publishers are seeking to supplant traditionally free kinds of access to information, such as library borrowing and "fair use" excerpting, with pay-per-use regimes. There are even attempts to get libraries to pay licensing fees for using the Dewey Decimal Classification System.[6]

What these various skirmishes add up to is an attempt to overturn the "cultural bargain" that lies at the heart of copyright and patent law. As mandated by the U.S. Constitution, copyright is a *limited* right granted by Congress to authors and inventors. Even though copyright is a grant of monopoly rights, it has been limited by a fixed term (originally 28 years, now extended to a lifetime plus 70 years) and by fair use rights (consisting chiefly of the right to quote and reproduce protected works for criticism, news reporting, teaching, scholarship, and research), among other limitations.

The property rights granted to authors, in other words, are balanced by the right of public access to the work and its preservation in the public domain once the copyright term expires. Copyright's primary purpose is to serve the public—in the words of Congress, "to facilitate the flow of ideas in the interest of learning." The primary objective of our copyright laws is not to reward the author, Congress has declared, "but rather *to secure for the public* the benefits from the creations of authors" (italics added).[7] Copyright protection is granted to authors chiefly to fulfill that purpose.[8]

Increasingly, however, industries have arrogated to themselves the moral and legal rights that we associate with individual authors. Through the "work for hire" doctrine, for example, media companies have claimed the prerogatives of authorship while, as large corporations, also using copyright law as an instrument of monopoly and censorship. Their essential strategy is to claim copyright as a plenary right without limits and thereby suspend the terms of the cultural bargain that copyright law embodies. By equating intangible copyrighted works with physical property, copyright industries incorrectly portray copyright as an *unlimited permanent right* to control all access to, distribution, and use of a copyrighted work.

The false presumption is: "It's *my* property." On that basis, publishers argue that libraries are the nation's leading pirates of "private property" and suggest that the public domain and fair use are inconsequential.[9]

Through such willful contortions, a system of law originally designed to bring new works to the public by rewarding authors is being morphed into a market protectionist system. Instead of preserving an open public space accessible to all and influenced by democratic processes and social norms, recent copyright initiatives, if fully implemented, will transform the Internet into a gigantic pay-per-use vending machine. Owners of intellectual property want their Barbie dolls, cartoon characters, corporate logos, and software programs to be *ubiquitous* in the culture, but never to be *freely usable* by the culture. They want to sanction only a controlled, consuming relationship with the products introduced into commerce, not an open, interactive one of the sort we associate with a democratic culture.

Using Intellectual Property Law to Enclose the Public Domain

Because it has been regarded as residual and not something with its own affirmative value, the public domain has always been something of "a dark star in the constellation of intellectual property," writes law professor David Lange in a landmark essay on the topic.[10] The public domain has also been neglected, he argues, because copyright law holds great esteem for individual "originality" as the basis for granting property rights in intangible creative works. Meanwhile, it virtually ignores the vast universe of "background material" in a community or culture—the commons—that is needed to develop any new creative work.

Copyright law assumes, for example, that such "originals" as Groucho Marx emerged full-grown out of thin air, when it was an open secret in vaudeville that everyone stole material from everyone else and built upon on other people's routines while developing their own *schtick*.[11] In vaudeville as in so many other arenas, creativity was the product not just of individual genius but of a *community* of people working in a shared tradition. In our time, Jerry Seinfeld performed in the same clubs as Richard Pryor, who was admired by Roseanne Barr, who was inspired by Norman Lear, who once worked for Danny Thomas, who worked in the same venues as Danny Kaye ... and so on.

The same dynamic drives creativity in any field. New works do not simply arise fully realized and wholly original from a single author, as copyright law implicitly holds. Creativity has its wellsprings, as well, in the sharing that takes place in a cultural commons.

Historically, copyright law has evaded this truth by asserting that while no one can own an *idea*, a person can own a particular *expression* of an idea. Alas, the practical meaning of the idea/expression dichotomy has proven maddeningly elusive. It is not so easy to tell when ideas that belong to everyone suddenly reach a threshold of individual originality and thus exclusive ownership.

A more astute analysis of the problem comes from law professor James Boyle, who contends that the idea/expression dichotomy amounts to:

> a moral and philosophical justification for fencing in the commons. [It gives] the author property in something built from the resources of the public domain—language, culture, genre, scientific community, or what have you. If one makes originality of spirit the assumed feature of authorship and the touchstone for property rights, one can see the author as creating something entirely *new*—not recombining the resources of the commons.[12]

So it is today, as a powerful array of copyright industries—books, news media, music, film, information—treat their own "original works" as fully deserving of property rights while the public domain is regarded as a limitless resource that will somehow take care of itself. This is a fundamental philosophical error in copyright law. It is one reason why the public domain is under siege as never before. In 1981, Professor Lange wrote that the growth of copyright law at the expense of the public domain had become "uncontrolled to the point of recklessness." In the two decades since then, copyright imperialism has blossomed into brazen rapaciousness. In one venue after another, copyright industries are using intellectual property laws to propertize information that was previously available to everyone in the "information commons."

Impoverishing the Public Domain

Future creativity and the public's end of the copyright bargain were dealt a severe blow in 1998 when Congress enacted the Sonny Bono Copyright Term Extension Act. The law extended by twenty years the legal protection of cultural works copyrighted after 1923. Tens of thousands of works, such as *The Great Gatsby*, the film *The Jazz Singer*, the musical *Show Boat*, and works by Robert Frost and Sherwood Anderson, will not enter the public domain until 2019.[13] Significantly, the character Mickey Mouse was due to enter the public domain in 2003, a prospect that gave the Walt Disney Company a good reason to agitate for the new law. (It is a rich irony, of course, that a company built on appropriating stories from the public domain—Snow White, Pinocchio, Br'er Rabbit, and so on—should protest so strenuously about surrendering its own copyrighted works to the public domain after 75 years of monopoly protection.)

The Sonny Bono Act is a clear case of corporate welfare for major corporations and a sheer windfall for authors' estates. After all, the constitutional rationale for copyright is to encourage authors to create new works. A retroactive benefit to dead authors (most of whose rights were acquired years ago by media corporations) cannot possibly help achieve that goal. The Supreme Court has consistently held that copyright's primary purpose is to enhance the public domain, which is precisely the opposite result achieved by the Bono Act. The net effect of the law is to delay thousands of works from entering the public domain and to force consumers to pay hundreds of millions of dollars more for access and use of creative works and characters that rightfully belong to them.

The law also amounts to a tax on the freedom of speech of authors who want to use the public domain to create new works. One such author is

Alice Randall, whose novel *The Wind Done Gone* sought to comment about plantation life in the South from a slave's perspective. Randall used characters and plotlines from the Margaret Mitchell novel, *Gone With the Wind*, a book whose copyright would have expired but for the Sonny Bono Act. But since the copyright term had been extended, Mitchell's estate claimed that Randall's book violated its copyright, and sought an injunction in federal court to prevent its publication.[14] The case became a *cause célèbre* because it pitted the public's obvious interest in commentary and parody, revolving around a much-loved cultural story, against the rights of copyright holders to control public uses of works and strike lucrative licensing deals in other media.

The extension of copyright term also eradicated the creative rights of Eric Eldred, a hobbyist who had launched a Web site of public domain literature, including many out-of-print books.[15] Eldred's Web site was getting 20,000 hits a day, and the National Endowment for the Humanities recognized it as one of the twenty best humanities sites on the Web. But the Bono Act forced Eldred to remove a number of works from his site. With the help of Professor Lawrence Lessig and the Berkman Center for Internet and Society, Eldred has launched a constitutional challenge, *Eldred v. Reno*, which is now wending its way through the federal courts.[16]

Using Technolocks to Control Information and People

One of the most aggressive attempts to expand property rights over information is the Digital Millennium Copyright Act, or DMCA, enacted by Congress in 1998. This law goes well beyond traditional copyright principles by making it illegal for anyone to overcome a technological measure that restricts access to digital works. The DMCA also makes it illegal and possibly criminal even to *share* information about how to defeat a technological lock. A consumer violates the law by deciphering the encryption keys that control access to DVD movies, for example, or by sharing information about DVD encryption with anyone.

Why is this bad? Because it allows copyright holders to control later uses of the product, even uses that would normally constitute legal, fair use activities. All a company needs to do is to assert its own terms of usage for consumers and then put a "technology lock" around the information—even a weak, nominal lock. If a paying consumer then circumvents the lock for any reason or shares information about the lock itself, a violation of the law has occurred.

The effect of the anticircumvention provisions of the DMCA is to authorize large copyright industries to stifle competition and innovation and prevent the widest possible dissemination of creative works. This, of course, runs directly contrary to the very constitutional purpose of copyright: to advance and diffuse knowledge. Worse, industries are able to assert their copyright claims through legal intimidation of alleged violators, enabling a form of private censorship without even a prior court review.

The most celebrated prosecution under the DMCA is a lawsuit pending against a teenage Norwegian programmer who wrote a program that can run Hollywood's DVD movies on Linux operating systems (and not just on Windows-based DVD players). This innovation alarms the film studios because DVD makers are paying them license fees; any alternative distribution channels for DVD movies (such as Linux-based players) would upset Hollywood's strict control of the market and its pricing prerogatives. But copyright law is not intended to protect content-owners from any and all forms of market competition. No matter. The DMCA is providing film studios with an effective tool for preventing the fair use of digital products—without even a copyright violation alleged!—in order to stymie independent distribution of creative works.

The DMCA is also being used to stifle free speech. It inhibited a Princeton computer scientist from presenting a paper about flaws in the record industry's Secure Digital Music Initiative encryption methods; he is seeking a declaratory judgment that publishing the code is protected by the First Amendment.[17] The DMCA has also been used to criminally prosecute a Russian graduate student who made available on the Internet software that can deencrypt electronic books made by Adobe Systems.[18]

Microsoft has used the law to demand that Slashdot, a Web site forum for programmers, remove materials that criticize the technical specifications for Microsoft's Kerberos software. Microsoft grudgingly agreed to post the specifications to Kerberos on its Web site after the programming community criticized it as yet another Microsoft trick to substitute a closed, proprietary Web standard for an open standard. But in granting access to the code, Microsoft first required that users click on an "End User License Agreement" that stated that the software specs were proprietary trade secrets that could not be used or disclosed without Microsoft's permission. When Slashdot subscribers nonetheless posted the specs on the Slashdot Web site—a classic fair-use copying of material for the purposes of criticism and comment—Microsoft charged copyright infringement and insisted that the material be removed.

If this precedent is allowed to stand, warns Georgetown law professor Julie E. Cohen, "a publisher can prohibit fair-use commentary simply by implementing access and disclosure restrictions that bind the entire public. Anyone who discloses the information, or even tells others how to get it, is a felon."[19]

But some content industries are trying to use technology alone to bypass the cultural bargain of copyright law. The idea is to devise closed technological systems so that hardware systems—DVD players, audio players, and so on—will not record or play content that is not tagged with a watermark (controlled by film, music, and other content providers.)[20]

One of the starkest examples of using copyright to suppress information occurred when the *Washington Post* and *Los Angeles Times* sued to stop a right-wing Web service called Free Republic from sharing news stories as part of an online opinion forum. The newspapers argued that this usage was illegal and not a legitimate fair use of copyrighted material. (The case was on appeal in the 9th Circuit Court of Appeals in 2001). That two of the nation's leading newspapers, champions of the First Amendment, would seek to shut down robust political discourse in the name of copyright suggests how copyright and First Amendment values may be coming into greater conflict.

The broader issue is the future legality of hyperlinking on the World Wide Web. The ability to embed links within a Web page is a tremendous aid to users in locating and sharing information, and has made the Web the most participatory communications media in history. Increasingly, however, commercial enterprises want to control who can use their trade names and create hyperlinks to their Web sites.[21] This amounts to an enclosure of the Internet commons, which by custom has regarded the very creation of a Web site as an implicit grant of permission to others to create hyperlinks to the site.

As these examples suggest, the rampant propertization of information has far-reaching implications for free speech and the diversity of information sources in our society. As NYU law professor Yochai Benkler has pointed out, granting property rights in information "require[s] the state to prevent people from speaking in order to increase information production in society.... [Furthermore], the mechanism of property rights tends to favor a certain kind of increased production by a relatively small number of large commercial organizations. This, in turn, conflicts with the First Amendment commitment to attain a diverse, decentralized 'marketplace of ideas.'" [22] The Supreme Court, Benkler points out, has long held that it is central to our democratic processes "that we secure 'the widest possible dissemination of information from diverse and antagonistic sources.'"

Locking up E-Books and Public Facts

Encryption and licensing might be used in the future for an even more ominous purpose: the revocation of freedoms traditionally associated with books. Makers of the so-called e-book—handheld appliances that are being developed by a number of media giants—are likely to invoke the DMCA to "lock up" the digital text. The harm to free speech and our culture could be severe. Encryption locks on e-book content could eliminate free or cheap public access to texts (through libraries, for example) and wipe out the fair use rights of readers.

Traditionally, of course, readers can share their books with whomever they want. This right derives from the "first-sale doctrine," which limits the right of vendors to control their products after the first sale. (This doctrine enabled the videotape rental business to emerge independently of the film studios). Would the first sale doctrine apply to e-books, allowing content to be freely shared in subsequent uses, or would it be illegal for a young girl to share the e-version of *Harry Potter* with her brother? Would the DMCA apply to e-books, thereby preventing fair use of the text and its passage into the public domain?[23]

Such possibilities are already being explored. When Simon & Schuster experimented with an online sale of a new Stephen King novella, the e-book was not available to public libraries under any license, nor was it available to computers that did not run on Windows operating systems. The novella had essentially "gone private," shedding any responsibilities for providing public access while retaining full copyright protection. The cultural implications of these developments are chilling—yet virtually unknown to the reading public or policy-makers.

As computer technologies have made it possible to assemble huge numbers of facts into searchable databases, they have created new quandaries about how to protect the commercial value of the aggregated information. Vendors who assemble databases of book prices, CD titles, scientific research, or statistics generally want to have tight proprietary control over their compilations. It would be patently unfair for a freeloader simply to download one vendor's database for free and then resell it with impunity. On the other hand, there is a serious danger if facts—which have never been eligible for copyright protection—can suddenly be owned and removed from the public domain. Much of education, scientific research, journalism, and civic life could not function if *facts* can be owned and their free flow restricted. Yet the privatization of public facts—sports scores, stock quotes, research data, even news events—is now an imminent reality.

The American public had a foretaste of this future during the Summer Olympics in 2000, when the Olympics Committee claimed property rights in news of sporting events, raw tabulations of the results of competitions, and even real-time diaries of Olympic athletes that hometown newspapers wanted to publish.[24] One reason for the clampdown: Olympics officials feared that the news media's free use of sports data would undercut the commercial value of its Web site, sponsored by IBM and Swatch, especially given the time difference between Australia and the United States. This was not an isolated case. At the Masters' golf tournament, reporters were actually charged for access to a Web site with up-to-the-minute statistics.

Database vendors have tried for the past eight years to persuade Congress to give them rights of "authorship" in databases and so enable them to prevent people from extracting or reusing database information. The most recent legislative vehicle, the Collections of Information Antipiracy Act, would significantly overprotect database compilations in a way that exceeds traditional copyright principles. Scores of universities, academic societies, search engines, and telecom companies have criticized the database legislation for creating "an unprecedented right to control transformative, value-added, downstream uses of the resulting collection or of any useful fraction of that collection."[25]

Proprietary claims to public facts are also being claimed under novel common-law theories as well. The online auction house eBay complained in 1999 that Bidder's Edge, a service that helps shoppers identify the lowest prices for goods and services, was using Web-crawling software "bots" to compile comparative price data from dozens of Internet auction sites, including eBay. Even though eBay's price data are accessible to anyone via the Web, eBay claimed that the "spidering" represented a "trespass" on its personal property (its servers) as well as a form of copyright infringement and trademark dilution. A federal judge agreed with eBay's complaint in May 2000 and ordered Bidder's Edge to stop gathering data from eBay's site. That ruling is now on appeal.

Trademark law is also being used to extend corporate control over any uses of a company or product name, even for traditional free speech purposes. Much of this trend can be attributed to passage of the Federal Anti-Dilution Act, which holds that a person can be liable for using someone else's mark even if consumers are not deceived or confused as to the source of goods or services. All that matters is that the distinctive quality of the mark is "blurred" by the unauthorized usage, thereby "tarnishing" the mark's value. This legal argument has allowed the U.S. Olympic Commission to prohibit the use of the term "Gay Olympics" by gay and lesbian athletes but allow the use of "Special Olympics" by athletes with disabilities.[26] It has allowed companies to go after Web sites that use their names in domain names (the ubiquitous "sucks" Web sites), cultural commentary sites (e.g., parodies of Mattel's Barbie doll), as well as Web-crawling bots.

Trademark law has even allowed McDonalds to claim ownership in 131 different words and phrases, such as "Black History Makers of Tomorrow," "America's Favorite Fries," and "Healthy Growing Up."[27] As Professor James Boyle has pointed out, now that flag-burning is a constitutionally protected form of expression, trademark law has made commercial icons—the Golden Arches, Mickey Mouse, the Taco Bell Chihuahua—the sole remaining venerable objects in our law.[28]

The danger, of course, is that the new attempts to claim proprietary control of public facts and words are shutting down all sorts of creativity and discussion. Excessive ownership rights in images and information are impeding scientific research, limiting academic dialogue, and stifling political life. Not surprisingly, it is also raising prices for information. Intellectual property scholars J. H. Reichman and Pamela Samuelson cite the case of Landsat satellite images, which many scientists use to "map and monitor" terrestrial ecosystems for agricultural and environmental purposes. After this databank was privatized, prices soared from $400 to $4,400 per image, bringing academic research in these areas to a complete halt.[29] Beyond this stifling of research, new copyright laws are giving information vendors monopoly control over their markets, with all the pricing abuses and anti-innovation effects that that entails.[30] The fundamental beauty of the Internet—the cheap and easy ability to find and aggregate information on a vast scale, and the blossoming of collaborative creativity and accountability—is being quietly, incrementally subverted.

The Rise of a Copyright Police State

The expansion of copyright protection into new areas has a disturbing correlate: intrusive new surveillance of people's reading and viewing habits. In a pay-per-use environment, after all, a single unauthorized use constitutes "piracy." Now that the technology can feasibly detect such "violations," copyright industries have every incentive to step up their monitoring of readers/viewers. The right to be an "anonymous reader" is being superseded by corporate interests in "digital rights management."[31]

In order to control market distribution and use more tightly, new software technologies are being devised to allow copyright holders to keep precise track of who accesses what digital works and under what circumstances. Copyright enforcement is only one goal. Digital rights management also enables a company to institute new regimes of discriminatory pricing for different market segments (individuals, companies, libraries, etc.). It can also collect valuable consumer usage data to refine its own marketing strategies or to resell or lease to third-party vendors (advertisers, market research firms, etc.). The rise of "geolocation technology," which can pinpoint a user's geographic location for the purposes of targeted marketing or political control, is another means of "top-down" Internet management.[32]

This represents a logical end point for the new Internet management systems: a tightly managed regime of metered access subject to centralized control and surveillance monitoring. It is a model of perfect control and the antithesis of the Internet today and of our open, democratic norms.[33] It is also the business model for Prodigy and Compuserve that was already failing miserably in the early 1990s before the wide open Internet paradigm exposed it as a sterile, claustrophobic model of online life.[34] The very assumptions of copyright law in a digital environment tend to advance a user-identification system of control—a system that requires greater surveillance of users, the balkanization of the Internet into regulated enclaves, and the loss of creativity and diversity that can only flourish in a commons that enjoys the free, unmetered exchange of information.

That is why we prize public libraries, academic freedom, and open societies with First Amendment protection. They provide the white space in which new experimentation and creativity can occur. Excessive copyright protection in the digital environment tends to inhibit such exchange and erode the robustness of the information commons.

Patents on Business Methods

The overpropertization of the commons is being played out in another arena as well: the patenting of business methods. Until recently few such patents were issued, because most innovations in business processes were embedded in the technology itself. But in 1981, the federal courts allowed a computerized method of molding tires to be patented. A 1998 court ruling that a method of managing mutual funds could be patented triggered an avalanche of new business-method patent applications, many of them involving computerized processes. Amazon.com won a patent for its "1-Click" shopping system, which allows purchases with a single click of a computer mouse. Priceline.com received a patent for its "name your own price" online auction process. British Telecom now claims a patent on hyperlinking.

The rise of business patents represents an ominous new trend of propertizing knowledge that has traditionally been shared and public. Knowledge about medical procedures, information distributed by libraries, genetically engineered crops, basic biological knowledge, mathematical algorithms, basic chunks of software code—all of these types of knowledge are being claimed by private owners through the patent system.

While patent holders argue that they are simply getting their just rewards for their inventiveness, critics reply that the out-of-control patenting of knowledge is allowing the "first mover" to corner the market and monopolize any future creativity in that field. A cautionary example from history is the Wright brothers' broad patent on their airplane. For nine years they defended their patent, thereby inhibiting the progress of American aviation while Europeans surged ahead. Finally, in order to help the U.S. war effort during World War I, the U.S. government forced the Wrights to license their technology.[35]

So it is today that patent rights have become so complicated and far-reaching—"a kudzu-like thicket," says Professor J. H. Reichman[36]—that new creativity is being inhibited. Companies are aggressively acquiring patents not only to preempt potential markets but to acquire bartering chits for cross-patenting licensing negotiations. Patent claimants make the same arrogant presumption that copyright holders often do: that their innovations have nothing to do with the collective knowledge, traditions, and resources that have been generated by communities of researchers over decades.

The breadth of new business-method patents has reached such extremes that even many high-tech leaders are publicly expressing alarm, and the U.S. Patent Office is reviewing its practices. But this may be too modest to solve the larger problem. "What is needed," writes Seth Shulman, author of *Owning the Future*, "are guidelines about when the overriding public interest requires restrictions on private capture of formerly shared knowledge assets. Unless we tackle the issue head on, proliferating private claims will choke productivity, magnify current inequities, and erode our democratic institutions."[37]

Neutering the Internet through International Law

For companies seeking to maximize gains from their intellectual property, the international arena opens up entirely new vistas of opportunity. The legal norms governing electronic commerce across national borders are still fairly undeveloped, and few organizations representing the interests of citizens (as opposed to government and business) are invited or allowed to participate in treaty negotiations. It is not surprising, then, that most Internet users have not heard about an arcane treaty, under negotiation by dozens of nations since 1992, dealing with cross-border jurisdiction in international legal disputes. While hardly the stuff of front-page headlines, the Hague Convention on Jurisdiction and Foreign Judgments could radically change which nation's laws shall apply to a person using the Internet—and could over time alter the very functioning of the Internet.

In the pre-Internet world, it was easier to track the transborder flow of physical goods and information and so to establish recognized boundaries for national laws. But now that the Internet allows transactions to occur anywhere, and information and commerce exist in a vast global matrix, the idea of giving each nation the right to impose its laws on the rest of the world is highly problematic. Yet that is the general effect of the proposed Hague treaty. Each nation would be able to apply its own domestic legal standards—for consumer protection, privacy, libel, copyright, and other civil laws—to anyone using the Internet. A small country with highly restrictive laws for free speech—Iran or China, say—could demand that the United States enforce foreign legal standards on American Internet users.

American film studios and record companies love the idea of the Hague Convention because it would allow them to collect royalties in foreign nations and crack down on pirated versions of their movies and CDs. As one commentator put it, the Hague treaty would help copyright industries in their "global game of Whack-a-Mole, where copyright violators are shut down in one country, only to pop up in another."[38] For their part, many nations with special cultural concerns like the proposed treaty because it would enable them to go after Web sites with "offensive" subject matter: in France, Nazi paraphernalia; in Iran, pornography; in China, criticism of the Communist Party.

Unfortunately, the Hague treaty would also allow companies to do some egregious "forum shopping" to maximize their advantages in any court litigation. If a company wanted to sell products online that were defective or dangerous, for example, it could stipulate in the sales contract where any disputes will be resolved (i.e., a nation with weak consumer protection law) and then insist that any lawsuits be adjudicated there. If a software company wanted to go after programmers who "reverse engineer" its products—a practice legal in the United States—it could sue Americans from a country where reverse engineering is illegal. Foreigners could sue Internet Service Providers for libel and defamation based on the more restrictive laws in their own countries.[39] Book publishers and film studios could even use the Hague treaty to try to override the first-sale doctrine in the United States, the copyright rule that allows public libraries to lend books for free and video stores to make royalty-free video rentals.

If Hollywood studios think their intellectual property rights would trump these adverse effects, one of the treaty's leading critics, James Love of the Consumer Project on Technology, points out that Cuba could decide to grant copyright protection for the "Cuban beat," demand five percent royalties from anyone who sold "Cuban" music, and then invoke the Hague treaty to force the U.S. government to enforce its claims.

"In a nutshell," Love points out, "the Hague treaty will strangle the Internet with a suffocating blanket of overlapping jurisdictional claims.... It will lead to a great reduction in freedom, shrink the public domain, and diminish national sovereignty."[40] Since the substantive provisions of the Hague treaty have only recently reached the public after nearly ten years of semisecret negotiations, there may yet be hope that the tide could be turned. But if it proceeds, the Hague treaty could impose some of the most sweeping changes on the Internet since its origins; a commercial enclosure of international scope.

Copyrights, Patents, and a Free Society

The ominous expansions of new intellectual property protections force us to confront, as a matter of law and social practice, what kind of society we will be. Will property rights become so prized that they will trump traditional rights of free speech science and scholarship? Will the commercial interests of the Big Content oligopolies be allowed to prevail over our interests in privacy, diversity of expression, localism, and innovation? Professor Lessig warns about "the power through property to produce a closed society—where to use an idea, to criticize a part of culture, to quote 'Donald Duck'—one will need the permission of someone else. Hat in hand, deferential, begging, a society where we will have to *ask* to use; *ask* to criticize; *ask* to do all those things that in a free society—in a society with an intellectual commons, in a society where no man, or no corporation, or no soviet, controls—one takes for granted."[41]

Overly expansive intellectual property rights also threaten to bring about "the medievalization of our national system of innovation," in the words of legal scholar J. H. Reichman.[42] In medieval times, wayfarers on the Rhine River had to pay a tribute or tax at every castle along the way—a tremendously inefficient balkanization of commerce. Now we are on the cusp of a similar regime in the information economy, where market tribute must be paid at every tollgate that someone manages to erect. The resulting losses to the commons of public knowledge have far-reaching implications for our economy, technological innovation, and our entrepreneurial, open culture.

If we are to avoid this fate, Americans will need to shake off the runaway dreams of propertized control through copyright and patent law, and begin to rediscover the functional and cultural value of openly shared knowledge and culture. This alternative vision is no utopian dream. It can be seen in the history of the Internet and in the growing power of free and open source software. It is apparent in the many gift cultures scattered throughout our society—in scientific disciplines, in academia, in local communities, in countless Internet venues. But the challenge facing us may actually be more complex than rediscovering the commons of public knowledge. We must learn new ways to enable the gift economy and market economy to coexist while invigorating each other constructively and retaining the integrity of each. That is the unmet challenge.

9.

Enclosing the
Academic Commons

Higher education is changing profoundly, retreating from the ideals of liberal arts and the leading-edge research it always has cherished. Instead, it is behaving more like the $250-billion business it has become.

—*Business Week*, December 22, 1997

There was actually a time, not so long ago, when academic researchers regarded the patenting of their discoveries as unseemly—a contemptible affront to the mission of science. Jonas Salk, Albert Sabin, and John Enders did not seek to claim ownership of their pioneering polio vaccine research in the 1940s and 1950s. Cesar Milstein, who shared a Nobel Prize for helping develop monoclonal antibody technology in 1975, did not even ask if the method should be patented.

Stanford University's Stanley Cohen and Herbert Boyer gave no thought to patenting the gene-splicing techniques they developed in 1973 until a university attorney urged them to do so. "My initial reaction, said Cohen, "was to question whether basic research of this type could or should be patented and to point out that our work had been dependent on a number of earlier discoveries by others." Cohen later agreed to file for a patent, but only if the university would be named as the exclusive beneficiary.[1]

Times have changed.

In the course of one generation, the public-spirited ethic of the academy is being challenged by a frankly acquisitive ethic that aggressively seeks private ownership and profit from the fruits of university research. This has not been without its benefits. The commercialization of promising scientific research—"technology transfer"—has in fact accelerated, bringing forth a great many useful products and biomedical advances of significant benefit to humanity. And a handful of universities have reaped bonanzas that may help them fortify and expand their educational missions.

Higher education plays a unique role in our democratic society by discovering new knowledge and transmitting it from previous generations to the next—and to all segments of contemporary society. But the rampant propertization of knowledge is subverting the purpose, institutional design, and culture of the university. Its intrusion into the academy is raising new questions about the integrity of research. The long-standing scholarly ethos of collaborative sharing is giving way to a more proprietary, market ethic, thanks to the blandishments of corporate sponsors: lucrative consultancies, generous research grants, royalties from patents, corporate stock, and conference honoraria and junkets.

As business spending at universities has soared from $850 million in 1985 to $4.25 billion less than a decade later, the new piper is calling some new tunes.[2] Instead of setting their own research agendas, particularly with regard to basic science and undirected research, universities are chasing the money. While the humanities and the social sciences go begging, university administrators enthusiastically shovel funds to disciplines that promise greater returns on investment, such as molecular biology and computer science. Business interests are not only influencing the *kinds* of knowledge that universities are generating, they are demanding ever-greater *control* over who may have access to that knowledge and on what terms. Increasingly, researchers are being asked to sign agreements that prevent them from sharing their results and that allow the sponsoring companies to delay or squelch publication of research. As more knowledge is marketized, it is becoming legally compartmentalized.

"There's been a paradigm shift," admits a high-ranking University of Southern California administrator. "There was a time that this kind of work—and the idea of making money from your research—was not acceptable at universities, including ours."[3] Now, however, "the kept university"—as Eyal Press and Jennifer Washburn document in their pioneering reporting and synthesis on the topic[4]—is becoming far more common. Few university administrators care to speak candidly about how market enclosure is transforming the academy; most of them are too eager to capitalize on industry partnerships. Yet the distressing truth is that the marketization of the academy is eroding its historic commitment to the public interest. It is undermining the fabulously productive gift culture of the university and precipitating a greater array of conflicts of interest and ethical misbehavior. One cannot blame a wary public for wondering if universities are still reliable, trustworthy public institutions or a new breed of corporate shill.

The University as a Commons

The scientists of previous generations who refused to patent their break-through discoveries were neither naïve nor saintly. They were members of a flourishing gift culture, the academy, which presumed (and still presumes, for the most part) that data, research tools, and other scholarly resources should be widely shared and openly scrutinized. There is an expectation that members of a scholarly community will adhere to certain standards of rigor, candor, and ethics, and that a discipline's work should serve a larger public interest.

Gift-exchange plays a crucial role in nurturing these values, as we saw in Chapter 2, because it nurtures *internal* commitments that cannot be easily maintained through *external* rewards such as money or sanctions. As sociologist Georg Simmel has written, gratitude to a community "establishes the bond of interaction for the reciprocity of service and return service, even where they are not guaranteed by external coercion."[5] In a society besotted by the market, it is sometimes hard to understand that the progress of science depends critically on its integrity as a cooperative venture. "Those who produce [scientific knowledge]," writes University of California at Berkeley law professor Robert P. Merges, "understand that the community always has extensive claims on it, because without shared knowledge, research techniques and even biological materials, there would often be no results, no progress, and hence nothing to argue about." It is important for scientists to share, he notes, because "a lab that always 'takes' research results, but never 'gives' in return … is like a municipality that pumps water as fast as it can, at the expense both of its neighbors and ultimately of rational water use."[6]

Science is a commons in a more familiar economic sense as well. The federal government provides about 59 percent of funding for academic research, or $15.6 billion in 1998.[7] Furthermore, many colleges and universities receive extensive state funding. Educational institutions are exempt from taxes because it is assumed that they are doing work for the public good that is not being addressed by the market. Serving the public is one reason that the land-grant colleges were created in the nineteenth century, and why government agencies look to academics for expert guidance. It is also why higher education has generally been considered a respected, independent voice in our democratic society.

The corporate invasion of university life over the past twenty years is calling into question this proud legacy. As Ronnie Dugger puts it, a growing number of business/university partnerships seek "to turn students into consumers, education into training for jobs, professors into hired-out consultants and researchers, and campuses into corporate research and profit centers."8 Business/university collaborations can be respectful and productive, to be sure. But such a relationship requires a university to maintain strict control over its core values and autonomy; corporate influence must be kept at an arm's distance. More and more, this is not the case.

Surrendering Public Science to Private Interests

A key moment in the enclosure of the academic commons occurred in 1980, when Congress enacted the Bayh-Dole Act. Intended as a way to accelerate the commercialization of academic research, the law would have profound implications not just for the public control of science but for the very identity of universities as institutions dedicated to public service.

Since World War II, there had been a broad consensus in American life that the intellectual property rights of federal research should stay in the public domain, or at least be licensed on a nonexclusive basis. That way, the American people could reap the full measure of value from their collective investments. In the late 1970s, however, large pharmaceutical, electronics, and chemical industries, restive at such restrictions, mounted a bold lobbying campaign to reverse the presumption of public ownership of federal research.[9] Large companies such as General Electric and Monsanto and trade associations such as the National Association of Manufacturers and the Electronics Industry Association argued that government discoveries were sitting idle and never making it to market because companies did not have sufficient incentives to commercialize them. Exclusive patent rights would change that, they claimed. They also insisted that foreign competitors should not be allowed to benefit from U.S. government research. (But note the contradiction: if foreign competitors were poised to exploit U.S. government research, why were incentives to commercialize government research needed at all?)

As the Bayh-Dole legislation was being debated, Representative Jack Brooks objected that the new law would "violate a basic provision of the unwritten contract between the citizens of this country and their government; namely, that what the government acquires through the expenditure of its citizens' taxes, the government owns. Assigning automatic patent rights and exclusive licenses to companies or organizations for inventions developed at government expense," Brooks argued, "is a pure giveaway of rights that properly belong to the people. . . . The federal government has the equivalent of a fiduciary responsibility to the taxpayers of the country.[10]

Congress thought otherwise and proceeded to enact the Bayh-Dole Act in 1980. In the years that followed, President Reagan signed a number of related laws and executive orders that weakened the public's control over government research in subtle but important ways.[11] By the end of the 1980s, federal technology transfer to the private sector had become a massive giveaway of taxpayer-sponsored R&D worth billions of dollars.[12]

It is not surprising that the private sector should look to government to perform all sorts of basic research. It is usually economically prohibitive for an individual firm to pursue costly, high-risk, basic research, particularly when the benefits may not accrue to any single company. And there are sometimes good reasons to give companies exclusive patents to public technologies—significant postpatent investments to commercialize research, for example, or compelling social needs. But none of this justifies the routine giveaways of government science at a fraction of its market value. It forces the American people to pay twice—first, as taxpayers reaping a lower return on their government's investments, and second as consumers paying inflated prices for the resulting technologies and products. (Chapter 11 examines this dynamic as it applies to federally funded drug research.)

From a short-term perspective, the Bayh-Dole Act has certainly fulfilled its purpose of accelerating the use of university research. The efflorescence of biotechnology parks and silicon corridors in university towns— Cambridge, Austin, Palo Alto, Raleigh-Durham—testifies to this fact.[13] According to the Association of University Technology Managers, academic research labs since 1993 have garnered an average of 1,600 patents annually, and in recent years, more than 2,000.[14] Dozens of important new drugs, medical technologies and other advances have been brought to market.

But these undeniable economic gains have come at long-term costs and inequities that many universities prefer not to confront: a sweeping privatization of publicly funded knowledge, a ceding of research agendas to the private sector, and an erosion of public confidence in the independence of university research.

The Marketization of the Academy

Because the *process* by which knowledge is generated and distributed is so abstract, it can be hard to appreciate why the marketization of academic knowledge can be so pernicious. Consider that basic research eventually resulting in the genetics and computer revolutions was federally funded in the years *before* enactment of Bayh-Dole. It was therefore in the public domain, open and available to all. This was critical in enabling other researchers to gain free access to basic scientific knowledge and come up with new discoveries and breakthrough inventions.

Now, imagine if all this knowledge had been privately owned—by universities, individual researchers, and sponsoring companies—and considered a proprietary secret. That, in essence, is what is occurring today as a result of the new norms encouraged by the Bayh-Dole Act and related rules. There is no longer a general presumption that research will flow into the public domain and be free to use. Instead, huge swathes of knowledge are fenced off into privately owned plots. This is an ominous trend because, if we recall Norbert Weiner's insight that opens Chapter 7, scientific knowledge only achieves it full value "with its further application by many minds and with its free communication to other minds." Marketization of knowledge can strangle the circulation of knowledge that is indispensable to good science.

This fear animated protests against the University of California at Berkeley's deal with Novartis (now known as Syngenta), the pharmaceutical and biotech company. In return for $25 million, Berkeley agreed to give Novartis the first rights to negotiate patent licenses on up to one third of the research produced by the Department of Plant and Microbial Biology.[15] While this deal may or may not be necessary to speed technology transfer, it cannot help but alter research priorities at the university and privatize more of the scientific knowledge it generates.

The marketization of university research is now becoming institutionalized. Many schools have opened special technology-licensing offices to obtain patents and collect royalties. Others have started venture capital funds to invest in business start-ups that "buy" university research. Stanford University has actually started its own brand-name product in order to extend its revenues beyond patent terms.[16]

While the logic of cashing in on university research may seem impeccable, a working group at the National Institutes of Health (NIH) warned NIH director Harold Varmus that creeping propertization was jeopardizing the free exchange of research data and tools in biomedical research.[17] The working group found that university contracts "present just about every type of clause that universities cite as problematic in the [contracts] ... they receive from industry." Among the restrictions: university review of manuscripts prior to publication; publication delays so patents can be filed; university ownership of future scientific discoveries; the right to refuse to license follow-on discoveries to other parties; and the right to prevent sharing of material with others.[18] It seems that a great many universities, beset by rising research costs, declining federal science funding, and declining state support for higher education, have jettisoned their academic scruples and turned themselves into brash marketeers.

Far from fostering new knowledge, overpropertization may in fact be *stifling* life-saving innovations, according to legal scholars Michael A. Heller and Rebecca S. Eisenberg. They call it the "tragedy of the anticommons"—a situation in which a scarce resource [biomedical knowledge] is seriously *under-used* because "multiple owners each have a right to exclude others … and no one has an effective privilege of use." Once an anticommons emerges, write Heller and Eisenberg, "collecting rights into usable private property is often brutal and slow."[19]

The implications can be especially severe as property rights reach further "upstream" into the research process to privatize knowledge whose utility is not yet known. If one researcher or company can patent raw segments of the human genome, for example, it means that many future researchers simply will not dare to "trespass" upon a patentee's "privately owned" knowledge. Since biomedical research requires the use of many inputs from preceding scientists—specialized processes, reagents, genetically distinct organisms, and so on—locking up upstream research introduces legal complexities that can have tragic results: "Researchers and their institutions may resent restrictions on access to the patented discoveries of others, yet no one wants to be the last one left dedicating their findings to the public domain," write Heller and Eisenberg.[20]

As the propertization of once-shared knowledge continues apace, scientific research seems to be ratcheting itself toward paralysis. A new kind of rice genetically engineered to resist a tropical virus cannot be sold because approvals must first be obtained by as many as 34 different patent holders.[21] About 45 percent of plant breeders at U.S. universities say their research has been impeded by difficulties in obtaining seeds from private companies.[22] Others complain that research on improving crop yields in developing nations is grinding to a halt because it is not an attractive market. This phenomenon is likely to replicate itself in many research fields as public-sector science shrinks in size, resources, and influence.

Once researchers at land-grant colleges and universities generated discoveries that belonged to the public domain, which catalyzed a robust field of follow-on innovation and commercialization. As private research eclipses public spending, the five major agricultural biotech firms are in a stronger position to introduce genetically engineered foods that (they hope) might supplant basic food crops. Proprietary knowledge aspires to neuter and replace common knowledge.

It is impossible to quantify the amounts of knowledge lost to the public and researchers because of marketization, but certain statistics are suggestive. "More than 90 percent of life-science companies now have some type of formal relationships with academic scientists," reports author David Shenk, "and 60 percent of those report that they have achieved new patents, products and sales as a result."[23] According to a study in the *Journal of the American Medical Association (JAMA)*, the universities' share of gene patents rose from 55 percent to 73 percent between 1990 and 1999.[24] Crudely put, these patents represent knowledge that would otherwise have entered the public domain and been available for others to use.

The Rise of Market Lysenkoism

Trofim Lysenko was a Soviet biologist and agronomist of the 1940s who was the embodiment of politically motivated science. Contemptuous of orthodox genetic doctrines, Lysenko outlawed their instruction and use, and insisted that Soviet scientists pursue only his outlandish, politically sanctioned theories. The entrance of market norms into the American academy has been nowhere as sweeping or crazy, but neither has it been benign or apolitical. Corporate-sponsored research in universities has led to the suppression of research and dismissals of scientists who reach discomfiting conclusions. It has skewed research agendas and thrown a veil of proprietary secrecy over important scientific projects. Not surprisingly, conflicts of interest and ethical abuses have become more common.[25]

One of the most remarkable instances of these dynamics involved Betty J. Dong, a clinical pharmacist at the University of California, San Francisco. Knoll Pharmaceutical paid $250,000 for a study that it hoped would show the clinical superiority of Synthroid, a popular thyroid drug. In its contract for the study, the company stipulated that it would have the right to design the scientific protocols for the study, the right to review results before publication, and the right to delay or suppress publication if desired—all common clauses in sponsored research. According to a 1997 survey by David Blumenthal, 58 percent of companies that sponsor academic research require researchers to delay the release of results for six months or more—even though the National Institutes for Health recommends no more than one or two months.[26]

When Dong reached the conclusion that Synthroid performed about the same as three cheaper medicines, the company suppressed publication of the study lest it jeopardize the drug's lucrative market. Dong's study was eventually published, years later, in *JAMA,* but not before the company had sought to discredit Dong's study through a major publicity campaign. The study inspired a class-action lawsuit against Knoll by Synthroid users, who claimed the company had defrauded them out of hundreds of millions of dollars. Knoll offered to settle for nearly $100 million, but that sum was "but a small fraction of the profits the company made from Synthoid during the years it was suppressing the study," writes author David Shenk.[27]

Such stories are not unusual. A Canadian drug company, Apotex, threatened to sue liver specialist Nancy Olivieri for breach of contract if she warned her patients or published her findings that the company's drug, L1, had dangerous side effects.[28] When researchers at the University of California, San Francisco, published a study that found no clinical advantage in the use of Remune, an AIDS drug, the sponsoring company, Immune Response Corp., sued the university for $7 to $10 million in damages.[29]

A Brown University specialist in occupational medicine, David Kern, wanted to publish disturbing evidence of a new and potentially fatal lung disease that he had discovered at a local manufacturing plant. But both the company and Brown University sought to prevent him from going public. After Kern did present his research, Kern's university contract was not renewed and his occupational health program was terminated. But the Centers for Disease Control ended up recognizing the new disease Kern had discovered, Flock Worker's Lung.[30]

Public trust in university research took a real dive in 1999 when it was learned that researchers at the University of Pennsylvania had taken ethical shortcuts in the course of experimental gene therapy—shortcuts that were fatal for one of the test subjects. Isolated abuses are inevitable, some may argue, but it did not help that the professor involved, a dean, and the university itself all had equity stakes in the company sponsoring the clinical trials.[31]

When universities own stock in the companies sponsoring research, it can lead to the kind of squalid episodes that occurred at the University of South Florida in the mid-1990s. Claiming that an undergraduate researcher had stolen research for a potentially lucrative invention (increasing the ammonia-absorbing capacity of a substance used in kitty litter), the university in 1996 prosecuted Petr Taborsky, who was convicted of a felony, sentenced to a three-and-a-half year sentence, and initially assigned to work on a chain gang. Following his release from prison, a flurry of bitter civil suits contesting ownership of the patents ensued.[32]

Why did the university have the stomach for such an ugly and expensive spectacle? Because it feared that *failing* to punish Taborsky and secure the patents might alienate future corporate sponsors.

"Is Academic Medicine for Sale"?" asked Marcia Angell, M.D., in an editorial in the *New England Journal of Medicine*. "I believe the claim that extensive ties between academic researchers and industry are necessary for technology transfer is greatly exaggerated, particularly with regard to clinical research," Angell wrote in May 2000. Such ties are supremely useful for exploiting the talent and prestige of universities, especially for marketing purposes, she said. But "it is highly doubtful" that consultancies, equity stakes in companies, travel to industry-sponsored symposia, meals, and other gifts "facilitate technology transfer or confer any other social benefit," Angell argued.[33]

Nonetheless, research universities have not been eager to grapple with these concerns. A 2000 study published in *JAMA* found no consensus among universities about appropriate conflict-of-interest policies, and very few formal safeguards are in place. Only 55 percent of the 100 universities surveyed required any disclosures of conflict-of-interest, for example, and only 19 percent specified any limits on researchers' financial ties to companies sponsoring their research. Only 12 percent of universities surveyed tried to limit corporate-dictated delays on the publication of research.[34] If the nation's universities are too timid to address corporate influence of academic research, the world's most prominent medical journals are not. Nearly a dozen of them jointly adopted editorial policies to reject studies that do not allow researchers to have full access to data and the freedom to report findings.[35]

Meanwhile, research priorities at universities, many of which are publicly funded, are being shifted to privilege the research needs of corporate sponsors. According to a pilot study in 1998, about 25 percent of 100 research facilities surveyed were changing their research agendas due to fears of intellectual property lawsuits and other actions.[36] A larger survey of 1,000 research organizations is now underway. When companies direct research goals, marketing interests may favor trivial work to develop "me-too" products, and avoid more meaningful lines of research. Then there are research areas that are socially important but commercially unattractive. A university that cedes its research priorities to corporate sponsors is not likely to pursue questions that have no patentable outcomes—say, research on sustainable agriculture or natural pest control. Medications to prevent or treat sleeping sickness or malaria, vitally important to millions of people, but unfortunately not lucrative markets, are not as likely to be pursued. Whole vectors of inquiry are more likely to be underfunded and marginalized.[37]

The proprietary "fences" created by marketization of research also disrupt the efficiency of scientific inquiry. "Ineffective or even dangerous drugs are not revealed as such at the earliest possible moment," writes David Shenk. "Avenues of research already known to be fruitless by some are needlessly pursued by others, wasting money and time and ultimately hindering scientific progress."[38] In many instances, patents are shutting down entire fields of potential research. Disease genes, for example, are rapidly being patented, resulting in a monopolization of knowledge about certain genes, their mutations, and the only available diagnostic testing services and therapies.

According to bioethicist Jon F. Merz, this fairly recent development "is at fundamental odds with good medical practice" because "patents should not be used to limit the practice of medicine in any way." Merz found that the monopolization of disease gene patents "threatens to restrict research activities; creates unacceptable conflicts of interest; may reduce patient access to testing; may lead to inequitable extensions of patent terms on tests and related discoveries; and grants to patent holders the ability to dictate the standard of care for testing, and to otherwise interfere with the practice of medicine."[39]

As if to rewrite the ethical standards by which science and medicine will be judged, the pharmaceutical industry is channeling significant money to bioethicists in academia. The influx of cash, consultancies, and prestige is changing the substantive ethical judgments of the profession in insidious ways, as Carl Elliott, a philosopher and bioethicist, has shown. "If bioethics is seen as an activity that can attract industry sponsorship, university administrators strapped for cash will inevitably look to industry as a financial solution," writes Elliott. "All that remains is for bioethicists themselves to dispense with the ethical roadblocks."[40]

The University as Market Resource

The marketization of the academy is not restricted to research, of course, but extends to a great many quarters of college life. Many companies regard campuses as a rich marketing venue to reach the next generation of consumers; capture the brand loyalties of the 20 million consumers between the ages of 18 and 24, many of whom are in colleges and universities, and a larger revenue stream is assured for years.

This is one reason that the Nike swoosh has become ubiquitous in college sports through branding deals with sports departments. Computer companies are aggressively trying to capture the "mindshare" of students, particularly student programmers. Soda and snack companies seek out exclusive vending contracts to ply their junk foods. Emulating the "in your face" captive advertising of the CNN Airport Network, the newly formed College Television Network has placed more than 2,000 TV monitors in the cafeterias, fitness centers, and other high-traffic areas of some 800 campuses.[41] Universities have also thrown open their doors to aggressive credit card solicitations even though many students, without jobs or income, end up deeply in debt.[42]

Innocuous on its face, the marketing invasion of college campus may reveal its pernicious aspects only if and when objections are raised. Microsoft's discounted deals on software, for example, are an attempt to prevent non-Microsoft programs, particularly Linux and free and open source software, from gaining a larger following. Nike does not want campus groups to raise a public fuss about foreign sweatshops that produce its sportswear.[43] Marketing to college students has gained such a foothold in part because university administrators and alumni groups have been bought off with a slice of the action. They like the extra revenues they reap from co-branding deals with credit-card banks and from granting soda vendors and the College Television Network access to a captive, demographically distinct consumer cohort.

What may be most disturbing is how university administrators have so thoroughly internalized market values into their management outlooks. It only stands to reason that most of them would regard course curricula as new profit centers to be exploited through distance education technology.[44] Few have shown the leadership of MIT in suggesting that the intellectual bounties generated by higher education—much of it financed by taxpayers—ought to be made publicly available on the Web for free. This was one motivation for MIT's new OpenCourseWare project.[45]

Universities who regard their enterprises chiefly as businesses—and thereby see the world through the scrim of market share, consumer satisfaction, marketing, and public relations—are subtly changing the very identity and mission of higher education. "As we in the academy begin to use business-speak fluently," warns Michele Tolela Myers, president of Sarah Lawrence College, "we become accustomed to thinking in commercialized terms about education. We talk no longer as public intellectuals, but as entrepreneurs. And we thus encourage instead of fight the disturbing trend that makes education a consumer good rather than a public good."[46] The humanistic and ethical values that should lie at the heart of higher education—the commitment to free and independent inquiry, wherever that may lead, and the ideals of service to a democratic culture—recede into the shadows as secondary, even discretionary concerns.

It is a measure of how much we have lost that the Jonas Salks and Cesar Milsteins of this generation would probably not leave the fruits of their labor in the academic commons. They would not regard their achievements as gifts to their colleagues and the American people and a gift outright to future generations (repaying the debt they owe to their predecessors). Nowadays, the gift culture in academia is under siege. Smart money wants to make darn sure that its precious knowledge is locked up in equity shares.

10.

The Commercialization
of Culture and Public Spaces

The American apparatus of advertising is something unique in history....
It is like a grotesque, smirking gargoyle set at the very top of America's
skyscraping adventure in acquisition *ad infinitum*. It is never silent, it drowns
out all other voices, and it suffers no rebuke, for is it not the voice of America?

—James Rorty, *Our Master's Voice*, 1934[1]

Once described as "the science of arresting human intelligence long
enough to get money from it," advertising is the vanguard machinery for
securing public support for enclosures of the commons, or at least a sullen
acquiescence. Now conflated with marketing and public relations, advertising is an indispensable tool for building public awareness of product
brands, expanding market share, and neutralizing public misgivings about
products and businesses.

A colossal business marketing machine has come to dominate
American culture over the past generation. In the early 1980s, cable television, VCRs, personal computers, and a host of other new technologies
began to upstage broadcast television and make electronic media even
more ubiquitous in the culture. Large national audiences that once
huddled around three TV networks soon splintered among dozens of
niche media. In hot pursuit of a fragmenting audience, marketers began
to pioneer new forms of targeted marketing, assisted by the computeriza-
tion of demographic data. To compete with the growing clutter in the
public sphere that their own efforts were creating, marketers developed
still other techniques and venues for selling. Over time the crush of
marketing has generated an ominous new discipline, the "economics of
attention," which regards human consciousness as a fugitive animal to be
hunted down and trapped.

Myriad noncommercial arenas—the arts, public education, sports, civic
life, public spaces—have been transformed into vehicles for marketing.

We now suffer from a dwindling supply of "unbranded" no-sell havens in our culture, perhaps replicating in humans the feelings that the snail darter and other endangered species must experience: a physical and psychic claustrophobia.[2]

At a pivotal moment in history, the surrender of the public's airwaves to commercial broadcasters was a giveaway that not only cost the American people untold billions of dollars, but consigned great swatches of artistic endeavor, science, politics, religion, and education to the periphery of American life. Following this critical event, business advertisers have invaded the public schools, "branded" countless civic spaces, and seduced a number of public institutions—journalism, art museums, public television, government services—whose integrity has historically stemmed from a certain insulation from the marketplace.

The marketing excesses raise an inevitable question: Can a society whose culture is so given over to incessant commercialism ever function as a deliberative democracy? Can the public find and develop its own sovereign voice, or has its character been so transformed by commercial media and the boundaries of its permissible discourse been so limited that public life will forever be a stunted thing?

Broadcasters Win Control of the Airwaves

The loss of a public commons in broadcasting must be counted as one of the great civic and cultural losses of the twentieth century. Broadcasting, after all, is one of the primary means by which our society communicates with itself. The loss of the airwaves to market enclosure, first achieved through 1927 and 1934 legislation and significantly extended through sweeping deregulation in the 1980s and 1990s, meant that commercial values would dictate the evolution of our culture.

Broadcast spectrum was originally so plentiful that the government granted radio licenses to anyone upon request. But by the 1920s, the proliferation of broadcasters was causing a cacophony of signal interference. This prompted a debate about how to allocate control of the electromagnetic spectrum. As RCA, General Electric, and other corporations owning commercial radio networks sought to gain exclusive control of the airwaves, educators, organized labor, religious groups, and politicians worried that their free speech rights in the new medium would be wiped out. Accordingly, they wanted a system of common carriage, which would require any broadcaster to sell airtime to anyone at nondiscriminatory rates. Broadcasters stoutly resisted this idea because it would diminish their editorial control and commercial opportunities.[3]

In the end, the broadcast industry prevailed upon Congress to enact the

Radio Act of 1927 and then a successor statute, the Communications Act of 1934. Cast as a compromise, the 1934 Act, still the charter for broadcasting today, banned common carriage regulation (a victory for broadcasters) while requiring broadcast licensees to operate in the "public interest, convenience and necessity" (an ostensible victory for civic, educational, and religious groups).

The idea was that broadcasters would serve as "public trustees" of the airwaves—enlightened hosts of the broadcasting commons. "It is as if people of a community should own a station and turn it over to the best man in sight with this injunction: 'Manage this station in our interest,'" declared the Federal Radio Commission.[4] The Supreme Court later elaborated that a licensee must "share his frequency with others and conduct himself as a proxy or fiduciary with obligations to present those views and voices which are representative of his community and which would otherwise, by necessity, be barred from the airwaves."[5]

And so the bargain was struck: broadcasters would receive free use of the public's airwaves in return for vague standards of public service. Broadcast licenses would not entail any ownership or property rights in the airwaves, and licenses could be terminated for a breach of public duty.[6]

Unfortunately, the public's end of the bargain has been more of a useful fiction than a meaningful dividend. From the start, Congress gave no particular definition to the "public interest, convenience and necessity," an egregious shortcoming in legal draftsmanship that no business person would ever accept. Some scholars considered the "public interest" standard to be an expedient gesture to make the government's licensing powers constitutional. After all, the U.S. government was choosing to give preferential free speech rights to some people—broadcasters—over others.

Congress and the FCC in the 1960s and 1970s did enact a number of specific requirements to help assure public and political access to the airwaves. Candidates for federal office were granted the right to buy airtime to reply to their opponents, and the right to free replies to any station's political attacks or candidate endorsements. The public was given nominal access to the airwaves through the Fairness Doctrine, which required broadcasters to cover "controversial issues of public importance," and allow opposing views to be heard. At one time the FCC actually had guidelines to prod broadcasters to provide diverse programming, children's programming, and local public affairs programming. A failure to comply with any of these requirements could theoretically result in the government's revoking a broadcaster's license.

In practice, however, most of these and other attempts to enforce a muscular standard of public trusteeship on broadcasters were doomed. Standards were vague, enforcement was irregular and highly legalistic, and political pressures on the FCC to coddle broadcasters were constant.[7] Over the past 68 years, fewer than half a dozen licenses have ever been revoked. Broadcasters are too powerful an industry to cross (what politician running for reelection wants to be on the wrong side of the local TV station?), and too much money can be made selling airtime to advertisers for public service to be a serious priority.

While the networks in the 1960s and 1970s occasionally mounted admirable productions and public affairs initiatives, these were tolerable sacrifices for a lucrative three-company oligopoly. When cable television and independent television stations stepped up the competitive pressures in the 1980s and 1990s, however, TV programming that did not garner maximum ratings—particularly public affairs, local programming, children's educational TV, and public service broadcasts—was severely cut back.

Industry consolidation allowed by the Telecommunications Act of 1996 made broadcasters even less eager to carry out "unprofitable" public service goals. Through a series of deregulatory moves in the 1990s, the practical meaning of the "public trust" in broadcasting was eviscerated, making virtually any sort of programming synonymous with the public interest.[8] (Indeed, some broadcasters once claimed in formal submissions to the FCC that *The Jetsons* and *Leave It to Beaver* constituted "educational programming.")[9]

The evolution of television over the past generation is not without its high points; never before has there been as much high-end news, arts, and public affairs programming, at least on cable television. But cable subscribers pay for these services, and they are not available to all Americans. Broadcast television is meant to serve all Americans, largely because station owners use the public's airwaves for free. The question is: What are broadcasters giving the American people in return?

A regulatory scheme based on broadcasters serving as conscientious stewards of the public interest had, by the 1990s, effectively morphed into outright ownership of the spectrum. A juggernaut of race-to-the-bottom programming—leering talk shows, tabloid news, salacious dramas, and incessant station promos—had been unleashed, and the fiction of broadcasters serving as stalwart public trustees had grown embarrassingly thin.

Broadcasters now consider even the most basic sorts of public service, such as probing coverage of political elections, too expensive a burden. Issue coverage of the 2000 presidential race on the nightly news declined by 27 percent over 1996, and two of the four major networks chose not to air a presidential debate live. In the month before the "Super Tuesday" primaries in 2000, the national networks and their local affiliates aired just 36 seconds a night of candidates addressing issues.[10] Fewer than 7 percent of the nation's 1,300 stations agreed to try voluntarily to provide five minutes a night of candidate-centered discourse in the 30 days before the election. Even fewer stations met that goal.[11] Only 0.3 percent of total commercial time in 24 broadcast markets during a typical two-week period in 1990 was devoted to local public affairs programming.[12]

Airtime has become so lucrative that broadcasters simply do not want to surrender it for purposes that do not generate maximum revenue. TV stations sold between $600 million and $1 billion in paid political advertising in the 2000 election season—a record and more than six times the ad revenues collected in 1972. Much of this windfall came from simple price-gouging. The Alliance for Better Campaigns found that "local television stations across the country systematically gouged candidates in the closing months of the 2000 campaign, jacking up the price of their ads to levels that were far above the lowest candidate rates listed on the stations' own rate cards. They did so despite a 30-year-old federal law designed to protect candidates from such demand-driven price spikes."[13]

With political ads generating more money for TV stations than fast food in 2000, broadcasters are the main reason that political candidates have to raise such huge sums of money from special interests, with the predictable corruptions of the democratic process. Instead of the public having some modest form of free access to its own airwaves to hear candidates speak, broadcasters have privatized the broadcasting commons for their own considerable gain. For an asset that as currently organized would probably sell for $80 to $100 billion, or about $700 to $900 if distributed equally to every American household, citizens might understandably question the returns they are reaping from their investment.[14]

The enclosure of the public's airwaves has found a farcical repetition in the broadcast industry's successful appropriation of another 6 megahertz slice of spectrum for digital television. "It is one of the great ripoffs in American history," said Senator John McCain of Arizona. "They used to rob trains in the Old West, now we rob spectrum."[15] In the early 1990s, broadcasters lobbied Congress to give them new spectrum so that free over-the-air television could develop high-definition television (HDTV) to compete with cable and satellite television. The idea was that better video and sound quality, along with many more channels, would usher in the next generation of TV. As part of the Telecommunications Act of 1996, Congress agreed. It gave existing broadcasters a large new slice of spectrum space—estimated value at the time, $70 billion—for free. No additional public-interest obligations were imposed.[16] Moreover, Congress allowed broadcasters to hang on to both portions of their spectrum—analog and digital—until 2006, or until 85 percent of American households had digital TVs, whichever came later.[17]

It could be a long wait. By 2000, TV manufacturers had sold only 50,000 digital TV sets at $5000 or more apiece, and broadcasters were not broadcasting much high-definition video programming: a classic chicken-and-egg situation. The HDTV market is not developing very quickly, nor are broadcasters especially aggressive about moving ahead with HDTV. In fact, many broadcasters are instead investigating lucrative nonbroadcast uses of the spectrum, such as cell phones and wireless e-mail. (Congress conveniently did not require the spectrum to be used for HDTV.) In October 2000, then-FCC Chairman William Kennard likened the situation to each broadcaster having two rent-controlled apartments on Manhattan's Upper East Side, with the second one left empty. To force a more productive use of the public's assets, he proposed a "spectrum squatter's fee" that would escalate yearly, starting in 2006, to prod broadcasters to complete the transition to digital TV and return the analog spectrum to the American people.[18]

Meanwhile, broadcasters' lockup of this valuable bit of spectrum could seriously affect the nation's long-term economic competitiveness. The U.S. wireless industry, one of the most robust sectors of the economy, is clamoring for spectrum space in order to develop new markets and catch up with European and Japanese technology. But the congressional giveaway of digital spectrum now precludes such moves, and a political firestorm would ensue if Congress were to try to reclaim spectrum from broadcasters.

So it is that market enclosures tend to be expansively self-reinforcing. This is seen not just in broadcasters' hammerlock on the digital spectrum space but in their successful campaign to stymie the development of low-power community radio stations.[19] In an attempt to democratize radio, counter industry concentration, and foster diversity of programming, the FCC in 2000 proposed granting a new class of noncommercial FM radio licenses that would allow schools, churches, and dozens of other community organizations to run their own radio stations. The FCC received more than 1,200 applications for low-power licenses, but in December 2000 the Senate intervened on behalf of the broadcast industry (including National Public Radio) to sharply cut back the number of potential stations, chiefly in urban areas, by as much as 75 percent. Broadcasters argued that the stations would interfere with existing radio signals, but critics charged that the real concern was protectionism—a charge given credence by a Senate amendment ordering the FCC to study the "economic impact" of low-power radio on "incumbent FM radio broadcasters."

The exile of the noncommercial sector from television has been a tremendous disenfranchisement that the rise of public television in the late 1960s did little to offset, particularly now that even public television is increasingly commercializing itself. Jerold Starr's *Air Wars* describes how public television stations have betrayed their core mission of local service and innovative programming in pursuit of corporate sponsorships and marketing partnerships.[20] Instead of fulfilling the early predictions that television would become a liberating instrument of public enlightenment, television has instead become the "vast wasteland," in Newton Minow's famous phrase—a "boob tube" filled with sensation, diversion, and idiocy, punctuated only occasionally with bracing performances or intelligence.

Fortunately, the principle of auctioning spectrum space is becoming more widely accepted, offering leverage for obtaining a fair return on public assets and perhaps new vehicles for public-interest programming. Since 1994, the FCC has conducted more than two dozen auctions for frequencies dedicated to wireless personal communications services, accepting bids that total over $36 billion. As demand for spectrum for wireless services soars, even higher sums are likely to be paid, as seen in the $46 billion in bids for German 3G wireless licenses and $35 billion in bids accepted by the British government in March 2000. Spectrum auctions at least allow the public to gain a financial payback for use of their assets; whether the public interest will simply be converted into money or whether it will be actualized through noncommercial content and other public projects is another question.

The commercial colonization of public spaces and culture is not confined to the airwaves. The remainder of this chapter examines how it is transforming childhood, sports, civic institutions, and assorted public spaces.

The Corporate Branding of Children

"There's been a shift in the predominant way our society thinks of children," observes Gary Ruskin, director of Commercial Alert, an advocacy group that fights an array of commercial excesses in American life. "Not long ago we considered children vulnerable beings to be nurtured. However, today, we increasingly see kids through an economic lens. In our business culture, children are viewed as an economic resource to be exploited, just like bauxite or timber."[21]

Having discovered that children are one of the most underexploited market segments, marketers in the 1990s made up for lost time by developing all sorts of ingenious ways to persuade impressionable youngsters to buy. According to one marketer, there is the "primary market," the $24.4

billion a year that kids directly spend; the "influence market," the $300 billion of adult spending that kids directly or indirectly influence; and the "future" market, which is the lifelong spending that kids will do based on brand loyalties they develop while young.[22]

"Branding kids for life," is how one marketer puts it. "If you own this child at an early age, said the president of Kids-R-Us, a clothing chain, "you can own this child for years to come. Companies are saying, 'Hey, I want to own the kid younger and younger.'"[23] Businesses were once satisfied with market share; today's companies realize that the real payoffs come from owning *mindshare*—the personal attitudes and loyalties of children.[24]

This motivation to insinuate brand names into children's identities has led to commercials in every imaginable crevice in a child's daily life. Video games plug Pepsi and McDonald's. McDonald's has created such videos as "Mac and Me," and "McTreasure Island," a crude adaptation of Robert Louis Stevenson's "Treasure Island." Content and advertising are now blurring, creating new forms of cryptomarketing. *Back to the Future II* featured more than two dozen brand-name products slyly integrated into the story, and *Space Jam*, a star vehicle for basketball star Michael Jordan, himself a product, set a new standard for blending a putative film with outright advertising.[25]

Commercial tie-ins between movies and toys have existed since Mickey Mouse was first licensed in 1934. But commercial substitutes (think Disney) have virtually replaced the characters of classic literature, and cross-media promotion now spans a spectrum that includes film, toys, video games, fast-food restaurants, action figures, and books. With an average weekly diet of 40 hours of media a week and 20,000 commercials a year, childhood is being turned into one seamless web of commercialism.[26]

It should not be surprising that children are adopting the values peddled by advertisers. Severe obesity among young children has doubled since the 1960s, and childhood diabetes is also on the rise—trends aggravated in no small part by advertising by fast-food restaurants and candy companies.[27] Ads exploiting young girls' fears about their body image have contributed to one third of twelve-year-old girls trying to lose weight through diets, vomiting, laxatives, or diet pills.[28]

An obvious target for innovative marketers is the public schools. Where else can such a large, age-specific cohort of children be found in one place, as mandated by law? Since outright advertising would be too blatantly unacceptable in a public institution dedicated to learning, marketers have had to develop a variety of clever subterfuges.

One of the most ambitious projects to turn public education into an advertising venue has been Channel One, the pseudo-news program for teenagers founded by Chris Whittle in 1989. By "donating" satellite dishes, VCRs, and TV sets for every classroom in participating schools, Channel One wins the right to show a daily twelve-minute video program containing two minutes of ads. Through this novel means, the company has created a whole new marketing platform for reaching a captive audience of eight million teenage students in 12,000 public and private schools.[29]

An equally ingenious scheme was hatched by ZapMe!, a company that gave a free package of computers, software, and Internet access to schools in exchange for the right to show online advertising to students. They also tracked children's every move on the Web, correlating the results with their age, gender, zip code, and other identifying information. Despite the invasion of privacy of a captive audience, some 5,000 financially beleaguered school districts signed up with ZapMe! in 1999 to receive some $90,000 of equipment per school. While some schools rationalized that kids are already exposed to plenty of advertising—why quibble about a little bit more?—others objected to public education being so crudely commandeered for commercial purposes. Due largely to agitation by Gary Ruskin's Commercial Alert and prominent congressional critics, ZapMe! abandoned its free equipment giveaways in November 2000, effectively scuttling the venture.

Such failures are unusual in the annals of corporate marketing via the public schools, however. Dozens of companies distribute slickly produced "educational" materials that give generous space to corporate logos and political propaganda. Shell Oil waxes eloquent about the virtues of the internal combustion engine, and Exxon congratulates itself for its role in restoring the ecology of Prince William Sound (while omitting mention of its role in the Exxon Valdez oil spill).[30] Textbook publishers have used brand-name products in math books, ostensibly to make the lessons more relevant to students.

Coca-Cola and Pepsi have paid millions of dollars to convince school districts to give them exclusive onsite vending contracts. Soft drink companies gain a prime sales location, the implicit endorsement of the school, a ban against competitors (which has led to higher prices), and access to a captive audience of thirsty teenagers. A Coca-Cola spokesman primly described the arrangement as a "value-added partnership." Critics have called it a betrayal of the public schools' mission, and their noisy protests finally persuaded Coca-Cola in 2001 to stop pressing its bottlers for such "partnerships" with schools.[31]

The marketing invasion of schools even reaches into higher education, where companies such as General Motors, Time Warner, Bristol-Myers Squibb, and Wells Fargo & Co., have underwritten college marketing classes where students spend a term pitching products to fellow students on campus. Some classes have thrown promotional parties for the local Chevy dealership, while others have promoted Saturn cars around campus—all for academic credit.[32]

Fortunately, public concern about commercialization in the schools is growing, even prompting a U.S. General Accounting Office survey of how well states and local school boards protect students from marketers. The answer: not very well. Only 19 states have any statutes or regulations that deal with school-related commercial activities, and these rules are partial in fourteen of the states.[33]

The Commercialization of the Public Sphere

It seems almost quaint. In 1975, in an arrangement with *Esquire*, the Xerox Corporation gave a no-strings-attached grant of $40,000 to journalist Harrison Salisbury to write a major article about his travels throughout America. What Xerox saw as a bit of enlightened sponsorship, the journalistic establishment saw as a shocking surrender of editorial integrity to advertising—a specific article sponsored by an advertiser![34]

A generation later, this kind of moral hand-wringing seems downright priggish. The monetization of civic institutions, public spaces, and public reputation is often celebrated as a "win-win" scenario—so long as the price is right. Selling and selling out have become something of a national obsession, boosted no doubt by the frenzied entrepreneurial climate of the 1990s. In any case, public institutions that were once regarded with reverence and respect have become, in the words of one marketer, "terrific, leverageable assets." In fact, the more unsullied it is by commercialism— "virgins" in the trade—the more attractive sponsors regard the "asset."

The process has clearly gotten out of hand in professional sports, which is now a prime venue for marketers. The real breakthrough event in the branding of sports, according to author Naomi Klein, was the partnership between Michael Jordan and Nike, the sneaker company. "A company that swallows cultural space in giant gulps, Nike is the definitive story of the transcendent nineties superbrand," writes Klein:

> More than any other single company, its actions demonstrate how branding seeks to erase all boundaries between the sponsor and the sponsored. This is a shoe company that is determined to

unseat pro sports, the Olympics, and even star athletes, to become the very definition of sports itself. . . . By equating the company with athletes and athleticism at such a primal level, Nike ceased merely to clothe the game and started to play it.[35]

The Nike marketing paradigm has been widely imitated, transcending moral qualms by making them seem irrelevant. Through sheer ubiquity, corporate branding creates an entirely new universe of images, products, celebrities, and companies. Brands now live and breathe in a parallel reality that renders moot any lines between content and commercial or integrity and cynicism.

Michael Sorkin explains the aesthetic as exemplified in one of the most brand-intense locations on earth, Times Square: "Think of the teenager in the Tommy t-shirt or the tourist in the MSNBC baseball cap. A deal has been cut here. By agreeing to wear the brand, we express our willingness to surrender our identities and be seen as . . . advertising. This provides a thrill, of sorts. It is the closest we get to being like real celebrities, who are recognizable enough to be their own brands, logos for themselves."[36] The commodification of personal identity and experience through branding is a epochal story of our time, with many subplots.[37]

Behind the branding phenomena is an attempt to appropriate the commons of everyday experience—identity, tradition, street vernacular—by transforming it into a salable product. The more intensely emotions are felt, the more attractive they are to brand creators. It accounts for Starbucks' embrace of jazz, Levi Strauss's celebration of street hipsters, and the Body Shop's championing of progressive causes in its marketing.

It is also why sports is such an irresistible marketing vehicle for companies. The Polo Grounds, Forbes Field, Tiger Stadium, Fenway Park, the Boston Garden, and Candlestick Park conjure up a long and cherished sports history rooted in those cities' lives and shared from one generation to the next. What company wouldn't want to own that rich set of feelings and images?

As it happens, many cities and sports franchises have been only too willing to marketize the community's fan culture by auctioning off stadium names. The result has been a series of icy names devoid of authentic emotions or context: the FleetCenter (formerly the Boston Garden), Continental Airlines Arena (the Meadowlands), 3Com Park (Candlestick Park) and FedEx Field (Washington, D.C.), Enron Field (Houston), and the new Staples Center (Los Angeles). How much is fan culture worth? A stadium-naming consultant estimates that naming deals on sports stadiums alone are worth $3.2 billion.[38]

A heartening backlash has emerged, however. Even though the City of

Denver was offered millions of dollars to sell the naming rights to a new $400 million stadium, for which taxpayers paid three quarters of construction costs. The city's Bronco fans wanted to retain the beloved old name, Mile High Stadium. "Why would you sell an identifiable icon, even for millions of dollars?" asked Mayor Wellington E. Webb. "We're a western city, a new city that doesn't have many icons. Once they're gone, they're gone. Not everything should be for sale."[39] Even though the naming rights were eventually sold for $120 million to an investment company, Invesco Funds Group Inc., many fans and one of Denver's daily newspapers are insisting upon calling Invesco Field by its historic name.[40]

Broadway theaters are also selling their evocative traditions for cold, hard cash. Upon its refurbishment, the Selwyn Theater, home to the nonprofit Roundabout Theater Company, became the American Airlines Theater. The Winter Garden Theater may become the Cadillac Theater, and other theaters may soon sport corporate marquees as well. Hasbro, a toymaker, donated $2.5 billion to have a Providence, R.I., children's hospital named after it, and a museum of African-American art in Detroit is named after General Motors.[41]

What makes perfect sense from an economic point of view serves to eradicate the distinctive identity and regional uniqueness of a public place. Naming a storied theater after an airline, for example, sends a clear message that local traditions and history itself can be "owned" by whatever distant corporation may want to buy them. The company may have no intrinsic interest in the sport or theater or city. With the sense of entitlement of a feudal lord, it may simply want to buy access to an attractive consumer demographic.

The enclosure of public spaces for business advantage has reached some rather dramatic extremes in recent years. For $6 million in cash and services, the City of Huntington Beach, California, gave Coca-Cola exclusive rights to use municipal property to sell its soft drinks, making the city one of the first branded cities.[42] The City of Sacramento has actually considered selling corporate sponsorships of "an official car rental partner," a "preferred ice cream," a "preferred coffee," and "an official undergarment supplier for city police, fire, and security." Estimated earning stream: $2 million to $5 million.[43] The Texas Parks and Wildlife Department declared the Chevrolet Suburban "the official vehicle of Texas State Parks" in return for two of the vehicles, $230,000, and some Chevy ads in the park agency's magazine. "This is part of the overall corporatizing of public parks, not only in Texas but all across the country, as park officials seek to jack up their revenues by commercializing the public domain," said author and commentator Jim Hightower.[44]

All sorts of public festivals and events—annual occasions with long traditions and brimming with regional pride—are also being bought up by corporate sponsors. According to one marketing expert, fewer than 25 percent of such festivals had corporate names attached to them fifteen years ago. Now 85 percent of festivals have corporate titles such as the Hooters Hula Bowl, the AT&T Rose Bowl, and the Kodak Albuquerque International Balloon Fiesta. Described by some critics as "the McDonaldization of local events," the corporate naming of events essentially dispossesses the local community of its sense of ownership of the tradition. The same dynamic has even affected the venerable Macy's Thanksgiving Day parade, which had built up a reservoir of hometown pride over the decades. While the parade was always intended as a marketing vehicle for Macy's, the store has recently turned it into a full-bore marketing juggernaut, charging corporate sponsors $200,000 and more to get their mascots made into massive balloons.[45]

The Rise of Captive Audience Advertising

In their indefatigable pursuit of human consciousness, advertisers in recent years have developed cunning new venues to ambush people when they think they are alone and free from commercial intrusion. Coca-Cola recently came up with a 900-foot "flip-book" series of images pasted on the underground tunnels of Atlanta subways. Another firm is pioneering the installation of TV monitors on public buses to force-feed advertising to hapless bus riders.[46] A mortgage company has sent thousands of "spam" messages to cell phones that receive text e-mails.

Space Marketing Inc., having succeeded in getting a Pizza Hut logo on the side of a Russian Proton rocket, is apparently continuing its quest to place a mile-long, half-mile-wide "billboard" made of reflective mylar plastic into orbit. "If allowed to happen," said Rep. Ed Markey, "this scheme would turn our morning and evening skies, often a source of inspiration and comfort, into the moral equivalent of the side of a bus."[47]

Some movie theaters now show as many as 20 minutes of preshow trailers and ads.[48] Dozens of radio stations are now using a new digital software program, appropriately named "Cash," to eliminate brief pockets of silence between words and so squeeze four extra minutes of advertising into each hour.[49] Programmers are so obsessive about selling that they are putting text on the bottom of TV screens during programs to plug upcoming shows. The "snipes," as they are known in the industry, represent a new form of "screen clutter" that was started when network logos and content ratings began to appear on screens.[50]

Captive-audience advertising now extends far beyond theaters and school rooms, ambushing people as they use public restrooms, gas pumps, elevators, and ATM machines. Telephone customers placed on hold are forced to listen to audio ads. Even ordinary reality is being supplanted to insert advertising. Disturbed to find an NBC logo and Budweiser ad in its video backdrop of Times Square, CBS News digitally obliterated the offending images and inserted in their place a digitally generated CBS News logo on a digitally generated billboard.[51] The same technology is used by sports broadcasters to insert corporate logos digitally on otherwise empty soccer fields and on panels behind home plate at baseball games. It has also been used to create a virtual street banner for Denny's and ad logos on sidewalks for Ford and MasterCard as movie stars arrived at the Grammy Awards.[52] An entirely new genre of "virtual advertising" is coming to supplant ad-free reality.[53]

Public Space and Civic Culture

The commandeering of shared public spaces for marketing is part of a larger project to convert community spaces into marketplaces. The basic idea is to elevate consumer obsessions over civic identity. Shopping malls may represent the purest example of this dynamic—a triumph of commercial control over the social messiness of Main Street. A mall is aesthetically soothing, homogenized, and safe. Main Streets can be loud, motley, and unpredictable.

Why does this matter? Because public spaces are one of the few places where strangers can meet and communicate in ways that do not involve selling or buying. It is a place where free speech—and all the civic and democratic benefits that flow from it—can flourish. Anyone can go to Main Street and speak their mind to strangers. That is not possible in most shopping malls.

Under a long line of U.S. Supreme Court cases, the First Amendment does not apply to shopping malls because they are considered private, not public, facilities. Now that most aspects of American life take place in the suburbs, automobiles, malls, and on television, there are almost literally no free public spaces left in which meaningful civic dialogue can occur. This is troubling because, as Margaret Kohn has argued, democratic discussion does not just occur in academic journals, direct mail, and letters to the editor. It occurs when we can encounter other citizens—solicitors for Greenpeace, homeless people, union picketers, and ordinary people who might otherwise be insulated from their fellow citizens. "For a robust democracy we need more than rational deliberation," writes Kohn. "We need public places that remind us that politics matter."[54]

We also need public spaces to have convivial neighborhoods and public life. Here, too, through sprawl development and gated communities, open, public spaces are disappearing. In New York City, hundreds of office towers and apartment buildings have received special zoning privileges (such as approval to build higher structures) in return for providing plazas, arcades, and atriums that are legally open to the public. Such spaces are at a premium for New Yorkers and represent a vital community resource. Yet as Jerold Kayden discovered when he systematically surveyed the City's 503 "privately owned public spaces," 41 percent can hardly be used by the public. They have been rendered "marginal" by locked gates, missing chairs and tables, "usurpation by adjacent commercial activities" such as delivery zones and outdoor cafes, among other actions.[55]

In isolation, few of these enclosures of public spaces, either physically or via advertising, may seem significant. This is a capitalist nation, after all, and what's the harm of a landowner squeezing a few more bucks from his property? What's the harm of a few Burma Shave signs on the roadside or naming a show the Kraft Television Theater? By ones and twos, such actions generally *are* inconsequential.

In the aggregate, however, the sheer pervasiveness of commercialism in public spaces and contemporary life has reached nearly totalitarian dimensions. "Gotcha" advertising in men's urinals and instant messaging, sports stadia and local hospitals, has the malodorous whiff of a corporate Big Brother. What may seem minor and annoying in isolated instances becomes, through its recurrence in hundreds of nooks and crannies of daily life, a defining framework of cultural values. It should come as no surprise that Internet sites during the 2000 presidential campaign invited people to sell their votes, and that tattoo parlors do a brisk business in the Nike swoosh—the branding of flesh.

The signs are still modest, but an incipient movement is stirring. Counterattacks such as Commercial Alert and the Center for Commercial-Free Public Education have beat back some excesses, most notably ZapMe!, in the process raising consciousness about lines that should not be crossed.[56] Organized protests such as "Buy Nothing Day" (on the Friday after Thanksgiving) and "National TV-Turnoff Week," sponsored by TV-Free Network, are also beginning to pique the American mainstream.[57] Even amidst the conspicuous excesses of the 1990s, the "voluntary simplicity" movement has gained quite a following among Americans trying to reclaim some peace amidst a clamorous, intrusive market economy.

While some resisters pursue ascetic or puritanical visions, many others simply want to carve out quiet, no-sell zones in which to live their lives.

They desperately want more opportunities to participate in an authentic civic and cultural commons, untainted by commercial intrusions. This was a significant force behind the Seattle protests against the World Trade Organization in 1999. The demonstrations may have been directed against various abuses caused by globalized commerce, but there is no doubt that they were also directed against the "brand bullies," as described by Naomi Klein in *No Logo*. In that sense, Seattle was an important salvo of the emerging movement to reclaim the cultural commons.

11.

The Giveaway of Federal Drug Research and Information Resources

Such a deal! The taxpayers pay to invent a promising drug, then give a monopoly to one company. And the company's role? To agree to sell it back to us.

—James Love, Consumer Project on Technology[1]

Drug expenditures in the U.S. have doubled since 1993, and are expected to double again by 2004[2]—a troubling trend that provoked politicians in the 2000 campaigns to quarrel about how to make prescription drugs more affordable. Strangely, the hand-wringing over exorbitant drug prices has ignored the federal government's role in *giving away* its most promising drug research and development (R&D) for a fraction of its actual value. Drug companies then charge whatever prices the market will bear. It is a sweet deal for drugmakers but an outrage for millions of American taxpayers and consumers.

Call it a hidden subsidy to the highly profitable drug industry, the kind of corporate welfare seldom tallied in the accounting books or remarked upon in Washington salons. Yet some of the most important drug break-throughs of the past fifty years have been generated by the National Institutes of Health and other government-funded researchers. These include drugs to fight cancer and treat HIV and AIDS, and treatments for genetic disorders, depression, and diabetes, among many others.

It is a scandalous fact that the fruits of risky and expensive scientific work typically do not accrue to the sponsors/investors, the American people, until drug companies have extracted huge markups of their own. Invaluable research is routinely given away for a fraction of its potential market value. The American people pay twice: first, as taxpayers, reaping a lower (or nonexistent) return on their investments, and second as consumers, paying higher drug prices charged by pharmaceutical companies.

This long-standing arrangement in drug R&D is now replicating itself in genetic research. Public science is paying the bills for the breakthroughs while private players are allowed to rush in and acquire patent monopolies that raise prices, stifle competition, and inhibit future research.[3]

Corporate Free Riding on Federal Pharmaceutical Research

The federal government's role in sponsoring basic research and developing new drugs is extensive and expensive.[4] The government funds the discovery of new therapeutic agents, sponsors clinical testing of drugs in humans, and develops and refines drug manufacturing techniques. Throughout the life of a drug, publicly funded research provides a rich source of fundamental knowledge for discovering new drugs, designing drugs that have already been discovered, and providing clinical guidance for new indications for drugs already approved.[5]

When government does the preclinical testing of a new drug, the most difficult and risky aspect of new drug development, it is shouldering some 65 to 70 percent of the total development costs. The key role left to industry, when using federally sponsored research, is to meet the requirements of a New Drug Application (NDA), from the Food and Drug Administration (FDA) in order to market the drug. While this can be a costly process, it pales in comparison to the research already sponsored by taxpayers. The pharmaceutical industry has claimed that it spends more than $500 million on R&D for every new drug developed. But a 2001 report by Public Citizen, the consumer group, found that once taxpayer-funded research and tax credits are calculated in, actual R&D costs are about $110 million per new drug. The federal government paid for at least 55 percent of the published research that led to the discovery and development of the five top-selling drugs in 1995, (Vasotec and Capoten for hypertension, the antiviral drug Zovirax, Prozac and Zantac), according to an internal NIH document obtained by Public Citizen.[6]

Numerous studies have confirmed the paramount role of government research in developing the most medically significant drugs. An MIT study in 1995 found that eleven of the fourteen new drugs that industry identified as the most medically significant over the preceding 25 years had their origins in work sponsored by the government. A study of 32 innovative drugs introduced before 1990, reports the Senate Joint Economic Committee, found that approximately 60 percent of the drugs would not have been discovered or would have had their discoveries markedly delayed, but for government funding.[7] The invaluable role of public science is reflected as well in medical patents. More than 70 percent of the scientific papers cited on the front pages of U.S. industry patents were products of public science—government or academia—according to a study commissioned by the National Science Foundation, while only 17 percent were industry sponsored.[8]

When Love and Nader looked at the government's role in developing new cancer drugs, they found that the federal government was involved in the preclinical development of 28 of 37 drugs developed since 1955.[9] For cancer drugs that reached the clinical stage of research, the National Cancer Institute (NCI) was involved in 34 of the 37 cancer drugs developed.[10]

One of the most lucrative drugs has been paclitaxel, also known under its brand name, Taxol, which is used to treat cancer of the breast, lung, and ovaries. Using Pacific yew trees on federal lands, the NCI spent fifteen years and $32 million to develop paclitaxel, before inviting pharmaceutical firms to enter into a Cooperative Research and Development Agreement. The agreement sets forth the terms of government-industry collaboration, including up-front guarantees of exclusive patent rights even before any discoveries were made. In the case of paclitaxel, NCI chose Bristol-Myers (now Bristol-Myers Squibb) over three other applicants, giving the company exclusive access to government-funded research, including raw data and new studies.

Although the agreement had a "fair pricing clause," there were no clear criteria by which the NCI could enforce it, according to records obtained by Love through the Freedom of Information Act.[11] The actual cost of manufacturing paclitaxel, according to Love, is about $500 per patient for an 18-month treatment regimen. Bristol-Myers Squibb charges more than twenty times that, earning between $4 million and $5 million a day on Taxol, Love estimates.[12] In 1999, the drug generated an estimated $1.7 billion in sales for the company.

Bristol-Myers Squibb claims that it spent $1 billion to bring Taxol to market. But in light of the government's significant role in discovering and developing the drug, that claim seems dubious, according to Love's analysis.[13] The government did most of the drug development, the company bought the yew bark at discount prices from the federal government, and the NCI itself says the chief reason Bristol-Myers Squibb was selected was for its marketing expertise in selling cancer drugs.[14] Three other drug companies were interested in bringing paclitaxel to market, which suggests that an exclusive license for the drug was probably unnecessary.

A similar story can be told about Xalatan, an eyedrop-administered drug for glaucoma that was initially developed at Columbia University using $4 million in NIH money. The Pharmacia Corporation bought the patent to the drug from Columbia for no more than $150,000 and a share of future royalties. Pharmacia claims it then spent tens of millions of dollars to bring the drug to market.

When Xalatan finally hit the market, it charged from $45 to $50 for a tiny bottle that lasts for six weeks, or about $1 a day. Given that the key ingredient costs only 1 percent of the revenue it generates, Xalatan represents "liquid gold" for Pharmacia, in the words of one reporter.[15] In 1999, company sales of the drug amounted to $507 million, of which Columbia University received about $20 million in royalties. The federal government receives nothing.

Government officials have defended the exclusive licensing of Xalatan, saying that the reward to taxpayers is the drug itself. But to the two million Americans who suffer from glaucoma, many of whom are older people living on fixed incomes and can ill afford high-priced drugs, such arguments probably seem weak. Not only have taxpayers received nothing for their investment, they must pay an inflated price for a drug that their taxes financed.

These are not isolated stories. There are many other important drugs that were developed with federally funded research, and for which companies later charged handsome prices. These drugs include Prozac (for clinical depression), Capoten (for hypertension) and a variety of HIV- and AIDs-related drugs such as AZT, ddI, ddC, d4T, Ziagen, and Norvir.[16] That companies have charged high prices for such drugs, despite the government's primary role in shouldering the major costs, has naturally stirred great resentment among patients.

For years, drug companies nominally had to abide by a "reasonable pricing" clause in federal law. Any new drugs developed with federal funds were supposed to bear some "reasonable" relationship to the costs of development. But the NIH believed that the clause discouraged drug companies from collaborating with the government, and urged Congress to strike the clause, which it did in 1995. Fortunately, Rep. Bernie Sanders succeeded in reinstating the clause in June 2000.[17] Enforcing the provision may be the real challenge.

Enforcement may be difficult because the U.S. government does not even keep careful records of what new discoveries and inventions its funding has catalyzed. As many as 22 percent of discoveries financed by the federal health institutes go unreported, according to the Department of Health and Human Services, despite a law requiring universities receiving federal money to make such reports.[18] The U.S. General Accounting Office has concluded that the reporting system is "inaccurate, incomplete and inconsistent."

The political clout clearly belongs to the pharmaceutical industry, which actually tried to eliminate "notice and comment" requirements for exclusive drug licenses in 1999. The law currently allows the public to learn basic economic information about a drug's development and sale, such as royalty rates paid on licenses, subsequent development costs, and sales figures. The government must disclose such information, and allow the public to object to the granting of a license. Fortunately, the industry's attempt to throw a veil of secrecy over the granting of exclusive drug licenses failed.

Returning Drugs to the Commons: The Importance of Generics

Thanks to a 1984 federal law, the patent monopoly that the U.S. government grants to the makers of new medicines is not indefinite. When a drug's patent expires, other manufacturers can petition the FDA for permission to market a generic version that has the same active ingredients as the original drug and can achieve the same therapeutic results. This means that a proprietary drug becomes a commodity. Competitors can arise to sell the identical drug combination—without its brand name—at much lower prices. Much like the public domain in copyright, generic drugs represent the triumph of the commons.

Before the 1980s, generics were a fairly narrow slice of the drug market. A key reason was that would-be manufacturers of generic drugs had to undergo the same panoply of costly drug reviews that any new drug had to undergo. The Drug Price Competition and Patent Term Restoration Act, commonly known as the Hatch-Waxman Act, made it dramatically easier for generics to enter the market by streamlining the FDA's drug approval process. Instead of having to re-prove safety and efficacy, generic drug makers only have to demonstrate "bioequivalence"—that the drug has the same medical effects as the "innovator" drug. Because of Hatch-Waxman, the entry of generic drugs to the market became much easier and less costly.

In 1983, before this act was passed, only a third of the top-selling drugs had generic competition when the patents expired. Nowadays, virtually all drugs whose patents are expiring face generic competition. The market share of generic drugs has risen from about 19 percent in 1984 to 43 percent in 1996. Because generics are available, consumers saved an estimated $8 billion to $10 billion on prescriptions at retail pharmacies in 1994.[19] Prices are typically 25 to 50 percent less than brand-name equivalents.[20]

Predictably, a functioning commons is generally seen by proprietary enterprises as a threat. Proprietary companies are concerned that over the next five years, the patents of twenty blockbuster drugs with combined sales of $20 billion will expire. As this happens, the average top drug company is likely to lose 30 percent of its sales to generics by 2003, according to the Boston Consulting Group.[21] Alarmed by these realities, brand-name drugmakers have stepped up their efforts to stifle generic competitors. They are mounting new and creative court challenges to try to prevent new generic approvals, knowing that a delay even of a few months can be tremendously lucrative.[22]

Some proprietary drug maker contrive dubious patent lawsuits against generic competitors in order to gain as much as 30 months more patent exclusivity—and tens of millions in revenues. Others have filed "citizen petitions" at the FDA ostensibly to call attention to problems with a generic drug but in fact to delay FDA approval of the drug and thus its entrance in the marketplace.

In what may be seen as the ultimate tactic, some proprietary drug-makers have actually made payments to generic manufacturers to keep generic products off the market.[23] According to the Federal Trade Commission, Abbott Laboratories paid generic manufacturer Geneva Pharmaceuticals $4.5 million a month to delay its introduction of Hytrin, a drug used for prostate enlargement and high blood pressure. The move was apparently designed to extend the proprietary company's market monopoly while extending the generic company's legally mandated, competition-free 180-day head start in the marketplace.[24]

Still another tactic is to use political contributions and lobbying to win longer patent terms for proprietary drugs, sometimes on an *ad hoc* basis. In 2000, Schering-Plough, the maker of Claritin, the popular allergy drug, unsuccessfully sought a special three-year patent extension from Congress. The move would have cost consumers an extra $7 billion and set a precedent for extending the patents of other popular drugs such as Prozac, Prilosec, and Vasotec. The value of delay is significant. Prilosec reportedly earns $11 million a day for its manufacturer, AstraZeneca.

As a market that revolves around a type of common ownership of once-proprietary goods, the generic drugs market represents an important commons. In that capacity, generics have had a highly salutary effect on competition and prices without seriously affecting the R&D of top drug-makers.[25]

Squandering the Public's Information Resources

The U.S. government is the largest and arguably the most important publisher and owner of information resources in the world. It generates thousands of authoritative reports and hearing records each year, sponsors cutting-edge scientific research in dozens of fields, and manages a huge variety of comprehensive databases. Government agencies hold some of the most sophisticated information available about agriculture, food safety, chemical safety, the environment, financial markets, labor markets, and much, much more.

Are American taxpayers receiving good value for their huge investments in government information? The short answer is: it depends. Significant progress has been made in making government information more accessible to the public, particularly since the rise of the Internet in the late 1990s. But a great many collections of valuable government studies, hearings, databases, and other information remain largely inaccessible.

The primary issue here is not so much the brazen giveaway of resources, although that still occurs. Rather, it is a failure to provide citizens with easy, low-cost access to government information, despite the availability of excellent distribution methods such as the Government Printing Office, the World Wide Web, and the Federal Depository Library Program.

The reasons for this failure vary. Many agencies do not have the money, expertise, or will to put their documents online. At other agencies, the technical expertise and systems for making information available are often missing. Still other agencies reflexively give private vendors exclusive control over federal information resources, enabling them to charge high prices in noncompetitive markets.

The executive branch has failed to provide much leadership or coordination in developing more thoughtful, citizen-friendly information policies. Maybe that is because making high-quality government information easily available could trigger greater scrutiny of the government's performance. This is certainly the case in Congress, which has been scandalously resistant to making its hearing records, legislative bills, research reports, and even members' voting records available on the Web.

The upshot: not only are taxpayers denied ready access to information they have already paid for, but a vital element of democratic openness and accountability is being thwarted.

It took a struggle to force the Securities and Exchange Commission to make corporate financial data available in the early 1990s. At the time, in the pre-Internet world, it was standard procedure for government agencies to give away their valuable data and reports to private information vendors, who would then resell them—perhaps with minor value-added improvements—at exorbitant prices. Corporate clients could afford the tab, but ordinary citizens found themselves priced out of the market for information they had paid to generate.

It was business as usual as the SEC deliberately tried to forfeit control of EDGAR, a new electronic system for filing corporate disclosure reports, to a private vendor, Mead Data Central. Despite the SEC's $50 million investment in developing the database, taxpayers would not even own a copy of the database, and access to it would be subject to high fees. The government alone would pay $2 million a year to access the EDGAR database. Other companies would typically charge hundreds of dollars for a single online session and $15 or more per document.

A public-spirited Internet activist, Carl Malamud, challenged this model and established the precedent that government data should be available for free on the Web. Working with consumer advocate James Love, Malamud decided to put the SEC's data on his own Web server at his own expense (and later with a grant from the National Science Foundation), undercutting the potential market for raw SEC data compilations.[26] While industry critics complained that the government was competing with private information services, it was in fact reclaiming the public's information for the public commons. Business competition was simply being shifted to more sophisticated, value-added markets, where it could do the most good, while public access to government information was being equalized. Access to the data would not be restricted to large Wall Street law firms and stock brokerages, but could now be feasibly accessed by individual investors, small businesses, financial journalists, and scholars.[27]

The SEC precedent and the growth of the Web in the late 1990s— which made it relatively cheap and easy to put digital information online—helped sweep aside many of the government's retrograde information policies. There are now more than 20,000 government Web sites, enabling citizens instantly to call up a cornucopia of information on their computer screens. The State Department puts up transcripts and audio feeds of its daily briefings, and the EPA posts its Toxics Release Inventory database. The Supreme Court finally got around to opening its own Web site in April 2000, letting anyone read the court's rulings. The public was so interested in its *Bush v. Gore* ruling on December 4, 2000, that the site had to use nineteen servers to accommodate 1.1 million requests for the case in thirteen hours.

But serious problems in information policy remain. The fate of the National Technical Information Service (NTIS), a priceless repository of highly technical research reports spanning nearly fifty years, remains in limbo as Congress and the executive branch argue over which federal agency should oversee it and how cheap and accessible NTIS documents should be.[28] There are problems in assuring "permanent access" to documents that are put up on the Web, only to be taken down later without notice or explanation. Among some federal agencies, there are copyright or copyrightlike barriers to the public use of government documents, notwithstanding a statutory prohibition against the copyright of materials prepared by the government.[29]

The most retrograde set of information policies, fittingly enough, has to do with Congress. As Speaker of the House, the self-styled revolutionary Newt Gingrich promised to bring Congress into the information age by putting congressional documents online. At the time, the daily *Congressional Record* and the original text of bills were available. But much more was not.[30]

"Some of the most important texts of bills—discussion drafts, chairman's marks, manager's marks, committee prints—are rarely placed on the Internet," notes Gary Ruskin, a longtime critic of government information policies and director of the Congressional Accountability Project. "So while Washington lobbyists read the relevant drafts of bills, most Americans can only obtain antiquated versions."[31] *Roll Call*, the congressional newspaper, called this two-tiered system for distributing information "Info-Corruption" because it allows corporate lobbyists and committee chairmen to negotiate legislation behind closed doors, leaving the public frozen out of the process.[32]

Another egregious void in congressional information is the voting records of members. While individual members and congressional committees often have their own Web pages, filled with self-serving press releases and other fluff, there is no easily searchable Internet database of congressional voting records indexed by bill name, subject, and members' names.

Congressional hearings are a rich and timely reservoir of information, but each committee makes its own decisions about whether to make this information available online. Some do, many do not. As Congress dithers and delays, an entrepreneur, Philip Angell, launched HearingRoom.Com to sell near-real-time transcripts of hearings in all 192 congressional committees. Using a private, digital network of speech recognition software and audio- and video-streaming technology, the company delivers a synchronized stream of text and audio with 95 percent accuracy and on a five- to ten-minute delay. Real-time service will be $1,000 per hearing; a yearly subscription to transcripts via the Internet costs $5,000 to $15,000. Of course, the only people who can afford such prices are corporate lawyers, lobbyists, and other well-heeled special interests.

By failing to take the most basic steps to make its hearings accessible via the Internet, Congress has in effect created a special set of corporate skyboxes for its deliberations, leaving other branches of government and state governments to fend for themselves. The public, by Congress's reckoning, stands last in line. "Congressional hearings are public information," said Gary Ruskin. "We taxpayers paid for these hearings. We ought to be able to read them, on the Internet, for free."[33]

Congress not only grants special access to business, it helps shield corporate influence-peddling by refusing to put lobbyist disclosure reports on the Internet even though they are electronically stored. These reports disclose which lobbyists are paid how much by whom to work on a particular issue: politically explosive information that Congress does not really want the press or public to obtain readily. Anyone who wants the disclosure reports has to trek personally up to a little office in the Capitol building.[34]

A similar controversy, still unresolved, surrounds public access to special research on thousands of issues that come before it. Congress spends over $64 million a year on reports from the Congressional Research Service (CRS), but it refuses to make CRS reports available to the public except through special requests to members' offices. Traditionally, Congress has seen the CRS reports as a kind of precious largess to be dispensed to constituents as a favor. But a number of firms have arisen to sell bootleg versions of CRS reports; one such firm charges $49 per report.

Twice Burned ...

The federal giveaway of taxpayer assets may have a long and inglorious tradition in American life, but it is one that is grossly unbecoming to a democratic people. The "double payment" by Americans—first, as taxpayers, second, as consumers—is increasingly embarrassing and politically provocative. Not only do private companies reap a huge windfall from this arrangement, but they have little incentive to explore sophisticated, value-added innovations or new markets. Why should a company challenge itself to excel in new areas of public benefit, after all, when ample profits can already be had for so little effort?

The bigger loss, of course, is to the public itself. The privatization of the public domain of research and information impoverishes scientific research, journalism, civic and cultural public discussion, and the quality of political discourse. Now that the Internet is helping showcase the indefensible, it is time for Congress and federal agencies to give the American people a better return on their investments.

Part III.

Protecting

the Commons

12.

The Commons:
Another Kind of Property

The concept of the commons flies in the face of the modern wisdom that each spot on the globe consists merely of coordinates on a global grid laid out by state and market.... *Commons* implies the right of local people to define their own grid.

—*The Ecologist* magazine[1]

"Do communities have rights?" That question was once posed by Joseph Sax, the great legal proponent of the public trust doctrine.[2] His question points to one of the central quandaries explored by this book: that various commons are surprisingly powerful engines of economic, social, and personal value, yet they are depressingly vulnerable to enclosure. The problem is that we hardly have a vocabulary for articulating when a commons is threatened, let alone for selecting from an array of effective strategic responses.

This should not be surprising. It is an unexamined premise of our liberal market polity that individual interests are paramount, especially with respect to property rights, and that the strictest protection of these rights yields the common good. The idea of *communities* having sovereign, indivisible interests, and needs, especially when it comes to property, seems alien. Schooled as we are in market ideology, we have trouble understanding that *community wealth* can generate distinctive forms of value—economic, social, and personal—that the market cannot.

Upon reflection, however, this is partly what the American experiment in self-governance is all about: a project of constructing a common-wealth—a civic organism; a commons; one nation, indivisible—that works for the benefit of all. The commonwealth is dedicated not just to preserving individual rights in a market based on the ability to pay, but to promoting the *general welfare* based on an inclusive civic equality. The market needs to be understood as a mechanism that is inscribed *within* the commonwealth, not vice versa. At bottom, we know that the rambunctious, anarchic energies of the market can survive only if they can be tamed to behave within the edifice of our democratic republic.

Our American pragmatism confirms this. Consider how often we have been willing to suspend our market ideology and its "tyranny of small decisions"[3] to embrace collective solutions that work, from Social Security to national parks to environmental regulation. The problem is that the predominance of economic discourse, particularly over the past two decades, has eclipsed our traditional American reliance on collective solutions to collective problems. In the process, incessant market-talk has stymied the development of a more muscular public philosophy of the commons.

The next two chapters are a first step toward that much larger project. This chapter focuses on some of the conceptual barriers we must overcome in understanding the commons. Why is it so difficult for Americans to comprehend the dynamics of the commons? What rudimentary taxonomies might we use to classify the different sorts of commons encountered in the preceding chapters? What broad generalizations might be made about the commons?

This conceptual overview will be followed in Chapter 13 with a survey of specific strategies—legal, social, and cultural—that can help us construct and maintain the commons. The strategies do not presume to "solve" the dozens of enclosures described in this book. But they do sketch some promising ways that government, voluntary organizations, and diverse communities can help fortify the commons as a vessel of economic, social, and personal gain.

Public Trust Doctrine and "Inherently Public Property"

In reclaiming the commons, we might best begin by understanding that certain resources and dimensions of life ought to be regarded as inherently public. This idea has its roots in Roman law.[4] The Romans believed that some forms of property, by their very nature, should not be subject to individual ownership and control. These types of property were known as *res extra commercium*. By contrast, property that could only be used in common, because it was indivisible or "fugitive"—such as fish, game, waterways, and the ocean—were called *res communes*. The Romans even had a separate legal category, *res publicæ*, for property that was reserved for public use by civil servants and politicians. This included public structures, memorials, and furniture.

Drawing upon this tradition, American courts developed a distinct line of "public trust" analysis to recognize certain forms of property, such as natural resources,[5] roads, and navigable waters,[6] as inherently public property. In recent decades, the legal concept of the "common heritage of mankind" (*res communes humanitatus*) has been applied to deep seabed minerals, human genetic structures, the global atmosphere, and other resources which should not legally be appropriated by any one individual or state.[7]

It is revealing that public trust doctrine, while durable, has not been well developed. Like the commons itself, there is perhaps uncertainty about how to define it. Yet there is sufficient clarity to say that inherently public property belongs to the people, even if the state nominally owns and formally administers it. But this state ownership is not absolute. The people in common are considered the true owners, and the state is empowered only to act as a trustee for the public. This is not a mere formality but a substantive legal doctrine that limits the power of government to alienate the people's rights in the property.

In essence, there are two different versions of the public embodied in public trust doctrine: "[O]ne is the 'public' that is constituted as governmental authority, whose ability to manage and dispose of trust property is plenary," writes Professor Carol Rose. "But the other is the public at large, which despite its unorganized state seems to have some property-like rights in the lands held in trust for it—rights that may be asserted against the public's own representatives."[8] Thus, under one theory of public trust doctrine, the people are considered sovereign in their ownership, which means that neither government nor private parties can deprive the people of their beneficial interests in common property they own.

A primary use of public trust doctrine in the nineteenth century was to assure that roads and navigable waterways were open to an indefinite, open-ended class of users: the general public. If a single property owner could prevent the public from using a given stretch of road or waterway, then the scale returns that the public could collectively reap through commerce would be diminished. The cornucopia of the commons would be thwarted. In the twentieth century, this same reasoning has been applied to assure certain public interests with respect to beaches, water policy, public lands management, wildlife, and ecological resources in general.[9]

So while the commons, as a concept of law, has survived, its growth has been hobbled not just by political opposition but also by cultural prejudices. The very idea of a commons seems alien to our highly individualistic society whose economic orthodoxy revolves around "rational" actors using property to generate private wealth. After all, the commons focuses on collective well-being and not on individual enrichment. It places the social organism at the center. It is not just concerned with the "thingness" of property, as our market culture is, but also with the social management of commonly owned resources, be they property, information, or social values.[10]

There is a long tradition among property theorists and libertarians of regarding common property and private property as polar opposites.[11] The argument purports to find human beings "naturally" committed to rational self-interest and private property. Cooperation in pursuit of shared goals is discounted as a vestigial trait of little consequence.[12] According to natural-rights traditionalists, there is private property (sole ownership) and there is the commons (open access), and not much else in between. An entire edifice of political philosophy and *laissez-faire* economics is built upon this stark dichotomy.

But this narrative is highly misleading and contradictory. After all, a private-property regime cannot function unless people are willing to cooperate with each other in order to respect each other's property and make and enforce laws against theft, fraud, and so forth. A civil society, a commonwealth, is needed to administer any property regime. There must be shared cultural norms. But it has been pointed out that champions of strict private property rights—John Locke, William Blackstone, Richard Epstein, and Robert Nozick—cannot really explain how a mass of self-serving individualists can possibly get together to create a civil society. Such a project requires public-spirited cooperation among people who are supposedly incapable of it.[13]

The point of exposing this contradiction is to show how the classical story about property rights is really a polemical narrative, a foundational myth.[14] It is an attempt to deny the actual role of cooperation in ordering our society and structuring property rights. It seeks to skirt past the fact that our democratic commonwealth *enframes* any system of private property rights and takes precedence over it. Any functioning market system requires a range of public institutions and cultural norms to support it.[15] From this perspective, the free enterprise system is itself a kind of commons regime: a cooperative endeavor to enhance collective well-being based on rights of private property, contracts, and market exchange. But as the dozens of examples in this book demonstrate, there are other ways to advance collective well-being than through property, contracts, and market exchange. Call them the commons in its many permutations.

The Many Faces of the Commons

A number of distinctions are useful at this point. Under the rubric of "the commons," it makes sense to distinguish "public assets," "common assets," and the commons as a social regime.[16]

Public assets and services are owned and delivered by government and financed by taxes of various sorts. This property—buildings, objects, real estate—is what the Romans would have called *res publicæ*. But common assets are different because they are typically unowned, unpriced, and increasingly vulnerable to enclosure by private owners. These assets would be considered *res communes* in Roman law.

The distinction may seem minor but in fact it helps illuminate a central challenge in defending the commons. Public assets do not necessarily require new legal structures or property boundaries to be preserved; sometimes they simply need better government management or political oversight. But a key challenge facing "unowned" common assets is to devise new legal forms of common ownership and/or social practice. Without such protections, enclosures of the commons are more likely to occur.

One solution is to "assetize" a common asset through new structures such as stakeholder trusts, cooperatives, contractual clauses such as the General Public License, and boundaries on community membership. The idea is to make the resource "property on the outside, commons on the inside." Good examples would be land trusts and open-source-code software communities. Another (complementary) approach is to protect the commons by leveraging the social practices of the community itself. As scholars of common-pool resources have shown, people can come together to manage a scarce resource and pursue their shared interests as a group.

This is a third facet of the commons: the commons as a social regime, not merely as a physical asset. The gift economies examined in Chapter 2—scientific communities, New York's community gardens, blood donation systems—are examples. Through social means alone, it is possible for shared community practices to manage common resources and sustain certain values.

The problem today is that we have barely developed a mental framework for entertaining such vehicles as worthy alternatives to marketization. Curiously enough, the corporate charter for municipalities in early English law was actually used to affirm the sovereignty of a community.[17] Scholar Martha Hirschfield writes: "With respect to property, the charter defined a preexisting community by what it owned, not as a collective or a commons, but as an 'individual.' Corporate membership, in turn, was conceived not as an asset one could buy or sell, but as a non-fungible characteristic derived by virtue of one's belonging to the 'person' of the corporate community."[18]

The corporate charter, in this sense, legally recognized the indivisible community as a community. In time, of course, membership in that "community" became alienable. People could buy or sell shares in the corporate body, and the organic integrity of the community as a group of people with shared values and commitments dissolved. Reclaiming the commons requires us to imagine new kinds of "institutional DNA" that might resurrect the original goals of the corporate charter. The sovereignty of the community needs better legal definition.

An interesting case study in how the contemporary corporate form works against the interests of community can be seen in the Alaska Native Claims Settlement Act. To clear the way for oil drilling in Alaska in 1971, Congress forced Native American tribes to incorporate into profit-making corporations, a move intended to help them assimilate into modern life and benefit from oil revenues. But the corporations were not able to generate enough jobs or dividends, and the alienability of the corporate shares meant that outsiders could gain control of the Native Americans' corporate assets (especially their land) after twenty years. For Native American tribes, this is not just an economic misfortune; it amounts to a loss of their identity and heritage.[19]

This drama suggests that we need to find better ways to assure the long-term sovereignty of communities against the market's tendency to buy and sell anything. Ways must be found to take certain shared resources and values "off the market." Structures that foster the commons offer good chances for doing so. Why? Because the corporate DNA invariably seeks to maximize return on investment, chiefly over the short term. Shares are owned by the principle of one dollar, one share, and shares can be bought and sold. But in the commons, the goal is to maximize the long-term value of the asset and social stability. Shares are owned by the principle of one person, one share, and shares are inalienable. They can be "owned" only by authentic members of the community. It is difficult, even impossible, for members of the community to "cash out" at the expense of everyone else.[20]

The Misunderstood Commons

Because we are so immersed in the familiar categories and mythologies of the market, it helps to probe why the commons is so frequently misunderstood. Much of the problem might be traced to the formalism of economics and its inability to explain the complexities of social and personal behavior. Unlike neoclassical economic theory, a commons analysis does not imagine a formalized world of hyperrational, utilitarian exchange. It frankly acknowledges that the world is run by flesh-and-blood human beings who have a range of contradictory and subtle attitudes and behaviors. We are creatures who not only compete with each other, but cooperate as well. In this sense, the commons is a subject more suited to broad humanistic inquiry than narrow economic analysis.

To look at economic phenomena through the prism of a commons reveals a constellation of cultural facts that market theory flattens. The rich texture of shared social understandings—whether based on nationality, profession, local residency, or personal affinity—comes into focus. Individuals' choices are not existential and abstract, as market theory has it, but rooted in a dense history of personal and community relationships. The actors of a commons are not individuals who migrate from one isolated economic transaction to another seeking material advantage. They are situated in a more complex, enduring social order: "the dangerous, fluid, subtle generosities that bind members into crystallized orders of relation, in all dimensions of human life, from which they cannot easily be released," as John Frow puts it. "These patterns of obligation are, at the same time, in tension with the contractual rationality of the commodity, which produces quite different forms of the everyday."[21]

To Western societies, the property boundaries and operating rules of a commons are disconcertingly complex, blurry, and informal. The legal clarity is missing. Indeed, as a way of managing property, the commons seems to have too many variations. How can one begin to generalize about an institution that varies so greatly?

Our sense of the commons as a disorienting concept, then, is entirely understandable. Yet this does not make it an overbroad model. The conceptual orientation and vocabulary of the commons point to a different vector of human possibility from the market and, in this sense, implies a different metaphysical stance. Notions of "progress" and the future differ. And yet—and this is the interesting thing—the market and the commons are conjoined in subtle ways, and depend on each other, as we saw in Chapter 2.

The commons is also a perplexing concept because it is still an emerging realm of inquiry. There are few shared definitions. The term is applied to everything from air and water, wildlife, the Antarctic continent, academic communities, genetic structures, folk culture, among many other domains. The literature on the commons is sprawling and irregular.[22] Different disciplines—economics, political science, anthropology, sociology, environmental science—approach the subject with different premises and biases. A great many of them focus on small-scale commons in undeveloped countries, which are seen as having little relevance to the United States.

There is also a basic intellectual reason why study of the commons is a fragmented field of inquiry. Its premises cannot be universalized in broad, ahistorical ways—a "problem" that does not constrain conventional economics. Since the commons is essentially a social institution, its character naturally varies according to its resource base, legal regime, history, culture, and geographic setting. In so many instances, as *The Ecologist* magazine explains, the commons lives in a nether space between the market and the state:

> [The commons] provides sustenance, security and indepen-
> dence, yet (in what many Westerners feel to be a paradox)
> typically does not produce commodities. Unlike most things in
> modern industrial society, moreover, it is neither private nor
> public: neither commercial farm nor communist collective,
> neither business firm nor state utility, neither jealously guarded
> private plot nor national or city park. Nor is it usually open to
> all. The local community typically decides who uses it and
> how.[23]

The commons, *The Ecologist* authors continue, "is the social and political space where things get done and where people derive a sense of belonging and have an element of control over their lives."[24] It is a nonprivate realm that is readily accessible, openly shared, and governed by consensual rules among members who share a rough equity of interests. This is not necessarily the case in market regimes, where disparities of wealth are often great and where individual wealth can "buy" political and legal advantage.

Some Generalizations about the Commons

It is clear that there is not likely to be a unified-field theory of the commons any time soon. The taxonomies and approaches vary too much. But this very fact—the adaptability of the commons to local circumstances, from the Alpine meadows to lobster-fishing fiefs to Internet communities—accounts for its success as a governance regime.[25] It is not monolithic and rigid; it is versatile and flexible. This is a disconcerting idea: a single term, the commons, that sanctions an incredible diversity of phenomenon.

Still, much can be learned from investigating successful commons. One of the most influential theorists is Elinor Ostrom, whose pioneering study of small-scale "common-pool resource" (CPR) institutions, *Governing the Commons*, helped define the field. Ostrom identifies eight design principles for effective CPR regimes. These include clearly defined boundaries to the resource; usage rules tailored to the specific resource; a process of collective rule-making that involves all users; monitoring and accountability of usage; graduated sanctions for violations; and low-cost mechanisms for resolving conflicts.[26]

Other analysts have developed different, derivative, or overlapping frameworks for understanding the commons. Important books include *The Global Commons*, by Susan Buck,[27] *The Question of the Commons*, by Bonnie J. McCay and James M. Acheson,[28] *Common Property Economics*, by Glenn G. Stevenson,[29] and *Whose Common Future?* by the staff of *The Ecologist* magazine.[30] There are also a number of forums in which analysts and practitioners gather to develop a better understanding of the commons.[31]

This scholarship is invaluable, but it may or may not illuminate the commons examined in this book. The American democratic system has its own distinctive features which bear on how contemporary commons operate. I will not presume to propose a grand blueprint, but there are some general principles that seem to be present in the successful commons of American life.

Openness and Feedback

While any functioning commons must have boundaries, much of its effectiveness stems from a social "transparency" among its participants. This means that there must be clear and effective "feedback loops" about resources and relationships in the commons. Openness and feedback help keep everyone apprised of what is going on. They help participants modify their governance rules as circumstances change. Transparency also encourages frank and probing discussion, which improves management and accountability in the commons.

A familiar example of transparent norms can be found in scientific communities, whose members critique their peers' published research, find flaws, debate hypotheses, and build new research on previous work. Open dialogue helps move this process in more fruitful directions. Citizens of our Jeffersonian democracy, similarly, use the openness guaranteed by the First Amendment to root out error, provide feedback, and develop a political consensus for governing. In small-scale commons, to cite another example, openness allows sheepherders to monitor the amount of grazing that other animals do, helping to identify and sanction herders who violate the rules.

Collective Decision-Making

A commons is flexible yet hardy precisely because it draws information from everyone in a "bottom-up" flow. This means that the rules are "smarter" because they reflect knowledge about highly specific, local realities. Inclusive decision-making is more likely to be responsive and tailored to actual realities. This helps account for the durability of so many commonly managed fisheries and irrigation systems and for the ecological sensitivity of well-managed commons.

The effectiveness of collective decision-making in a commons is not really surprising. Rules informed by popular participation are more likely to have moral authority because everyone affected by the rules has had a say in formulating them. In addition, because the rules are not mere formalities, but robust social practices that are integrated into people's daily lives, the governance of a commons has great stability and depth.

Interestingly, complexity theory—the science of complex adaptive systems in nature, economics, computer networks, and other realms—holds that feedback mechanisms are crucial for evolutionary success. A complex adaptive system that has constant and subtle flows of information about the external environment—an organism, a business enterprise, a software system—is likely to incorporate that knowledge into its governance schema. When that "new knowledge" can be integrated into an organism's genes, a company's business strategy, or a software program's design, its adaptability, and therefore its ability to compete and thrive, will improve.[32]

It is in this manner that collective participation and decision-making in a commons are highly adaptive in the Darwinian sense. Rich feedback from decentralized sources yields high-quality intelligence that helps an organism adapt and thrive amidst changes in the external environment. A commons is not the communism of the Soviet Union, which brutally suppressed feedback mechanisms, but the commonwealth of the United States, which, in principle at least, honors open, robust feedback and democratic change.

Diversity within the Commons

While homogeneity within a commons provides some advantages, particularly with small-scale commons in rural settings—there are fewer conflicting interests to mediate—larger commons can become robust precisely because they have a "genetic diversity" among their members. In the theory of evolution, diversity within a gene pool means that there are greater opportunities for adaptive innovations to emerge. Just as biodiversity on the planet has led to the evolution of more sophisticated organisms and a hardy stability,[33] so the diversity of the American populace, *e pluribus unum*, is often cited as a reason for our nation's robust, innovative character. Diversity combined with openness can yield phenomenal creativity, as seen in the free-software community and other Internet groups.

There are practical explanations for why diversity is healthy for a commons. A varied number of perspectives can readily identify the most advantageous ways to grow and adapt. Subtleties of the locality or resource are more likely to be discovered. That is one reason many enlightened companies seek diversity within their workforces: it helps them adapt to changing market conditions. In the open-source software movement, there is a saying: "With enough eyes, all bugs are shallow." The idea is that the more participants in a software commons contributing their unique points of view, the more easily software bugs will be discovered.

Social Equity within the Commons

While a commons need not be a system of strict egalitarianism, it is predisposed to honor a rough social equity among its members. That is because everyone has a common stake in a shared future. For both social and practical reasons, no one can be too unequal or disenfranchised without destabilizing the regime. The American polity is predicated on a similar equality of all citizens before the law. A key goal of commons management is to democratize social benefits (e.g., freedom from pollution, safety risks, etc.) that can otherwise be obtained only through private purchase—an option unavailable to everyone.

In a market economy, serious inequality is not only common but to be expected and even celebrated. The average total compensation of the chief executive officers of the nation's largest 350 companies was 400 times greater than the average worker's ($12.4 million versus $31,000) in 1998, and moguls like Bill Gates and Michael Eisner are lionized.[34] Meanwhile, over the past two decades, the 20-fold disparity between the top quintile of American earners and the bottom quintile has doubled, and the wealth of the top 1 percent of households exceeds the combined wealth of the bottom 95 percent.[35]

To the extent that inequality becomes a structural feature of the culture, so the ability of the nation to act as a commonwealth declines. Disparities of interest become too entrenched and frozen in diverging class cultures. Robert Reich has written about the "secession of the rich," the affluent families who move to gated communities in the suburbs, attend private schools, fly first class, and in other ways isolate themselves from the general public.[36] Such trends are alarming because a healthy commonwealth is predicated on a fairly equal dispersion of wealth. John Adams warned that the people are free "in proportion to their property" and if "a division of the land into small quantities" allowed many to hold property, "the multitude will take care of the liberty, virtue and interest of the multitude, in all acts of government."[37]

Environmental Sustainability

A striking feature of some commons has been their durability over centuries without harming the environment. In her book, Ostrom examines a few of them: communal high mountain meadows in Törbel, Switzerland (operating since 1483), *huerta* irrigation regimes in Valencia, Spain (since 1435), and *zanjera* irrigation communities in the Philippines (since the 1600s).[38] This remarkable sustainability certainly has a lot to do with the isolation of these places, cultural norms, and specific design principles. But it can also be attributed to the ability of a well-designed commons to honor environmental sustainability and community stability over sheer material output.

A key premise of industrial societies is the pervasiveness of scarcity even though material wealth may be plentiful or increasing. "Inadequacy of economic means is the first principle of the world's wealthiest people," writes anthropologist Marshall Sahlins. "The market-industrial system institutes scarcity, in a manner completely unparalleled and to a degree nowhere else approximated. Where production and distribution are arranged through the behavior of prices, and all livelihoods depend on getting and spending, insufficiency of material means becomes the explicit, calculable starting point of all economic activity."[39] The market has been a fantastically productive engine for creating material wealth, otherwise known as "progress." It has also been a fierce colonizer of resources, with fearsome environmental effects.

Participants in the commons do not have a compulsion to produce and consume ever-growing quantities of output in order to sate culturally defined "scarcities." Social stability and interdependence are more urgent priorities. Ivan Illich once explained that people who organize themselves into a commons have essentially "designated an aspect of the environment that was limited, that was necessary for the community's survival, that was necessary for different groups in different ways, but which, in a strictly economic sense, was *not perceived as scarce.*"[40] The implications for ecological sustainability are obvious.

The commons may be not be as productive or efficient as a market regime—although this is not always so, and in any case, market metrics frequently fail to capture the actual externalities generated by markets. What matters more is that a commons is far more likely to take into account the long-term repercussions of its choices on the environment, social equity, and values. A commons *optimizes* rather than *maximizes*. It is more adept at internalizing the long-term external costs of its activities than markets are. In practice, markets tend to maximize private gain for short-term ends, while commons tend to optimize collective gain for long-term ends. There is a structural incentive for this phenomenon. As long as members of a commons cannot liquidate their interests and invest them elsewhere, their lives and long-term futures are bound up with the fate of the commons. Stewardship of resources, rather than development for private gain in the market, is structurally favored by a commons regime.

Sociability in the Commons: The Gift Economy

While market theory puts forward a cardboard facsimile of human beings in the form of the rational, acquisitive individual, the commons sanctions a far richer empirical model of human life. The commons forgoes quantitative modeling and frankly traffics in the social dimensions of people's lives. Not only cultural and local differences, but subtle shades of cooperation, competitive generosity, moral duty, and conscience can play powerful roles in propelling the gift economy of the commons.

■   ■   ■

I have sketched some of the compelling features of the commons, but it has distinct limitations as well. The commons does not typically give free rein to the kind of delirious entrepreneurial freedom celebrated in the market. Gift economies can be platforms for exceedingly creative achievement, to be sure, but radical individualism can be stifled by community norms. Also, the innovation that germinates within the commons—in academia, say, or the Internet—does not necessarily pay off in cold, hard cash. This can be a serious disadvantage, for obvious reasons. Some kinds of work can get done only through the market, and there is often no substitute for cash.

The commons in some settings may also be more static, and not as fiercely, calculatedly efficient and dynamic as the market. This can be regarded as good or bad. The market can produce destructive, short-term behavior and ethical abuses—and it can propel development of new technologies. While the commons may be less dynamic and volatile than markets, it may also be more environmentally benign because it is not as intent on achieving the maximum "throughput" of production and sales.

Nurturing a New Narrative of the Commons

If we are going to reclaim the commons, we need to begin to create some new narratives that show how the commons actually works—how it can foster a sense of meaning and belonging, how it can preserve important values, how it can succeed as a long-term economic and social proposition.

We gain a lot from such a project. Most immediately, we reclaim our ability to talk about the effects of enclosure—the social, cultural, moral, and even spiritual dimensions of life that are sometimes eroded by a market economy. The stability of families and households, citizens' concerns for the natural environment, consumers' aspirations for social leadership by business, struggles for human rights and worker protections in the Third World: such themes need no longer be marginalized as bothersome sidebars to the main action of economic discourse.

The commons allows us to resituate the market squarely in the context of society, in the intellectual tradition of economic anthropologists and institutionalists such as Karl Polanyi, Robert Hale, Thorstein Veblen, and others. The *informal* economy of human relationships is pulled out of the shadows and shown to be a highly influential force in the *formal* economy measured by money and bottom lines.[41] The commons allows us to see and explore critical networks of social reciprocity within households, nonprofit realms, scientific professions, Internet communities, work teams, and our democratic culture. It reveals how the informal commerce of human relationships creates economic value while building social vitality.

To talk about the commons, finally, helps us see how all sorts of important social movements—for the environment and conservation, for humane values in commerce and trade, for limits on commercialization in public spaces, and so on—are thematically related. They are all about defending the integrity of the commons and its various gift economies against the forces of market enclosure.

These are some of the conceptual issues that need to be confronted in advancing an agenda for the commons. But what about specific policy strategies and social innovations? We turn now to an array of strategies, some mature, others still emerging, that can help preserve the integrity and vitality of the commons.

13.

Strategies for
Protecting the Commons

The people need to "see themselves" experimenting in democratic forms.
—Lawrence Goodwyn, historian of Populism[1]

What are you going to do about it?
—William Marcy "Boss" Tweed, nineteenth-century
New York City political leader, responding to a critic

In contemplating the fate of the commons, the challenge that recurs is how to retain the surplus value generated within a commons. How can members of a commons prevent the appropriation of community-generated value by proprietary interests? A related challenge is how to prevent business enterprises from monetizing interests that members of a commons regard as inalienable. How can a commons ensure the integrity of its gift economy, whether it is a scientific community trying to maintain its open exchange of knowledge[2] or an Internet affinity group trying to resist corporate control of its social interactions?[3]

In our market-obsessed society, protecting the commons can be an ambitious, almost insurgent enterprise. After all, the culture of the market and proprietary activity is entrenched, powerful, and normative. It commands great resources and legal means to perpetuate its traditions. The commons, meanwhile, is too often regarded as an aberration. Common assets are seen as free and inexhaustible resources to be exploited and abused, not as shared wealth that can and should be preserved through effective group management.

Notwithstanding its many enemies, the commons—or at least the human impulse that gives rise to gift economies—is often a hardy flower. The personal and social impulses that came together in unexpected ways to create community gardens in New York City, develop the Linux operating system, sustain academic disciplines, and rally behind a declaration of "We, the People ..." testify to a surprisingly strong and abiding cooperative drive. Scholars of common-pool resources in developing countries have shown that communities can and do self-organize themselves to manage natural resources in sustainable ways (confounding neoclassical economic theory and the "tragedy of the commons" model). In recent years, the feasibility of managing a commons has found conceptual support in complexity theory, which has revealed the seemingly inherent tendency of biological organisms, societies, and online communities to self-organize themselves.[4]

The first prerequisite for any commons to arise is for a critical mass of people sharing common interests to find each other—a threshold that the Internet has made far easier to meet. What has impeded the creation of new commons, historically, have been the inability of latent communities to *express* their collective self-interests, find organizational vehicles that can persist over time, and secure the enduring support of institutions of law, government, technology, and/or social association. What follows below, then, is a survey of tools that may help nascent communities to construct and defend the commons.

How can "we the people" defend our natural resources, our democratic values, and the frontiers of scientific discovery? Despite the strength and success of the corporate onslaught, we can and must defend our common wealth through:

1. The role that government must play;
2. The social institutions that we can create voluntarily; and
3. The cultural norms that we need to nurture.

Government's Role in Protecting the Commons

Government is the steward of the public good, but that public good is not simply a matter of individual rights. It also entails the sovereign interests of "the people" as a whole—interests that are often best served through the commons. Practically, certain resources actually have greater value when they belong to an entire community and not just a few individuals. The national parks, the Internet, the regulatory apparatus, government research, and many other resources all yield greater returns from being *public* resources managed by government.

As a matter of democratic political theory, furthermore, government has an inalienable obligation to protect the public's resources and not surrender them to private interests.[5] That is why it offends the democratic spirit when the public's natural resources are abused by private interests; when the Library of Congress lets the Coca-Cola Corporation promote its carbonated syrup in its stately halls; when the Smithsonian lets private donors dictate the terms of its public exhibitions;[6] and when Anheuser-Busch is allowed to be the official sponsor of the 2000 presidential debates.[7] It is *wrong* for core democratic functions and assets to be privatized.

The ways that government can bolster the commons as a source of economic and social value are obviously a large and complicated topic. But there are six general strategies worth pursuing:

Structure Markets to Allow a Commons to Emerge and Flourish

The specific structures of markets are not preordained. Government has a great deal to do with defining who can compete and on what terms. This amounts to creating a social and ethical commons for market activity. Government in effect declares: "All transactions shall abide by certain minimal levels of safety, fair play, information disclosure, and so on." Government also influences the scope of the commons by deciding how to dispense intellectual property rights and grant access to public resources. Excessive copyright protection can erode the public domain, for example. Giveaways of publicly owned timber and minerals can defraud the American people and impoverish future generations.

A guiding principle for government in creating a vigorous market is to create a robust commons. Some of the healthiest markets became that way because of extensive public-sector involvement in setting rigorous ground rules and providing ongoing scrutiny. The financial markets are a prime example; few sectors of the economy are more tightly regulated—or healthier as a result. Markets flourish when government establishes a framework of fair and open standards for competition. When AT&T and the Bell companies controlled the technical standards for the telephonic network, no one else could compete. But once standardized interfaces were required to ensure interoperability—a commons as the foundation for that market—new competition could emerge, and all sorts of innovation in value-added products and services materialized. The same dynamic occurred once IBM's grip on computing was loosened, and the open standards of the Internet arose. A commons of technical standards and operating software gave rise to a rich ecology of market competition and innovation.

In the case of the desktop operating system, of course, there has been a large commons, the Windows operating system. The only problem is that this commons is owned by Microsoft, so the "scale returns" that it generates are being privatized by Microsoft shareholders and not shared by everyone in the commons. Microsoft's ownership of this commons has also allowed it significantly to influence what sorts of benchmark prices, innovation, technical standards, and terms of competition will generally prevail. It may not be entirely coincidental that as public sector involvement in the Internet and software wanes, the incidence of antisocial, anticonsumer activities may increase. And why should that not be? When control of the commons is vested in a private corporation and not the government or some social vehicle managed by members of the commons, one should fully expect a rise in self-serving anticompetitive tactics, industry consolidation, seller-side manipulations of consumers, and bolder attempts to privatize open standards.

The utter triumph of proprietary norms is not inexorable, however. Consider how the U.S. government sponsored the creation of the Internet, computing hardware, and various software programs. The commercial and cultural gains made from building on top of that collaborative edifice continue to this day, enabling robust market competition and innovation. Thanks to the Hatch-Waxman Act of 1984, the American drug market consists not just of proprietary drug firms; it also hosts a flourishing commons, the generic drug market, based on commonly owned intellectual property rights.

In the broadcasting industry, the U.S. government could have created a commons in which noncommercial constituencies would have access to the airwaves. Instead, as media historian Robert W. McChesney has shown, commercial broadcasters convinced Congress in the late 1920s and early 1930s to establish a pseudocommons: a system in which broadcast licensees would serve as "public trustees" of the airwaves.[8] In practice, of course, this has been mostly an empty gesture. The regulatory fictions for protecting the public interest were actually rescinded in the 1980s and 1990s, unleashing the wall-to-wall commercialism in broadcasting today. Local public affairs programming is scarce, and even the news, once considered a public service, brazenly imitates its tabloid and entertainment competitors. Had a real broadcast commons been established 68 years ago, American culture and political life in the twentieth century might have been quite different.

People have become so accustomed to the idea of "spectrum scarcity" and the correlate that spectrum must be licensed to a single entity that few have even entertained the possibility of creating a wireless broadcast commons using "spread spectrum" technologies. It is now possible, using new wireless technologies, to allow multiple users to use the airwaves spectrum on an as-needed basis, just as users now "share" access to the Internet without anyone having an exclusive license to the infrastructure. Instead of big media companies having exclusive control over the airwaves, spectrum could be allocated to let large numbers of users simultaneously use the spectrum as a commons. The new diversity of users would enhance the First Amendment values that ought to prevail in use of a public communications resource. It would also foster a flowering of innovation, much as the open, nonproprietary Internet has unleashed enormous creativity.[9]

It is important to note that a robust market and a flourishing commons are not antithetical forces; they are complementary. Indeed, the collapse of the commons (through enclosure or otherwise) frequently engenders stagnation in the market, or at least a narrowing of its range. Consider the moribund pace of innovation in word-processing software today, thanks to Microsoft, or the dismal state of telephony innovation under AT&T in the 1970s. As these examples suggest, government has a preeminent role in structuring markets so that the commons can constructively coexist with a market, provoking synergistic improvements in both.

Stop the Giveaways of Taxpayer-Owned Resources

A depressing symptom of our corrupted political life is the egregious giveaways of public resources that continue even after public exposure and calls for reform. The scandalous surrender of valuable mining rights that persists under an 1872 statute; the logging of national forests for a fraction of their market value and at great environmental cost; the cheap leasing of federal rangelands for cattle grazing despite its horrendous ecological consequences; the slippery accounting methods for oil leasing on federal lands that have shortchanged the public—these are the signs of a government captured by industry interests and insulated from popular accountability.

The plunder of taxpayer resources is replicated in many other important realms as well: pharmaceutical R&D, government information resources, government-funded university research, and intellectual property rights. All of these public-sector resources represent significant hidden subsidies for industries that purport to be free-market champions. Exposure of their use of public resources is important, but ultimately there is no substitute for public agitation for change.

Fortunately, the crusade against corporate welfare begun by Ralph Nader in the 1970s picked up considerable momentum in the 1990s as a number of conservative, libertarian-minded congressional leaders joined in the cry against government handouts. Yet even this pressure has had only a modest impact in reforming some of the worst giveaways of the public's natural resources and intellectual property. The circle of awareness and public action against retrograde government policies needs to be widened. As any business has certain fiduciary duties to its shareholders, so government must be made to manage the public's assets with the same conscientious attention.

Create Stakeholder Trusts and Other Legal Vehicles for Empowering Communities

One of the more imaginative and effective ways that government can build new commons is through stakeholder trusts that give all citizens a personal stake in public assets. The idea is to give individual citizens an identifiable economic stake in certain public assets so that they can reap personal dividends from them. When property rights and citizenship are linked together in this fashion, it can lead to greater social equity. Alternatively, stakeholder trusts can earmark their funds for important public purposes—conservation of land, public education, and so on—rather than distributing those funds to individual citizens.

Perhaps the most successful stakeholder trust has been the Alaska Permanent Fund, a state-run investment savings account that pays equal annual dividends to every Alaskan citizen. Created in 1976 by a voter-approved amendment to the state's constitution, the Alaska Permanent Fund is a public trust for oil revenues from drilling on the state's North Slope. With some $27 billion in assets, the fund is one of the 100 largest investment funds in the world. Nearly 18 percent of the $45.8 billion of state oil revenues has been saved as investment capital. In 2000, it generated $1.15 billion in dividends for the state's residents, or nearly $2,000 per person.[10]

State land trusts are another sort of common asset that have been used to generate revenues for state governments and citizens.[11] Twenty-two states have lands comprising 135 million acres held as state land trusts. When states joined the Union, starting with Ohio in 1803 and ending with Alaska in 1959, Congress granted the land to states in order to support common schools and other public institutions. The land has also been used by states to generate revenues. In 1996, about $3 billion in revenues were generated from leases for grazing, agriculture, timber harvesting, and mineral extraction.

Stakeholder trusts for natural resources do pose a special risk: they create new incentives for individuals to overexploit the resource. Alaskan citizens, for example, have strong reasons for wanting the maximum production of oil from state lands, as opposed to ecologically benign production.[12] But the risks of overexploitation can be mitigated by the ways that stakeholder trusts are structured in the first place, so that sustainable limits are observed.

The Alaska Permanent Fund has inspired at least two other notable stakeholder trust innovations: the Sky Trust, an idea developed by social entrepreneur Peter Barnes and the Corporation for Enterprise Development, and stakeholder trusts for young people, proposed by Yale law professors Bruce Ackerman and Anne Alstott.

The Sky Trust is an ingenious vehicle for giving all Americans a stake in the "scarcity rents" that polluters would pay for being allowed to emit carbon emissions into the atmosphere.[13] Instead of the government just giving away emission permits to polluters, the Sky Trust proposal urges auctions in which companies buy a limited number of emission permits. This process would naturally raise the prices for gasoline and other products that use burnable carbon. But it would also be a means to force companies to shoulder the actual costs of their pollution, rather than displacing it into the sky where it will cause global warming and other environmental and health problems. Furthermore, the Sky Trust would be a means for offsetting the higher prices that consumers would face. All citizens would receive dividends from the Sky Trust, derived from the revenues raised by the auction of emission permits.

"The formula driving the [Sky Trust] machine," writes Peter Barnes, "is, *from* all according to their use of the sky, *to* all according to their equal ownership of it. Those who burn more carbon will pay more than those who burn less. And, since every American receives the same dividend, households will come out ahead if they conserve, but lose money if they don't. This isn't only fair; it's precisely the incentive needed to reduce pollution."[14]

Another creative stakeholder trust is the one proposed by Ackerman and Alstott, who ask: Why should not each generation have an equal right to the patrimony of the previous generation? To help people just graduating from high school to invest in their futures, whether through education, training, or starting a business, Ackerman and Alstott propose an annual tax of 2 percent on the property owned by the richest 40 percent of Americans, generating a pool of some $255 billion a year. Every qualifying young adult would be entitled to a $80,000 stake.

Instead of expanding a paternalistic welfare system to deal with people's needs, the idea of this stakeholder trust is to encourage individuals to take responsibility for themselves while giving them the means to invest in their future. The authors explain that "stakeholding is a more democratic and more effective substitute for a declining institution: providing a social inheritance to the rising generation just when it needs it most."[15] While this particular stakeholder proposal is likely to be more controversial than others, it offers a glimpse into a paradigm worth exploring: using state-administered trust funds to share wealth more equitably or to channel dividends directly toward unmet public purposes.

A good example of the latter is the Land and Water Conservation Fund, which uses revenues from offshore oil and gas drilling to acquire land for parks, forests, and open spaces and to develop recreational projects. Since its creation in 1965, the fund has been used to acquire nearly seven million acres of park land and to revitalize the Everglades, Golden Gate Park, New York City's Central Park, as well as hundreds of smaller state and federal lands. Unfortunately, most of the $900 million in annual drilling receipts intended for the fund were diverted by the Reagan and Bush I administrations to the general treasury in the 1980s and used for entirely different purposes.[16]

President Clinton in 1999 launched a drive to reinvigorate the fund through legislation he dubbed the Lands Legacy Initiative. His legislation, the Conservation and Reinvestment Act (CARA), sought to channel more than $45 billion of Outer Continental Shelf oil royalties into an off-budget, dedicated trust fund over the next fifteen years. The fund is intended to support the Land and Water Conservation Fund as well as funds for endangered species, historic preservation, and coastal protection. Although the legislation did not pass, bipartisan efforts to enact some form of CARA continue.[17]

One of the more intriguing legal innovations in protecting community wealth is "compensatory liability," a model recently proposed by Duke Law professor J. H. Reichman. The goal is to solve the tragedy of the anticommons, in which "the weed-like thicket of exclusive property rights ... threaten[s] to throttle more innovation than they could ever possibly stimulate."[18] Under current patent law, of course, as the "first comers" are awarded exclusive property rights for their innovations, the effect is to "divide up the community's shared know-how into ever smaller parcels that are withdrawn from the public domain," writes Reichman. We saw earlier how this pathology affects innovation in software and new drug development.

Reichman proposes a new system of compensatory liability by which "first comers" cannot exclude others from building on their "sub-patentable" innovations (improvements that are not novel or significant enough to warrant patent protection). Any "second comers" are given a legal entitlement to build on the community know-how of predecessors. But these follow-on innovators are not allowed to be free-riders. They must pay fees to the first comer for a relatively short period of time (hence the term "compensatory liability"). This ingenious legal arrangement has the advantage of giving rewards to both the first comers and follow-on innovators without restricting access to the public domain or stifling the flow of new products. "With small amounts of tinkering," Reichman writes, "a compensatory liability regime could be adapted to encourage use of traditional knowledge without denying the relevant indigenous communities the right to a fair share of the proceeds." One can imagine compensatory liability being used to reward the "community knowledge" of software developers and indigenous peoples—while enabling follow-on innovations and an expansion of the public domain.

Capture Capital Gains from Public Infrastructure and Put Them to Public Use

Whenever new subway stops were built in Washington, D.C., and its surrounding suburbs, a funny thing happened to the value of real estate nearby: prices soared. No surprise here. When privately owned land is suddenly connected to a much larger universe of people—especially consumers and businesses—it becomes a more valuable commodity. But note that even though the government built the subway system, it did not directly reap the gains from rising real estate values (only indirectly, through a larger tax base). The big capital gains windfalls went to investors and speculators shrewd enough to own the land and buildings or influential enough to get subway stops built near their properties.

An imaginative government would explore ways that it could participate in the gains that its own investments help create. Two examples come to mind: the gains that private investors reap from taking a private stock public, and the gains that flow from the socially created value of land. In such cases, a costly public infrastructure showers considerable unearned gains on private parties. Why not recoup some of those gains for public purposes?

Take the huge popularity of initial public offerings of stock (IPOs) in the Internet era. One reason that entrepreneurs like to take their companies public is to reap fast, huge gains in the value of their privately owned stock. Much of this gain stems from the new ability to sell the company's stock to potentially millions of investors via a public market. The asset can be turned into cash—made liquid—much more readily. The liquidity that comes from a company's "going public" is worth at least 30 percent, entrepreneur Peter Barnes learned when he took his start-up company, Working Assets, public. That 30 percent premium, writes Barnes, did not come

> from the company itself, or from its CEO, but from society—
> from the public stock market and the entire infrastructure of
> government, financial institutions and media that backs it up. Yet
> this enormous socially created value is reaped by only two kinds
> of people: underwriters (who get fees) and private shareholders
> (who get large capital gains). Indeed it is fair to say that most
> fortunes in America are made by shareholders who make the
> magic leap from non-liquid private stock to very liquid public
> stock.[19]

So why should not the taxpaying public, or its representative, government, reap some of piece of the action for its role in maintaining the public markets? After all, taxpayers pay for the Securities and Exchange Commission, the Commodities Futures Trading Commission, and many other administrative and judicial bodies that make public markets open and trustworthy. Barnes proposes that the public should receive a royalty on every IPO for its role, as taxpayers, in maintaining the public markets. A given percentage of stock of all IPO transactions—say, 5 percent—could be placed in a public trust resembling a mutual fund. Shares in the trust would collectively belong to all American citizens, and could be redeemed upon retirement or at age 65.

While the principle of taxing private users of "socially created value" is unfamiliar to many people, it actually has a long history. A similar idea—land value taxation—was proposed by Henry George, the author of *Progress and Poverty*, in 1879, and has been enacted in a number of locations around the world.[20] George realized that the scarcity value of land owes little to individual effort but a great deal to the community, especially government.[21] For example, government maintains a civil infrastructure of roads, sewers, and police protection that makes it more attractive to use certain parcels of land, especially in cities. More people can live nearby, and more businesses find it attractive to set up shop there. This is socially created value.

To capture some measure of this value, George proposed taxing land, not the buildings or improvements upon it, as a way to discourage speculation in land (which produces an artificial scarcity in land and higher prices for it). Land-value taxation is a way to promote a more efficient land market, channel investment into more productive activity, simplify the tax system, and discourage urban sprawl (by deterring speculative landholding in cities). As the late William Vickrey, the 1996 Nobel Prize winner in economics, put it, land value taxation "guarantees that no one dispossesses fellow citizens by obtaining a disproportionate share of what nature provides for humanity."

In the places where local governments have adopted land value taxation (sometimes known as "site-value taxation")—Denmark, South Africa, some states of Australia, and Harrisburg, Pennsylvania, among others—the system has largely proven effective.[22] A number of United Nations bodies and prominent economists (including Milton Friedman, Herbert Simon, Paul Samuelson, James Tobin, James Buchanan, and Robert Solow) have endorsed land value taxation.[23]

It has been noted that the power to create money and earn interest from that power is another valuable public asset that has essentially been given over, for free, to private bankers. Whenever they lend money, banks must have 3 percent of the loan on hand in "reserve accounts" with the Federal Reserve Bank. But the remainder of the money, from which they earn revenues for their shareholders, comes "from assets they never bought, never owned, never even borrowed, but simply willed into being," writes Richard Behan.[24] He asks: Why should not government receive a greater share of direct benefit from this power to create money, a value known as *seignorage*? The Federal Reserve could charge interest on the 97 percent share of loans that banks now claim as their own, and the federal government could reap billions of dollars in *seignorage* that could be devoted to public purposes or tax reduction.

Reaffirm Regulation as a Vehicle for Advancing Common Values

As much as government regulation is reviled for being inefficient and unpredictable, it remains an indispensable democratic vehicle for asserting common ethical and social values. Business enterprises can act with swift decisiveness, but regulatory agencies, as creatures of government, must respect the discipline of due process of law and politics. This naturally makes for a more cumbersome, unpredictable process. But a process that is governed by norms of public access and participation, scientific facts openly debated, and legal accountability to Congress and the courts is more likely to be seen as credible and legitimate. It is more likely to yield sound decisions than private business decisions based on short-term, narrow, economic self-interest and partial, self-serving information.

The regulatory process is thus a means for striking a balance between the economic priorities of the marketplace and the social and ethical norms of the commons. It sanctions an "incomplete commodification" of people's values, in the words of Stanford law professor Margaret Jane Radin,[25] because it makes both economic and ethical valuations of various hazards (air pollution, dangerous toys, hazardous chemicals). This may be why regulation is typically so controversial: it is an arena for resolving deep-seated disputes between the market and the commons. Business generally emphasizes the *economic* implications of regulation, even though the chief impetus for most health, safety, environmental, and some consumer regulation is *ethical and social*. As this suggests, the very meaning of regulation is often a contested matter. Much of the perennial debate about "reforming" regulation is, in fact, a debate about which set of values should prevail—market or commons—or in what hybrid combinations and calibrations.

Regulation is a tool for enhancing the commons in another respect. It confers benefits on everyone, not just those who can afford it. Ability to pay—the preeminent criteria for expressing one's preferences in the marketplace—is not the controlling factor (theoretically, at least) in regulation. Any citizen has the right to petition her government, request answers, and effect change. And everyone, not just those who pay, benefit. A commonwealth has a different constitutional logic from a market, a fact that is reflected in the regulatory process. While many steps can and should be taken to make regulation more efficient and less onerous, at bottom regulation has a different set of objectives from the market.

Bolster Democratic Rights to Participate in Power

If the essence of freedom is "the ability to participate in power," as Cicero held, then a key goal of the American commonwealth should be to bolster democratic rights. The commons is a healthier place when its membership is inclusive, its decisions open to public scrutiny, and its actions accountable to the people. These are broadly stated goals, admittedly, but they might be defined as policies that encourage access and participation in government and stronger guarantees of due process of law.

These ideals were advanced by a strong wave of civic reforms in the 1970s. Numerous laws were passed to require that government meetings be open and held with advance notice; that government documents be accessible through the Freedom of Information Act and other means; that members of federal advisory committees not have conflicts of interest; that the names of contributors to political campaigns be disclosed; and that citizens have the right to sue federal agencies that fail to perform their statutory duties.

Today, one can imagine other legal principles that could fortify the democratic commons further. An expansion of the scope of the public trust doctrine could help defend community interests in the environment and beyond, as Joseph Sax has proposed.[26] Federal policies that enfranchise ordinary people to vote without impediment and to run for office without being a millionaire—achieved through new voting rights protections and campaign finance reform—would also enhance the democratic commons. Laws that strengthen the public domain and fair use in copyright would enhance civic culture and the free exchange of knowledge. The list could surely be expanded. The point is that government can do a great deal to enhance the participatory strength and accountability of the American commonwealth.

Building Voluntary Commons in a Market Society

Whatever leadership government may provide in supporting the commons, individuals and social groups have an indispensable role to play. In the great tradition associated with Alexis de Tocqueville and with the "civil society" movement today, voluntary associations of private citizens can do a great deal to reinvigorate the commons in American life. It is tempting to believe that this role is mostly a matter of "getting people together" into new civic organizations and social clubs.

But commons do not just happen spontaneously, or through moral exhortation. Like markets, they emerge through an infrastructure of law, government agencies, and cultural support (as the Eastern Bloc countries are demonstrating in their struggle to create market societies from scratch). They require well-designed organizational structures and institutional and cultural supports. Otherwise, the social relationships and voluntary work that people bring to the enterprise will not accrue to the commons over the long term, but will dissipate or be appropriated through enclosure. Ways must be found to retain the surplus value generated by the commons within the commons.

New legal vehicles must be designed, perhaps along the lines of "property on the outside, commons on the inside." Effective self-governance principles for contemporary commons need to be devised, a task that, happily, is made easier by the Internet's ability to organize people. New vehicles for collective ownership also hold great promise, as do new vehicles for sharing and collaboration among the members of a self-selected community. Innovation in each of these areas is already burgeoning (even if the diverse projects under way are not usually seen as related).

Here are some of the more exciting homegrown legal and social strategies for devising new commons.

Explore New Innovations in Private Law

One of the most remarkable legal innovations for preserving the commons of software development is called the General Public License, or GPL, the contractual license sometimes called "copyleft," discussed in Chapter 2. The GPL, it should be recalled, guarantees that the creative energy that is committed to the commons in the form of new source code will remain free and available to everyone in perpetuity. It is worth pondering the GPL as both an inspiration and a model for other legal innovations that can preserve commons from proprietary plunder.

One example, a proposed Creative Commons, using a GPL-like license, is described below. There may be technological equivalents to be invented. In the online world, software has been devised that can identify free riders and exclude them from participation in a cooperative venture. For example, software could exclude from the commons any users in peer-to-peer file sharing (such as Gnutella) who freely download other people's files but refuse to allow others to upload their files.[27] This tool may have promise, although it might easily impose strict norms on a gift economy that usually operates according to a more informal, "who's counting?" ethic.

The outright purchase of land by land trusts is an increasingly popular vehicle for protecting the commons of nature. It was the strategy used by the Trust for Public Land to acquire the community gardens in New York City. Land trusts have also used conservation easements to great effect in purchasing the "development rights" to land in order to prevent its development. A conservation easement is a voluntary legal agreement between a landowner and a land trust or government agency. The landowner can gain tax benefits and keep the land in private hands while the public benefits from the open space, wildlife habitat preservation, and other benefits of an intact natural ecosystem.

Create Local Commons to Manage Finite Resources

Over the past fifteen years, a growing corps of scholars and practitioners has pioneered new insights into the commons as a governance structure for local, small-scale, common-pool resources. These include fishery grounds and grazing pastures, water supplies and game hunting, land tenure and lobster fiefs. While the social systems for managing finite natural resources vary immensely from culture to culture, making broad generalizations risky, scholarship on the commons has shown that social institutions can be created to manage common property successfully and sustainably. The tragedy of the commons is not inevitable. There is more than an either/or choice between government intervention and privatization.

Unfortunately, this scholarship has been mainly focused on small-scale resources in developing nations, a fact that might lead the casual observer to believe that the commons has little relevance here. This is not true, either historically or in the present. In one notable example, Elinor Ostrom examined how various municipal bodies came together in the 1960s with legal incentives from the state to manage access to a series of fragile groundwater basins beneath the Los Angeles metropolitan area.[28] Contemporary case studies have looked at commons governed by lobster fishermen in Maine,[29] cattle ranchers in northern California,[30] users of the Edwards Aquifer in south central Texas,[31] and Alaska halibut fishermen,[32] among many others.

Not only is there a growing awareness that local commons are feasible alternatives to traditional policy approaches, but new initiatives specifically designed to promote reliance on commons regimes are emerging. Michael M'Gonigle, a cofounder of Greenpeace, has proposed government chartering of regional or local "ecosystem trusts" to get local stakeholders to come together and manage a natural resource in sustainable ways. If such a legal vehicle existed, he writes:

> native and non-native fishers, tourist operators and local forestry operations would have a reason to talk. After all, if something could be worked out among members of the community, they *could* act—and the government would be *required* to support them. And what could be the objection if ecosystem sustainability and community health terms are set out in the provincial trust charter, thus ensuring that local action protected the "public interest"?[33]

One of the more ambitious projects to foster commons is the Chaordic Commons of Terra Civitas (formerly the Chaordic Alliance), which seeks to foster the proliferation of self-organizing commons on a global scale.[34] Already the group has helped develop the Northwest Atlantic Marine Alliance to manage fisheries and other marine resources through a community-based approach.[35] It has also facilitated the Appleseed Centers, a network of community-based law firms, and the Community Alliances of Interdependent AgriCulture, a set of commons to advocate for local agriculture.[36]

Other novel initiatives are being launched to manage local resources for the public good. Brian Donahue has written about towns, especially in New England, that have reinvented and reclaimed community farms and forests.[37] Ithaca, New York, Madison, Wisconsin, and a number of other towns have created local currencies designed to bolster their local economy and community spirit.[38] There is a renewed attention in many communities to reclaiming an actual physical commons in the centers of towns—urban parks and open spaces—as a shared community space.[39]

The goal that unites these seemingly disparate projects is the desire of local communities to have greater self-determination, control, and accountability over their immediate environment and economy. There is also a realization that one of the best ways to achieve these goals is by developing a new skein of social relationships, values, and trust at the community level. While no community can function as an island, especially in today's global economy, it is entirely possible to create more self-reliant communities through new socially based institutions and practices.[40]

Develop New Vehicles for Collective Ownership

Our democracy requires a rough equality of wealth among all citizens, or at least no huge structural inequalities. Thomas Jefferson, for one, believed that decentralized wealth and self-responsibility were the best foundation for the American republic, and that concentrated ownership of wealth is dangerous to self-government. While there are any number of government strategies for promoting this goal, the focus of this section is on voluntary private vehicles for promoting collective ownership.

There are both personal and societal reasons for promoting such vehicles. At a time when property ownership is becoming more concentrated, a new kind of "participatory capitalism" comprised of millions of citizen-owners can yield a new social contract. Jeff Gates outlined what this might look like in his book, *The Ownership Solution*:

> My hypothesis is simply this. People are likely to become better stewards of all those systems of which they are a part—social, political, fiscal, cultural and natural—as they gain a personal stake in the economic system, with all the rights and responsibilities that implies.... Current ownership patterns not only offend our collective conscience; they also endanger our capacities by reducing decision-making to the lowest common denominator."[41]

The cooperative movement is one way by which collective ownership can be fostered. Co-ops have a long and glorious history of enabling consumers to band together to maximize their purchasing power and assure higher levels of safety, ecologically benign practices, and localism. Employee stock ownership plans (ESOPs), and profit-sharing plans are another way through which individuals have gained an equity stake in their companies. Empirical studies have shown that aligning the interests of managers, shareholders, and workers and giving them opportunities to collaborate on the job have measurable effects on productivity and stock values.[42] Land trusts are also a proven vehicle for protecting and augmenting community interests in land. Dozens of communities have used publicly owned lands to generate new revenues, build affordable housing, and preserve open spaces.[43]

One of the most stellar testimonies to community ownership may be the Green Bay Packers, the only team in the National Football League (NFL) owned by the fans. Incorporated as a private, nonprofit organization in 1923, the Packers are officially "a community project, intended to promote community welfare." Fans literally own the team's stock, even though the stock offering warns: "It is virtually impossible for anyone to realize a profit...." While there are fewer than 200,000 people in the Green Bay metropolitan area, Packer games have been sold out for thirty consecutive seasons and the value of the Packer franchise is in the top five of all professional teams.[44] Community ownership has also prevented money-minded owners from threatening to move the team to another city or extracting taxpayer subsidies for new stadiums. Perhaps for these reasons—to assure strict private control and not allow democratic control—the NFL formally banned community ownership in 1961. Major-league baseball also prohibits fans and communities from owning teams. One provocative response has come from Rep. Earl Blumenauer of Oregon, who has introduced legislation to withdraw a sports' broadcast antitrust exemption unless it allows a community to purchase its local team.

Centralized control cannot be so easily imposed on the Internet, however, which is one reason why it is proving to be one of the most fertile seedbeds for new kinds of public ownership of information. The University of North Carolina is now the host of a rapidly growing Internet library known as ibiblio.org. Formerly called MetaLab, the archive and information-sharing site is one of the largest public sites containing Linux software and software documentation, as well as millions of documents of public-domain text, audio, and databases. Users can upload material to the library's collection by filling out the electronic equivalent of a card-catalog card, and enthusiast groups can manage their own archives, such as the collection of materials on Pearl Harbor. Ibiblio receives approximately 1.5 million requests a day.

Another type of public-domain library is the nonprofit Creative Commons now being organized by a number of law schools.[45] The new organization will encourage artists, writers, filmmakers, software writers, inventors, and others to donate their intellectual works to the public domain, or at least to license the works to the public on generous terms. (The model is the General Public License, or GPL, used by free software.) Currently, the transaction costs for securing rights to copyrighted works can so high that would-be users of the works simply decline to use them. By cultivating a new public commons for intellectual property, the founders of the Creative Commons hope to reduce substantially the costs of securing permissions and, in turn, to stimulate greater use of donated works.

Other legal innovations inspired by the GPL are cropping up in other realms. The Electronic Frontier Foundation now has an Open Audio License,[46] and a French organization has devised a "Free Art License."[47]

New open software technologies are being devised as substitutes for MP3 and multimedia applications to help asssure that "open content" can survive any further proprietarization of Internet creativity.[48]

Develop New Vehicles for Sharing and Collaborating

A commons of *users* can be created without there necessarily being collective *owners*. The lines between the two often blur. There is no better example for this than the collaboratively created software, digital documents, and affinity groups made possible by the Internet. No one "owns" the Linux operating system in any strict sense; it a collaborative creation "owned" by everyone. The artifacts of a commons are largely identical with the community that generates them. The digital documents just happen to be objectifications of the collective social knowledge.[50]

It is beyond the scope of this book to explore how civil society can be rejuvenated through more robust social connections (depictions of this challenge are poignantly sketched in Robert Putnam's *Bowling Alone* and Robert Lane's *The Loss of Happiness in Market Democracies*).[51] But one venue that holds great promise for facilitating new kinds of sharing and collaborating is the Internet. In fact, a great many of the user groups, Web sites, Listservs, and other software systems used on the Internet, especially the Web, operate according to some classic principles of the commons.

Amy Jo Kim's *Community Building on the Web* advises would-be Webmasters to follow three underlying principles of "community design" on the Web: design for growth and change, create and maintain feedback loops, and empower your members over time. She also identifies nine "timeless design strategies that characterize successful, sustainable communities," including defining and articulating one's purpose, building flexible, extensible gathering places, developing strong leadership, and encouraging appropriate etiquette.[52] These and other rules for designing online communities bear a very close kinship with the design principles identified by scholars of common-pool resources.

Many online communities have emerged precisely because various market vehicles did not allow the kind of authentic interpersonal exchanges and shared pursuits made possible by the Internet. Slashdot has become the premier Web site for software developers precisely because it hosts a wide-open sharing of information, analysis, and criticism of the latest software design issues, particularly for open-source-code software.[53] Websites such as BirdSource and Journey North have brought together more than 70,000 bird-watchers around the globe to track bird migration patterns with much greater accuracy than before. This is not only improving the quality of our knowledge about birds, it is changing people's stewardship of the environment in efforts to boost certain bird populations.[54] E-mail, Listservs, Web sites, and Web logs (idiosyncratic personal Web sites featuring links to online information) are highly efficient vehicles for sharing information with huge communities of people on a global scale.

What emerges from such sharing is not just new connections among like-minded people, but a kind of deep community knowledge that might not otherwise develop. Recall the mantra of the open-source software community: "With enough eyes, all bugs are shallow." So it is in many online communities, where the number and diversity of participants help generate highly reliable information. This is the principle behind the famous Zagat restaurant guides and the Firefly "collaborative filtering" software that aggregates user feedback to identify larger trends and preferences.

A new kind of bottom-up knowledge can emerge through various Internet venues, which in time creates a commons that is neither a creature of the market nor government, but truly a creature "of the people."

One of the next great advances in Internet collaboration is likely to be peer-to-peer networking (P2P). Unlike the hierarchical model of central servers interacting with huge numbers of "client" computers, the prevailing mode of computer interaction on the Internet today, P2P networking allows individual computers to be coequal computers capable of connecting to any of the others directly. Napster was a foretaste of what P2P networking may entail (although not a perfect example, because it required users to access a central database of indexed songs rather than connecting to other computers directly). Gnutella and other file-sharing technologies may represent the future direction for P2P.

P2P is not just a vehicle for sharing copyrighted materials. It can enable scientists and libraries to share information in far more efficient and imaginative ways. Already scientists in the SETI Project, the Search for Extra-Terrestrial Intelligence, are using P2P software to use the unused computing power of more than 350,000 participants in 203 countries.[55] The speed and "intelligence" of searching across the Internet is vastly increased by P2P technology and evades the kinds of centralized control that media companies generally have in mind.

Distressed at the compromises of market enclosures, a number of Internet communities are ready for such a leap. Many prominent scientists, for example, are so worried about the copyright and technology-protected lockup of scientific research that they are organizing a new Web-based library for research in the life sciences and medicine. "Why should scientists support the publishers' demands to maintain their monopoly control over the research articles that they have published?" ask the organizers of the Web site. Just as a midwife can earn a living without keeping the babies that she delivers, they argue, journals can make a living by controlling access to their articles for six months, and then putting them into a single, searchable repository of public domain articles: publiclibraryofscience.org. Organizers argue that the project will "vastly increase the accessibility and utility of the scientific literature, enhance scientific productivity and catalyze integration of the disparate communities of interest in biomedical sciences."[56]

Of course, online sharing and collaboration raise some profound questions about the foundations of intellectual property law, which assumes that useful creativity will emerge only through a sanctioned structure of markets, incentives, and contracts. This is too large and complex an issue to tackle here. Suffice it to say that the Internet's great success in generating profuse amounts of valuable content despite the most minimal copyright protections seems to refute most IP traditionalists.[57]

Building a Culture that Honors the Commons

Fostering the commons requires not just a policy agenda, but a larger vision of community and personal fulfillment. McCay and Acheson put it well in their collected studies of common-pool resources: "The problem of the commons is one of how society creates superordinate allegiance to something—the commons or the communal—that transcends people's immediate and everyday sense of reality."[58] Such broader allegiances are forged by creating "imagined communities" that knit together through myths, stories, and customs, our social experiences.

A culture that honors the commons will strive to:

Enable democratic participation. The greater the role that members of a commons have in decision-making, the more informed the governance. Outcomes that everyone can influence are seen as more morally legitimate and thus respected and enforceable.

Set limits on market activity and commercialization. Not all human needs can be met through the market, and even the market grows sterile if it cannot draw upon the commons. It is therefore important that there be "white spaces" where human imagination and spirit can run free, unregimented by the commercial matrix of the market.

Create protected public spaces in which civil society can thrive. At a time when the market has enclosed so many "white spaces" of democratic culture, it is imperative that we reinvent the vehicles by which people can interact with each other outside the market: the community gardens, the political grassroots, the Internet newsgroups, the cultural events at which strangers can mingle. To combat the "bowling alone" syndrome identified by Robert Putnam, there must be the physical places, noncommercial media, online forums, and public events for people to come together to share their common concerns.

Nurture gift economies. Public policy and institutions can greatly affect whether gift economies can emerge and flourish or whether competitive individualism will be the default social norm. The traditions of blood donation systems, academic communities, community gardens, and the free-software movement demonstrate that the altruistic and cooperative can work. But such models need to be institutionally and legally supported.

Americans have a long tradition of creating innovative vehicles for ensuring a fair return to the American people on resources they collectively own. This tradition has galvanized conservationists, land reformers, and advocates of municipal ownership of transport, water and energy systems. It motivated the architects of urban planning, the Tennessee Valley Authority and garden cities, and the land-grant colleges that over time resulted in world-class universities in Ithaca, Urbana, Madison, Minneapolis, and Berkeley. It inspired the health, safety, and environmental programs of the 1960s and the 1970s, the Land and Water Conservation Fund, the Alaska Permanent Fund, and the public rollout of the Internet.

It is time to revive this tradition of innovation in the stewardship of public resources and give it imaginative new incarnations in the twenty-first century. The silent theft of our shared assets and gift economies need not continue. But first it is important to recognize the commons as the commons and understand the rich possibilities for reclaiming our common wealth.

NOTES

Introduction

1. By a rough estimate made by the Consumer Project on Technology, based on a compulsory license that West granted to the U.S. Justice Department, the cost of renting access to a single year of federal court cases—some 15,000 cases—comes to $40,500 for a single user. "This is a high price to pay to simply avoid [public domain] numbering opinions and paragraphs," writes James Love. See http://cptech.org/legalinfo/cost.html.
2. The most comprehensive history of the struggle to break West Publishing's monopoly and institute a regime of universal citation for federal cases is an essay by Jol Silversmith, "Universal Citation: The Fullest Possible Dissemination of Judgments," originally published in the now-defunct *Internet Legal Practice Newsletter* in May 1997, now available online at http://www.thirdamendment.com/citation.html. Another overview, from the perspective of 1994, is Gary Wolf, "Who Owns the Law?" *Wired*, May 1994, p. 198.
3. Franz Kafka, *The Trial* (trans. Willa and Edwin Muir, New York: Schocken Books, 1995), cited in Silversmith, *ibid.*
4. See, e.g., Reuters, "Justices, Judges Took Favors from Publisher with Pending Cases," *Washington Post*, March 6, 1995; John J. Odlund, "Debate Rages Over Who Owns the Law," *Minneapolis Star Tribune*, March 5–6, 1995, reprinted in the *Congressional Record*, July 28, 1995 (Senate), pp. S10847–10855; Thomas Scheffey, "Feds and West Publishing: Too Close for Comfort?" *Connecticut Law Tribune*, March 1997; and Doug Obey and Albert Eisele, "West: A Study in Special Interest Lobbying," *The Hill*, February 22, 1995, p. 1.
5. *HyperLaw Inc. v. West Publishing.* See David Cay Johnston, "West Publishing Loses a Decision on Copyright," *New York Times*, May 21, 1997, p. D1.
6. The courts in Great Britain, however, have adopted a public-domain, technology-neutral citation system based upon paragraph numbering. See "Neutral Citation of Judgments System Is Introduced, *The Times* (London), January 16, 2001. For more on the fight in the United States to introduce a public domain citation system, see Courts.net at

http:// www.courts.net/pdcs.htm. On June 20, 2000, Lexis successfully sued an Internet startup company, Jurisline.com, that was distributing U.S. case law for free. See T. R. Halvorson, "Jurisline.com: It's All Over, Including the Shouting," Law Library Resource Xchange, June 20, 2000, available at http://www.llrx.com/extras/jurisline8.htm.

7. The constitutional dimensions of this theme are discussed by Jennifer Nedelsky in *Private Property and the Limits of American Constitutionalism: The Madisonian Framework and Its Legacy* (Chicago: University of Chicago Press, 1990).

8. See, e.g., Clifford Cobb, Ted Halstead, and Jonathan Rowe, "If the GDP Is Up, Why Is America Down?" *The Atlantic*, October 1995, pp. 2–15. See also Herman E. Daly and John B. Cobb, Jr., *For the Common Good: Redirecting the Economy toward Community, the Environment and a Sustainable Future* (Boston: Beacon Press, 1989), pp. 62–84.

9. The focus here is on tangible assets and property rights that belong to the American people, as opposed to government subsidies to business, which represent another form of corporate welfare. An excellent comprehensive overview of varieties of corporate welfare can be found in Ralph Nader's testimony before the Committee on the Budget, U.S. House of Representatives, June 30, 1999.

Chapter 1: Reclaiming the Narrative of the Commons

1. This quotation came to my attention via an essay by Lewis Hyde, "Created Commons," the Andy Warhol Foundation for the Visual Arts, Paper Series on the Arts, Culture, and Society, Paper Number 8 (1998), available at http://www.warholfoundation.org/article8.htm.

2. Wendell Berry, *Home Economics* (San Francisco: North Point Press, 1987).

3. See a Report by Brooklyn Borough President Howard Golden, *City-Owned Properties: A Post Conveyance Assessment*, office of Howard Golden, January 1999.

4. Anne Ravner, "Garden Notebook: Is This City Big Enough for Gardens and Houses?" *New York Times*, March 27, 1997, p. C1.

5. Sue Halpern, "Garden-Variety Politics," *Mother Jones*, September/October 1999, pp. 33–35.

6. David Gonzalez, "New Life, Far From the Bright Lights," *New York Times*, January, 25, 1998, p. 28.

7. Ravner, 1997.

8. Ibid.

9. Jon Crow, quoted in Anne Ravner, "Houses Before Gardens, the City Decides," *New York Times*, January 9, 1997, p. C1.

10. Dan Barry, "Sudden Deal Saves Gardens Set for Auction," *New York Times*, May 13, 1999, p. A1.

11. Carol M. Rose, "The Several Futures of Property: Of Cyberspace and Folk Tales, Emission Trades and Ecosystems," 83 *Minnesota Law Review*, 129 (November 1998), p. 144.

12. Garrett Hardin, "The Tragedy of the Commons," 162 *Science*, December 13, 1968, pp. 1243–248

13. Elinor Ostrom, *Governing the Commons: The Evolution of Institutions for Collective Action* (New York: Cambridge University Press, 1990), p. 7,

writes: "Policy prescriptions have relied to a large extent on one of these three original models [tragedy of the commons, the prisoner's dilemma, and the logic of collective action], but those attempting to use these models as the basis for policy prescription frequently have achieved little more than a metaphorical use of the models."

14. Ibid., pp. 2–8.
15. Prisoner's dilemma analyses typically assume that the "prisoners" cannot communicate with each other, obtain outside information about their situation, or learn to develop mutual trust and loyalty—factors that are critical to the success of actual common-pool resource regimes.
16. Mancur Olson, *The Logic of Collective Action: Public Goods and the Theory of Groups* (Cambridge, MA: Harvard University Press, 1965).
17. Elinor Ostrom, *Governing the Commons*, p. 12. Ostrom adds: "The key to my argument is that some individuals have broken out of the trap inherent in the commons dilemma, whereas others continue remorselessly trapped into destroying their own resources. This leads me to ask what differences exist betwen those who have broken the shackles of a commons dilemma and those who have not. The differences may have to do with factors *internal* to a given group. The participants may simply have no capacity to communicate with one another, no way to develop trust, and no sense that they must share a common future." p. 12.
18. As Justice Cardozo once wrote: "Metaphors in law are to be narrowly watched, for starting as devices to liberate thought, they end often by enslaving it." *Berkey v. Third Ave. Ry.*, 155 N.E. 58, 61 (N.Y., 1926).
19. *The Ecologist, Whose Common Future? Reclaiming the Commons* (Philadelphia: New Society Publishers, 1993) p. 13.
20. Glenn Stevenson sketches the distinctions between public goods and common property in *Common Property Economics* (New York: Cambridge University Press, 1991), pp. 54–56.
21. Margaret Jane Radin, *Contested Commodities* (Cambridge, MA: Harvard University Press, 1996).
22. University of California researchers filed a patent in 1981 for a cell line derived from the T-lymphocytes of John Moore, a patient they were then treating for leukemia. The market value for products derived from his genetic information was established to be over $3 billion in 1990. The dispute inspired *Moore v. The Regents of the University of California*, 793 P.2d 479 (Cal. 1990), *cert. denied*, 111 S. Ct. 1388 (1991). Similarly, the U.S. Department of Commerce tried to patent the genes of a Guyami Indian woman living in the forests of Panama who was unusually resistant to a virus that causes leukemia. The claim was abandoned after indigenous peoples vehemently protested. "Whose Gene Is It Anyway?" *The Independent* (London), November 19, 1995, p. 75.
23. See, e.g., Theodore Steinberg, *Slide Mountain, or the Folly of Owning Nature* (Berkeley, CA: University of California Press, 1995), who writes: "Solutions like TDRs [transferrable development rights] to preserve landmarks are not simply neutral social practices; they are ideologies. While claiming to solve some problems, they force the ideology of exchange into the marrow of daily existence." p. 154.
24. Thomas Frank and Matt Weiland, *Commodify Your Dissent: Salvos from the Baffler* (New York: W. W. Norton, 1997).
25. For a critique of the market's coercive capacities, see Barbara H. Fried,

The Progressive Assault on Laissez Faire: Robert Hale and the First Law and Economics Movement (Cambridge, MA: Harvard University Press, 1998). A classic essay on this topic is Robert Hale, "Bargaining, Duress, and Economic Liberty," 43 *Columbia Law Review* 603 (1943).

26. See "The Commercialization Effect: The Sexual Illustration," in Fred Hirsch, *The Social Limits to Growth* (New York: Twentieth Century Fund, 1976, 1999), pp. 95–101.

27. Market theorists deny this very possibility by insisting that *all* values can be adequately "translated" into market categories. Hence the proliferation of subdisciplines such as "contingent value," "hedonics," and "willingness to pay," which try to develop surrogate market values for intangible, unquantifiable human values. Ultimately, of course, popular conviction in the incommensurability of human dignity, social relationships, democracy, and so forth, is the only effective retort to such mandarin theories, which resemble the contorted epicycles used by Ptolemaic astronomers to salvage their earth-centered cosmology. In limited ways, the "market experience," as sociologist Robert Lane puts it, can enhance human development. But the full scope and net effects are subject to great dispute. See Robert Lane, *The Market Experience* (New York: Cambridge University Press, 1991).

28. Russell Mokhiber, *Corporate Crime and Violence: Big Business Power and the Abuse of the Public Trust* (San Francisco: Sierra Club Books, 1988), pp. 373–382.

29. Peter S. Green, "Czechs Debate Benefits of Smokers Dying Prematurely," *New York Times*, July 21, 2001 p. B2. Also, Gordon Fairclough, "Philip Morris Says It's Sorry for Death Report," *Wall Street Journal*, July 26, 2001.

30. Radin declares that "systematically conceiving of personal attributes as fungible objects is threatening to personhood because it detaches from the person that which is integral to the person." Philosopher Martha Nussbaum, quoted by Radin, finds "especially repellent" the reductionist notion of universal commodification because "to treat deep parts of our identity as alienable commodities is to do violence to the conception of the self that we actually have and to the texture of the world of human practice and interaction revealed through this conception." *Contested Commodities* p. 75.

31. The moral and practical complications of turning organ donations into a marketplace are thoughtfully explored in Michael Finkel, "This Little Kidney Went to Market," *New York Times Magazine*, May 27, 2001, p. 26. See also "Putting a Price on Organ Donation," *New York Times*, June 12, 2001.

32. See, e.g., Lori Wallach and Michelle Sforza, *Whose Trade Organization? Corporate Globalization and the Erosion of Democracy* (Washington, DC: Public Citizen, 1999).

33. Clifford Geertz, *Local Knowledge: Further Essays in Interpretive Anthropology* (New York: Basic Books, 1983), p. 173, cited in Theodore Steinberg, *Slide Mountain*.

34. Thedore Steinberg, *Slide Mountain*, p. 13.

Chapter 2: The Stubborn Vitality of the Gift Economy

1. For more on the importance of free and open source software, see a lengthy memorandum by David Bollier, "The Power of Openness: Why Citizens, Education, Government and Business Should Care about the Coming

Revolution in Open Source Code Software," available at http://www.opencode.org/h2o.

2. See Daniel Golden and John Yemma, "Harvard Amasses a $13 Billion Endowment," *Boston Globe*, May 31, 1998. See also Stephen Manes and Paul Andrews, *Gates: How Microsoft's Mogul Reinvented an Industry and Made Himself the Richest Man in America* (New York: Touchstone, 1993), pp. 77–79.

3. Stallman's philosophy of free software can be read at http://www.gnu.org.

4. Professor Eben Moglen, attorney for Richard Stallman's Free Software Foundation, explains: "Users of GPL'd code [software covered by the General Public License, a contract that prohibits the proprietization of the program's source code] know that future improvements and repairs will be accessible from the commons, and need not fear either the disappearance of their supplier or that someone will use a particularly attractive improvement or a desperately necessary repair as leverage for 'taking the program private.' This use of intellectual property rules to create a commons in cyberspace is the central institutional structure enabling the anarchist triumph [represented by free software programs]." Moglen, "Anarchism Triumphant: Free Software and the Death of Copyright," in the online journal, *First Monday*, vol. 4, no. 8 (August 2, 1999), available at http://www.firstmonday.org/issues/issue4_8/moglen.

5. Eben Moglen, "Anarchism Triumphant."

6. For an extensive ethnographic account of the development of Linux, see the lengthy paper by Ko Kuwabara, "Linux: A Bazaar at the Edge of Chaos," in the online journal, *First Monday*, available at http://www.firstmonday.dk/issues/issue5_3/kuwabara/index.html.

7. For a good history of the free and open source software movements, see the essay by Steve Weber, "The Political Economy of Open Source Software," Berkeley Roundtable on the International Economy Working Paper 140, E-conomy Project, Working Paper 15, June 2000, available at http://brie.berkeley.edu/~briewww/pubs/wp/wp140.pdf.

8. Eben Moglen, "Anarchism Triumphant," writes: "Ensuring free access and enabling modification at each stage in the process [of free software development] means that the evolution of software occurs in the fast Lamarckian mode: each favorable acquired characteristic of others' work can be directly inherited. Hence the speed with which the Linux kernel, for example, outgrew all of its proprietary predecessors."

9. The rise of "digital rights managements" encryption and tracking technologies, for example, is meant to privilege market transactions in information over collaborative sharing. A special nemesis is peer-to-peer file-sharing software. Copyright industries have also convinced Congress to enact the Digital Millennium Copyright Act of 1998 to sanction these technologies and criminalize the open sharing of information about them. This theme is explored in depth in Lawrence Lessig, *The Future of Ideas: The Fate of the Commons in a Connected World* (Random House, 2001).

10. Jonathan Rowe, "The Hidden Commons," *Yes!* magazine, Summer 2001, p. 15.

11. Marcel Mauss, *The Gift: Forms and Functions of Exchange in Archaic Societies* (New York: Norton, 1965).

12. The study of these different gift-exchange regimes, wrote E. E. Evans-Pritchard, helps show modern man "how much we have lost, whatever we

may have otherwise gained, by the substitution of a rational economic system for a system in which exchange of goods was not a mechanical but a moral transaction, bringing about and maintaining human, personal relationships between individuals and groups." E. E. Evans-Pritchard, in Introduction to Marcel Mauss, *The Gift*, p. ix.

13. Edgar Cahn and Jonathan Rowe, *Time Dollars* (Emmaus, PA: Rodale Press, 1992). Unlike other segments of the "barter economy," however, time dollars work by developing social bonds among people, while barter exchange can be wholly impersonal and disconnected from a community ethos.

14. Richard M. Titmuss, *The Gift Relationship: From Human Blood to Social Policy* (New York: Pantheon, 1971). An updated and expanded version of this book taking account of the AIDS epidemic was published in 1997 by The New Press, edited by Ann Oakley and John Aston.

15. Titmuss, pp. 154–156.

16. See Ann Oakley and John Ashton, "Introduction to the New Edition," *The Gift Relationship* (New York: The New Press, 1997), p. 6.

17. Titmuss, p. 225.

18. See the essay, "AIDS and the Gift Relationship in the UK," by Virginia Berridge in the 1997 edition of Titmuss's *The Gift Relationship*, pp. 15–40.

19. Titmuss, pp. 225–226.

20. Warren O. Hagstrom, "Gift Giving as an Organizing Principle in Science," in Barry Barnes and David Edge, editors, *Science in Context: Readings in the Sociology of Science* (Cambridge, MA: MIT Press, 1992), p. 28.

21. See also Jane E. Fountain, "Social Capital: Its Relationship to Innovation in Science and Technology," *Science and Public Policy*, vol. 25, no. 2 (April 1998), pp. 103–115.

22. Hagstrom, p. 31.

23. Hagstrom, p. 30.

24. See David Bollier, *Aiming Higher: 25 Stories of Companies that Combine Sound Management with Social Vision* (New York: AMACOM, 1996), chap. 12, pp. 169–182. Also, Jack Stack with Bo Burlingham, *The Great Game of Business* (New York: Doubleday, 1994); and John F. Case, *The Open-Book Experience* (New York: Perseus Books, 1999).

25. Roger E. Alcaly, "Reinventing the Corporation," *New York Review of Books*, April 10, 1997, pp. 38–43.

26. See Eric Raymond, "The Cathedral and the Bazaar," available at http://www.tuxedo.org/~esr/writings/cathedral-bazaar.

27. Richard Barbrook, "The Hi-Tech Gift Economy," published online in *First Monday*, available at http://www.firstmonday.dk/issues/issue3_12/barbrook.

28. Steven Weber, "The Political Economy of Open Source Software."

29. Eric Raymond, "The Cathedral and the Bazaar," p. 151.

30. Carol M. Rose, "The Comedy of the Commons: Custom, Commerce, and Inherently Public Property," originally published in 53 *University of Chicago Law Review*, 711–781 (1986), and reprinted in Carol M. Rose, *Property and Persuasion: Essays on the History, Theory, and Rhetoric of Ownership* (Boulder, CO: Westview Press, 1994), chap. 5.

31. See, e.g., Jeffrey Rohlfs, "A Theory of Interdependent Demand for a Communications Service," 5 *Bell Journal of Economics and Management Science* 16 (1974), cited in Carol M. Rose, *Property and Persuasion*, p. 160.

32. See, e.g., "Clio and the Economics of QWERTY," 75 *American Economic*

Review (Papers and Proceedings), 322, 335 (1985), cited in Carol M. Rose, *Property and Persuasion*, p. 160.

33. Larry Lessig brought this quotation to my attention. It is discussed in Lessig, *The Future of Ideas*, p. 93.

34. This insight is contained in Barbrook's essay, "The Hi-Tech Gift Economy."

35. This phrase comes from Lewis Hyde, *The Gift: Imagination and the Erotic Life of Property* (New York: Vintage Books, 1979), p. 4.

36. As Lewis Hyde writes: "Gifts are a class of property whose value lies only in their use and which literally cease to exist as gifts if they are not constantly consumed. When gifts are sold, they change their nature as much as water changes when it freezes, and no rationalist telling of the constant elemental structure can replace the feeling that is lost." Hyde, p. 21.

37. Bronislaw Malinowski, *Argonauts of the Western Pacific* (Prospect Height, IL: Waveland Press, reprint edition, 1984), cited in Lewis Hyde, *The Gift: The Erotic Life of Property* (New York: Vintage, 1979), pp. 12–16.

38. See, e.g., Andrew Delbanco and Thomas Delbanco, "A.A. at the Crossroads," *The New Yorker*, March 20, 1995, pp. 50–63.

39. Hyde, p. 22.

40. Paul L. Wachtel, *The Poverty of Affluence: A Psychological Portrait of the American Way of Life* (Philadelphia: New Society Publishers, 1989).

41. Hyde, p. 37.

42. See, e.g., Sheryl Gay Stolberg, "Patent Laws May Determine Shape of Stem Cell Research," *New York Times*, August 17, 2001. Also, Howard Markel, "Patents Could Block the Way to a Cure," *New York Times*, August 24, 2001; and Michael A. Heller and Rebecca S. Eisenberg, "Can Patents Deter Innovation? The Anticommons in Biomedical Research," *Science*, May 1, 1998, pp. 698–701.

43. Hyde writes: "It is quite possible to have the state own everything and still convert all gifts to capital, as Stalin demonstrated. When he decided in favor of the 'production mode'— an intensive investment in capital goods—he acted as a capitalist, the locus of ownership having nothing to do with it." p. 37.

44. Hyde, p. 23.

45. Russian prince Petr Kropotkin reviewed the evolutionary history of species in his classic 1914 book, *Mutual Aid,* and argued that "sociability is as much a law of nature as mutual struggle," and that cooperation "results in the development of intellectual and moral faculties which secure to the species the best conditions for survival." Petr Kropotkin, *Mutual Aid: A Factor of Evolution* (Boston: Extending Horizons Books, Porter Sargent Publishers, reprint of 1914 edition).

Chapter 3: When Markets Enclose the Commons

1. "The Wiring of America," *The Economist*, December 19, 1998, p. 42.

2. My synopsis of the enclosure movement draws upon several sources: Raymond Williams, *The Country and the City* (New York: Oxford University Press, 1973), chap. 10, "Enclosures, Commons and Communities," pp. 96–107; *The Ecologist, Whose Common Future?: Reclaiming the Commons* (Philadelphia: New Society Publishers, 1994), pp. 21–58; and W. E. Tate,

The English Village Community and the Enclosure Movements (London: Victor Gollancz Ltd., 1967).

3. Gary Snyder, "The Place, the Region and the Commons," in *The Practice of the Wild* (San Francisco: North Point Press, 1990), pp. 25–47.

4. *The Ecologist, Whose Common Future?* p. 25.

5. *The Ecologist, Whose Common Future?* p. 26.

6. G. Slater, "Historical Outline of Land Ownership in English," *The Land: The Report of the Land Equity Committee* (London: Hodder and Stoughton, 1913, p. lxxii, cited in *The Ecologist, Whose Common Future?*, p. 25.

7. Karl Polanyi, *The Great Transformation* (Boston: Beacon Press, 1944/1957).

8. An excellent review of the "moral economic" school of inquiry can be found in William James Booth, "On the Idea of the Moral Economy," *American Political Science Review*, September 1994, pp. 653–667.

9. Ibid.

10. Gary Becker, *"A Theory of Marriage,"* Economics of the Family, ed. Theodore W. Schultz (Chicago, University of Chicago Press, 1974), pp. 300–301.

11. Gary Becker, *A Treatise on the Family* (Cambridge: Harvard University Press, 1981), p. 106.

12. Richard Posner, *Economic Analysis of Law*, 4th ed. (Boston: Little Brown, 1992), p. 218.

13. See the entertaining and incisive book by Thomas Frank, *One Market Under God: Extreme Capitalism, Market Populism, and the End of Economic Democracy* (New York: Doubleday, 2000).

14. See, e.g., Robert Kuttner, *Everything for Sale: The Virtues and Limits of Markets* (New York: Knopf, 1997), pp. 55–59.

15. David Kunzle writes: "Disney was, as Gilbert Seldes put it many years ago, the 'rapacious strip-miner' in the 'goldmine of legend and myth.' He ensures that the famous fairy tales became *his*: *his* Peter Pan, not Barrie's, *his* Pinocchio, not Collodi's," Introduction to the English edition, Ariel Dorfman and Armand Mattelart, *How to Read Donald Duck: Imperialist Ideology in the Disney Comic* (New York: International General, 1975).

16. Margaret Jane Radin, *Contested Commodities* (Cambridge, MA: Harvard University Press, 1996), chap. 7, pp. 102–114.

17. Michael Pollan, "The Organic-Industrial Complex," *New York Times Magazine*, May 13, 2001.

18. Ronald Alsop, "Corporate Sponsorship at Gay Pride Parades Alienate some Activists" *Wall Street Journal*, June 22, 1001, p. B1.

19. The Federal Trade Commission, on April 2, 2001, accused leading pharmaceutical companies of illegally blocking generic drug manufacturers from producing generic versions of brand-name drugs. See also Gardiner Harris and Chris Adams, "Drug Manufacturers Step Up Legal Attacks that Slow Generics," *Wall Street Journal*, July 12, 2001, p. A1.

20. Bill Carter, "A Struggle for Control: Local TV Fears the Networks' Power," *The New York Times*, April 23, 2001, p. D1.

21. Julie Flaherty, "By the Book: Individuality vs. Franchising: Trading the Spark of Creativity for the Safety of Numbers," *New York Times*, February 17, 2001, p. D1.

22. Eric Schlosser, *Fast Food Nation* (New York: Random House, 2001).

23. Paulo Prada, "European Inns Take the Hilton Route," *Wall Street Journal*, April 23, 2001, p. B1.

24. Gregory S. Alexander, *Commodity and Propriety*, p. 29.

25. Ibid.
26. For a broader treatment of these themes, see Harry Boyte, *CommonWealth: A Return to Citizen Politics* (New York: The Free Press, 1989), especially chap. 2, "The Populist Commonwealth."
27. A. James Casner, ed., *American Law of Property* (Boston: Little Brown, 1952).
28. Gregory S. Alexander, *Commodity and Propriety*, chap. 3, "Descent and Dissent from the Civic Meaning of Property," pp. 72–88. Adam Smith's belief that economics is "intertwined with the life of sentiment and imagination" is argued in Emma Rothschild, *Economic Sentiments: Adam Smith, Condorcet, and the Enlightenment* (Cambridge, MA: Harvard University Press, 2001).
29. Robert Kuttner, *Everything for Sale: The Virtues and Limits of Markets* (New York: Knopf, 1997), p. 4.
30. Charles Lindblom, *The Market System: What It Is, How It Works, and What To Make of It* (New Haven, CT: Yale University Press, 2001).

Chapter 4: Enclosing the Commons of Nature

1. Theodore Steinberg, *Slide Mountain, or the Folly of Owning Nature* (Berkeley, CA: University of California Press, 1995), p. 10.
2. Paul Hawken, *The Ecology of Commerce: A Declaration of Sustainability* (HarperCollins, 1993), p. 13.
3. Yvonne Baskin, *The Work of Nature: How the Diversity of Life Sustains Us* (Washington, DC: Island Press, 1997), p. 13.
4. David Ehrenfeld, "Return to Sender," *Utne Reader*, Nov./Dec. 1999, p. 77.
5. One source is Jeffery A. McNeely, *Economics and Biological Diversity: Developing and Using Economic Incentives to Conserve Biological Resources.* (Washington, DC: Island Press, 1991).
6. Paul Hawken, Amory Lovins, and L. Hunter Lovins, *Natural Capitalism: Creating the Next Industrial Revolution* (Boston: Little, Brown, 1999).
7. Aldo Leopold, *A Sand County Almanac* (New York: Oxford University Press, 1949, 1981), p. 224–25.
8. Norman Myers, "Biodiversity's Genetic Library," in Gretchen C. Daily, ed., *Nature's Services: Societal Dependence on Natural Ecosystems* (Washington, DC: Island Press, 1997), p. 141.
9. Norman Myers, "Biodiversity's Genetic Library," p. 255. Myers notes that "crop breeders are increasingly dependent on genetic materials from wild relatives of wheat and corn. In common with all agricultural crops, the productivity of modern wheat and corn is sustained through constant infusions of fresh germplasm with its hereditary characteristics. Thanks to this regular 'topping up' of the genetic or hereditary constitution of the United States' main crops, the Department of Agriculture estimates that germplasm contributions lead to increases in productivity that average around 1 percent annually, with a farm-gate value that now tops $1 billion."
10. Charles H. Peterson and Jane Lubchenco, "Marine Ecosystem Services," in Daily, *Nature's Services*, pp. 177–194.
11. Rosamond L. Naylor and Paul R. Ehrlich, "Natural Pest Control Services and Agriculture," in Daily, *Nature's Services*, pp. 151–174.
12. Hawken, et al., *Natural Capitalism*, p. 5.

13. William Greider, "Business Creates Eco-Side!" *The Nation,* February 28, 2000.
14. An excellent exposition of this theme can be found in Yvonne Baskin, *The Work of Nature.*
15. Lewis Hyde, *The Gift: Imagination and the Erotic Life of Property* (New York: Vintage Books, 1979), p. 27.
16. A classic meditation on this theme is Thomas Berry, *The Dream of the Earth* (San Francisco, CA: Sierra Club Books, 1988). David Abram, a cultural ecologist and philosopher, also makes a powerful and eloquent case for the value of reciprocity with the "more-than-human" in his article, "Reciprocity," describing how the endangered salmon of the Pacific Northwest partake of a vast gift economy with the forests, mountains, ocean, streams, and human culture. The transgressions against the salmon are symptomatic of a larger assault against the nourishing gift economy of which the salmon are a part. *Tikkun,* May/June 2001, pp. 21–26, 54–56.
17. Wendell Berry, *Life Is a Miracle: An Essay Against Modern Superstition* (New York: Perseus Books, 2000), p. 40.
18. Carol M. Rose, "The Several Futures of Property: Of Cyberspace and Folk Tales, Emission Trades and Ecosystems," *Minnesota Law Review,* November 1998, pp. 129–182.

Chapter 5: The Colonization of Frontier Commons

1. Quoted in Andrew Pollack, "Selling Evolution in Ways Darwin Never Imagined," *New York Times,* October 28, 2000, p. C1.
2. See Susan J. Buck, *The Global Commons: An Introduction* (Washington, DC: Island Press, 1998).
3. Pollack, *New York Times,* October 28, 2000.
4. Ismail Serageldin, vice president of the World Bank, cited in Maude Barlow, *Blue Gold: The Global Water Crisis and the Commodification of the World's Water Supply* (report), (San Francisco: International Forum on Globalization, June 1999) p. 2.
5. Maude Barlow, *Blue Gold,* p. 32.
6. Barlow, *Blue Gold,* citing Jamie Linton, *Beneath the Surface: The State of Water in Canada* (Ottawa: Canadian Wildlife Federation, 1997).
7. David M. Halbfinger, "Private Sector Sets Water Sale to Californians," *New York Times,* December 26, 2000, p. A1.
8. Dennis Owens, "Water, Water, Everywhere, but Canada Won't Sell," *Wall Street Journal,* August 31, 2001.
9. Barlow, *Blue Gold,* p. 29, citing Wade Graham, "A Hundred Rivers Run Through It," *Harper's,* June 1998.
10. Maude Barlow, "Thirst of Justice," *Yes!* magazine, Summer 2001, pp. 24–25.
11. Barlow, *Blue Gold,* p. 16.
12. Otti Thomas, "Conference Fails to Establish Water as Basic Human Right," *Reuters* (wire service), March 23, 2000, describes deliberation by the Second World Water Forum in the Hague, Netherlands.
13. One of the best surveys of the Wise Use movement—its philosophy, leaders, goals, and tactics—is *Let the People Judge: Wise Use and the Private Property Rights Movement,* edited by John Echeverria and Raymond Booth Eby, (Washington, DC: Island Press, 1995).

14. An insightful account of Madison's 1792 essay on property can be found in Gregory S. Alexander, *Commodity and Propriety: Competing Visions of Prosperity in American Legal Thought, 1776–1970* (Chicago: University of Chicago Press, 1997) pp. 68–69.

15. Jon Roush, "Freedom and Responsibility: What We Can Learn from the Wise Use Movement," in John Echeverria and Raymond Booth Eby, *Let the People Judge*.

16. For an overview of Takings law, see Jed Rubenfeld, "Usings," *Yale Law Journal*, vol. 102, p. 1077–1163 (1993). See also the Web site of the Environmental Policy Project at http://www.envpoly.org.

17. For more, see John Echeverria, "Who Owns Wildlife?" *Defenders of Wildlife*, Winter 1999/2000, p. 22. For a legal analysis, see *Amicus curiae Brief of Putnam-Highlands Audubon Society in Support of Plaintiffs-Respondents in The State of New York v. Sour Mountain Realty, Inc.*, July 27, 1999, available with other related documents at the Environmental Policy Center's Web site, http://www.envpoly.org/takings/courts/briefs/sour.htm.

18. One of the best overviews of Monsanto's GM foods is Michael Pollan's "Playing God in the Garden," *New York Times Magazine*, October 25, 1998, p. 44, et seq., which is given fuller treatment in Michael Pollan, *The Botany of Desire: A Plant's-Eye View of the World* (New York: Random House, 2001), chap. 4.

19. Amory B. Lovins and L. Hunter Lovins, "A Tale of Two Botanies," *Wired*, April 2000, available at http://www.wired.com/wired/archive/8.04/botanies.html.

20. "An Interview with Pat Mooney," *Multinational Monitor*, January/February 2000, p. 33.

21. William Greider, "The Last Farm Crisis," *The Nation*, November 20, 2000, pp. 11–18.

22. " 'What happened was, a whole growing system evolved around color and shape, because that's what the big buyers wanted,' said Steve Fox, the marketing director of a fruit packing and storage company here in the heart of apple country [Washington State]. 'So they made the apples redder and redder, and prettier and prettier, and they just about bred themselves out of existence.' ... In creating an apple that packs well, looks terrific, shines to a glossy polish and can live year-round in cold storage, the growers have produced something that many of them no longer recognize." Timothy Egan, " 'Perfect' Apple Pushed Growers into Debt," *New York Times*, November 4, 2000, p. A1.

23. Jane Rissler and Margret Mellon, *The Ecological Risks of Engineered Crops* (Cambridge, MA: MIT Press, 1996).

24. Industry-financed studies in 2001 claimed to find "negligible" risks to monarch butterflies, but neither the Environmental Protection Agency nor biotechnology firms would allow the study to be made public. See Andrew Pollack, "Data on Genetically Modified Corn," *New York Times*, September 8, 2001.

25. Michael Pollan, "Playing God with the Garden."

26. Amory B. Lovins and L. Hunter Lovins, "A Tale of Two Botanies."

27. Jennifer Kahn, "The Green Machine," *Harper's*, April 1999, p. 73.

28. Monsanto ad in *Farm Journal*, November 1997, p. B5, cited in Martha L. Crouch, "How the Terminator Terminates," published by the Edmonds

Institute, Edmonds, Washington, and available on the Web site of the Rural Advancement Foundation International, http://www.rafi.org.

29. Lance Nixon, "New Technology Would Help Seed Companies Protect Research Investments," *Aberdeen American News*, August 8, 1999.

30. Mississippi farmer Fred Stokes, head of the Organization for Competitive Markets, said: "These farmers are so desperate for profitability they grab whatever is offered to them. Offering GM [genetically modified] seeds is like selling them a bag of cocaine." Quoted in William Greider, "The Last Farm Crisis," *The Nation*, November 20, 2000, p. 14. Leading critics of GM seeds include the Union of Concerned Scientists, the Center for Technology Assessment, and Rural Advancement Foundation International.

31. William Greider, "The Last Farm Crisis," *The Nation*, November 20, 2000.

32. A useful overview of bioprospecting and its impact on developing nations can be found in Shayana Kadidal, "Plants, Poverty and Pharmaceutical Patents," *Yale Law Journal*, vol. 103 (1993), pp. 223–258.

33. Rural Advancement Foundation International, *Conserving Indigenous Knowledge: Integrating Two Systems of Innovation* (United Nations Development Programme, no date), p. vii.

34. James Boyle, *Shamans, Software and Spleens: Law and the Construction of the Information Society* (Cambridge, MA: Harvard University Press, 1996), p. 128.

35. These examples are culled from "Appendix A: The North—Benefiting from Biodiversity," in RAFI, *Conserving Indigenous Knowledge,* pp. 58–71.

36. Vandana Shiva, *Biopiracy: The Plunder of Nature and Knowledge* (Boston: South End Press, 1997), pp. 69–72. See also Karen Hoggan, BBC News, May 11, 2000, at http://news.bbc.co.uk/hi/English/sci/tech/newsid_745000/745028.stm.

37. Saritha Rai, "India-U.S. Fight on Basmati Rice is Mostly Settled, *New York Times*, August 25, 2001.

38. Tom Wilkie, "Whose Gene Is It Anyway?" *The Independent*, November 19, 1995, p. 75.

39. Kim Griggs, "Tonga Sells Its Old, New Genes," *Wired News*, November 27, 2000, at http://www.wired.com/news/print/0,1294,40354,00.html.

40. Christine Haight Farley, "Protecting Folklore of Indigenous Peoples: Is Intellectual Property the Answer?" *Connecticut Law Review*, Fall 1998, pp. 1–57.

41. See "Panning for Drugs" in Seth Shulman, *Owning the Future* (Houghton Mifflin, 1999), pp. 127–152.

42. Lori Wallach and Michelle Sforya, *Whose Trade Organization? Corporate Globalization and the Erosion of Democracy* (Washington, DC: Public Citizen, 1999), pp. 106–112.

43. Timothy Pratt, "Patent of Small Yellow Bean Provokes Cry of Biopiracy," *New York Times*, March 20, 2001.

44. "Mapping the Human Genome: Human Genes Considered National Resources," *The Daily Yomiuri* (Tokyo), August 2, 2000. Also, "Pacific Island Nation Sells Its Gene Pool to Private Industry, *Bloomberg News*, November 23, 2000; Julian Coman, "Iceland's Blonds Help Team Trap Alzheimer Gene," *Sunday Telegraph* (London), September 3, 2000; and Andrew Pollack, "Company Seeking Donors of DNA for a 'Gene Trust,'" *New York Times*, August 1, 2000.

45. Matt Fleischer, "Patent Thyself!" *The American Lawyer*, June 21, 2001.

46. Gina Lotata, "Sharing of Profits Is Debated as the Volume of Tissues Rises," *New York Times*, May 15, 2999, p. A1.

47. Kristen Philipkoski, "Biology Yearns to Be Free," *Wired News*, April 20, 2001.

48. "Indigenous knowledge has gone unnoticed by the institutional innovation system [which relies on intellectual property rights] for so long because it is—not informal or disorganized, as some would claim—but cooperative and conducted within the pace of daily living. In particular, indigenous people's knowledge systems operate, often invisibly, within the context of their immediate agro-ecological environment." RAFI, *Conserving Indigenous Knowledge*, p. 3.

49. James Boyle, *Shamans, Software and Spleens.*

50. A fascinating perspective on this theme can be found in William P. Alford, *To Steal a Book Is an Elegant Offense: Intellectual Property Law in Chinese Civilization* (Stanford, CA: Stanford University Presss, 1995).

51. This theme recurs in a multitude of domains. In scientific research, computer programming, and artistic circles, for example, the author-centered regime of intellectual property law is expanding property rights to such extremes that the public domain is shrinking dramatically. This is preventing future creators from freely using the raw material they need because it is already "owned" by someone else. Innovation is thwarted.

52. Boyle, *Shamans, Software and Spleens.*

53. RAFI, *Conserving Indigenous Knowledge: Integrating Two Systems of Innovation*, p. 4.

54. This issue is discussed in fascinating detail by Joseph L. Sax, "Is Anyone Minding Stonehenge? The Origins of Cultural Property Protection in England," *California Law Review*, vol. 78 (1990), pp. 1543–1567.

55. Joseph L. Sax, *California Law Review*, p. 1559.

56. A number of such ideas are set forth in RAFI, *Conserving Indigenous Knowledge*, chap. IV, "Alternatives to Intellectual Property Rights," pp. 39–54.

57. Theodore Steinberg, *Slide Mountain, or the Folly of Owning Nature* (Berkeley, CA: University of California Press, 1995), p. 23.

58. Bill Joy, "The Future Doesn't Need Us," *Wired*, April 2000.

59. Wendell Berry, *Life Is a Miracle* (Washington, DC: Counterpoint, 2000), p. 76.

60. Gary Snyder, "The Place, the Region and the Commons," in *The Practice of the Wild* (San Francisco: North Point Press, 1990), pp. 36–37.

Chapter 6: The Abuse of the Public's Natural Resources

1. Richard W. Behan, *Plundered Promise: Capitalism, Politics and the Fate of the Federal Lands* (Washington, DC: Island Press, 2001).

2. An excellent overview of the Mining Act of 1872 and its history can be found in Carl J. Mayer and George A. Riley, *Public Domain, Private Dominion: A History of Public Mineral Policy in America* (San Francisco: Sierra Club Books, 1985), chap. 3. Other worthwhile overviews of the Mining Act are Carlos Da Rosa, *Overburdened*, (Washington, DC: Mineral Policy Center, 1999); Dale Bumpers, "Capitol Hill's Longest-Running Outrage," *Washington Monthly*, January 1998; and Congressional Research Service (Marc Humphries, Resources, Science and Industry Division), *The 1872 Mining Law*, January 22, 2001.

3. Mineral Policy Center, *The Last American Dinosaur: The 1872 Mining Law* (undated, MPC fact Sheet).
4. U.S. PIRG, "Green Scissors '98: Cutting Wasteful and Environmentally Harmful Spending," (report) (Washington, DC, 1998), p. 24.
5. Jonathan Dushoff, "Gold-Plated Giveaways: The Mining Act of 1872," *Multinational Monitor*, January/February, 1993, p. 18 and 19.
6. These estimates come from the now-defunct U.S. Bureau of Mines and are cited by Mineral Policy Cener, op. cit. and U.S. PIRG, op. cit.
7. USPIRG, *Subsidies for Sale: How Fat Cat Contributions Lead to Government Handouts for Polluters* (Washington, DC, April 1999), p. 20.
8. "The Great American Oil Rip-Off," *Los Angeles Times*, July 20, 1999, p. A12.
9. These include the oil depletion allowance (a 15 percent deduction on gross income of independent drillers), the "intangible drilling cost" deduction (an up-front 70 percent deduction of the costs of building a drilling operation rather than a depreciated expense over the life of the well), and the enhanced oil recovery credit (a tax subsidy intended to encourage domestic oil extraction).
10. The Project on Government Oversight (POGO) in Washington, DC, has issued a number of reports on underpayment of oil royalties. Two notable ones: "With a Wink and a Nod: How the Oil Industry and the Department of Interior Are Cheating the American Public and California School Children," March 1996, and "Wait! There is More Money to Collect. . . . Unpaid Oil Royalties Across the Nation," August 1996.
11. POGO, "With a Wink and a Nod," March 1996, p. 3.
12. Data from Center for Responsive Politics, cited by Morton Mintz, "#10 Big Oil: Cheating Taxpayers, Funding Candidates," at http://tompaine.com/news/2000/01/04/11.html.
13. See Harold K. Steen, *The U.S. Forest Service: A History* (Seattle: University of Washington Press, 1991).
14. Paul W. Hirt, *A Conspiracy of Optimism: Management of the National Forests since World War Two* (Lincoln, NE: University of Nebraska Press, 1994).
15. Hirt, *A Conspiracy of Optimism*, p. 135.
16. Hirt, *A Conspiracy of Optimism*, p. 294.
17. Barlow et al., Natural Resources Defense Council, *Giving Away the National Forests* (Washington, DC: NRDC, June 1980); U.S. General Accounting Office, "Congress Needs Better Information on Forest Service's Below-Cost Timber Sales," GAO-RCED-84–96; June 28, 1984; Perri Knize, "The Mismanagement of the National Forests," *Atlantic Monthly*, October 1991, pp. 98–112.
18. Hirt, *A Conspiracy of Optimism*, pp. 278–281.
19. Hirt, *A Conspiracy of Optimisim*, p. 297.
20. Paul Rogers and Jennifer LaFleur, "Damage Goes On—at Taxpayer Expense," one of a series of articles in a special report, "Cash Cows: Taxes Support a Wild West Holdover That Enriches Ranchers and Degrades the Land," *San Jose Mercury News*, November 7, 1999 (eight-page reprint edition).
21. Rogers and LaFleur, *San Jose Mercury News*, p. 2S.
22. USPIRG, *Subsidies for Sale*, p. 20–22.
23. Thomas Michael Power, *Lost Landscapes and Failed Economies: The Search for a Value of Place* (Washington, DC: Island Press, 1996), p. 186–189. See also Rogers and LaFleur, *San Jose Mercury News*, p. 3S.
24. Rogers and LaFleur, *San Jose Mercury News*, p. 3S.

25. See National Wildlife Federation, "Threat to Grasslands: Failed Steward-ship," available at http://nwf.org/grasslands/threattograsslands.html.
26. See George Wuerthner, "Livestock Industry Myths," at http://www.fs.fed.us/forums/eco/get/eco-watch/forestuse-forum/5/1.html.
27. A. J. Belsky, A. Matzke, and S. Uselman, "Survey of Livestock Influences on Stream and Riparian Ecosystems in the Western United States," *Journal of Soil and Water Conservation*, 1st quarter, 1999.
28. Todd Oppenheimer, "The Rancher Subsidy," *The Atlantic*, January 1996, pp. 26–38.
29. Cited in Susan Zakin, "Rivers of Crud: Grazing Saddles the West with a Heck of a Problem," *Grist Magazine*, August 26, 1999, available at http://www.gristmagazine.com/grist/maindish/zakin.82699.stm.
30. Julie Cart, "Deal Over Microbe Hunt at Yellowstone Draws Heat," *Los Angeles Times*, July 10, 2000. See also *Edmonds Institute v. National Park Service*, Docket No. 98-CV-0482 (D.D.C.).
31. Bill Sargent, "Blood Feud Biotech Firm that Catches Horseshoe Crabs off Cape Sues U.S. Government after Ban on Harvest," *Boston Globe*, May 13, 2000. See also the Audubon Society website at http://www.audubon.org/campaign/horseshoe/vaeconrpt.html.
32. USPIRG, *Subsidies for Sale*.

Chapter 7: Can the Internet Commons Be Saved?

1. Norbert Weiner, *Invention: The Care and Feeding of Ideas* (1954, MIT Press, 1993), p. 153, cited in Seth Shulman, *Owning the Future* (Boston: Houghton Mifflin, 1999).
2. This is the central theme of Lawrence Lessig's *The Future of Ideas: The Fate of the Commons in a Connected World* (New York: Random House, 2001).
3. Charles H. Ferguson, *High Stakes, No Prisoners: A Winner's Tale of Greed and Glory in the Internet Wars* (New York: Times Business, 1999), p. 13.
4. Janet Abbate, *Inventing the Internet* (Cambridge, MA: MIT Press, 1999), p. 46.
5. Ibid., p. 74.
6. Robert E. Kahn, "The Role of Government in the Evolution of the Inter-net," in *Revolution in the U.S. Information Infrastructure* (Washington, DC: National Academy Press, 1995), pp. 20–21.
7. For an excellent survey of government-sponsored computer innovations, see Nathan S. Newman, "Net Loss: Government, Technology and the Political Economy of Community in the Age of the Internet," Doctoral dissertation, University of California, Berkeley, 1998, especially chaps. 2 and 3, available at http://Socrates.Berkeley.edu/~newman. See also Douglas K. Smith, *Fumbling the Future: How Xerox Invented, Then Ignored, the First Personal Computer* (New York: W. Morrow, 1988).
8. J.C.R. Licklider, "Man-Computer Symbiosis," *IRE Transactions on Human Factors in Electronics*, vol. 1., no. 1, 1960, pp.4–11
9. Sendmail is the program that routes over 80 percent of all e-mail on the Internet; Apache is the most popular Web server software in use on the Internet; PERL is the programming language that allows dynamic features on many Web sites; BIND, the Berkeley Internet Name Daemon, is the *de facto* DNS server for the Internet.

10. In his famous essay, "The Cathedral and the Bazaar," Eric Raymond described two competing processes of software development. The "cathedral" represents the closed, proprietary shop of software professionals exemplified by Microsoft; the "bazaar" represents the free and open system of software collaboration embodied by the Linux community. See Raymond's essay at http://www.tuxedo.org/~esr/writings/cathedral-bazaar.

11. Charles Ferguson, *High Stakes, No Prisoners*, p. 49.

12. Ibid.

13. Nathan Newman, "Net Loss," chap. 3, p. 16.

14. Nathan Newman, "Net Loss," chap. 3.

15. Janet Abbate, *Inventing the Internet*, p. 145.

16. François Bar, Stephen Cohen, Peter Cowhey, et al. of the Berkeley Roundtable on the International Economy [BRIE], "Defending the Internet Revolution in the Broadband Era: When Doing Nothing Is Doing Harm," (Berkeley, CA: UC Berkeley, August 1999).

17. Ibid.

18. Lawrence Lessig, *Code and Other Laws of Cyberspace* (New York: Basic Books, 1999).

19. In creating the Ethernet LAN (local area network) technology, Bob Melcalfe of Xerox PARC helped formulate an equation for understanding the value created by adding one additional person n to an electronic network. Melcalfe's Law holds that that value of a network grows by the square the number of people on the network.

20. Tim Berners-Lee, *Weaving the Web* (San Francisco: HarperCollins, 1999), p. 71.

21. Berners-Lee, *Weaving the Web*, pp. 71–74.

22. Nathan Newman, "Net Loss," chap. 3.

23. Nathan Newman offers a wry postscript: "In the end, Netscape would argue that the beloved public village of standards was threatened by Microsoft, and Netscape had only destroyed the village in order to save it. And if saving the village made Jim Clark's Netscape a $9 billion company (at least on paper at its stock market high) and snatched leadership of Internet development away from Illinois back to Silicon Valley—well, this was just returning leadership of Internet-based computing to the region government support had made the leader in the first place." Nathan Newman, "Net Loss," chap. 3.

24. Berners-Lee, *Weaving the Web*, p. 76.

25. Tim Berners-Lee, the inventor of the Web, recalls his fear that its protocols would become proprietary, thereby preventing the Web from becoming a universal global medium. He was greatly relieved in April 1993 when he received a formal declaration from CERN "saying that CERN agreed to allow anybody to use the Web protocol and code free of charge, to create a server or a browser, to give it away or sell it, without any royalty or other constraint. Whew!" Tim Berners-Lee, *Weaving the Web*, p. 74.

26. Software designer Dave Winer makes these compelling claims in his newsletter, DaveNet, at http://davenet.userland.com/2001/04/10/the AmazingStoryof SoapAndMicrosoft, which is also reported in John Markoff, "An Internet Critic Who is Not Shy about Ruffling the Big Names in Technology," *New York Times*, April 9, 2001.

27. Microsoft rescinded the Smart Tags after an uproar, but critics still fear that Microsoft will use its market power to dominate new software applications and markets. The Windows XP operating system integrates many features

that were previously independent and unconnected, such as Internet telephony; instant messaging, videoconferencing and document sharing, a
media player (music, DVD movies and streaming video), a security firewall,
and speech recognition software. Many computer observers fear this aggressive integration of features represents Microsoft's latest attempt to dominate
the Web. Rebecca Buckman, "With Its Old Playbook, Microsoft Is
Muscling into New Web Markets," *Wall Street Journal*, June 29, 2001;
Walter S. Mossberg, "Microsoft Backs Off Plan to Add Its Links to Others'
Web Sites," *Wall Street Journal*, June 28, 2001.

28. "The Default Language," *The Economist*, May 15, 1999, p. 67.

29. The Halloween memos, dubbed Halloween I and II by Eric Raymond, were
written by Microsoft employee Vinod Valloppillil and are accessible at
http://www.opensource.org/halloween/.

30. Michael Heller, "The Tragedy of the Anti-Commons," *Harvard Law Review*,
vol. 111, no. 3 (January 1998).

31. For more on the value of patent pools, see Jeanne Slark, et al., "Patent Pools:
A Solution to the Problem of Access in Biotechnology Patents?" United
States Patent and Trademark Office, December 5, 2000, available at
http://uspto.gov/web/offices/pac/dapp/opla/patpoo/cova.html.

32. Yochai Benkler, "Free as the Air to Common Use: First Amendment
Constraints on Enclosure of the Public Domain," *NYU Law Review*, May
1999, p. 408.

33. Robert W. McChesney, *Rich Media, Poor Democracy: Communication Politics
in Dubious Times* (Urbana, IL: University of Illinois Press, 1999).

34. Patricia Aufderheide, "Walled Gardens or Enclosure Movement? The
Debate over the Public Interest in the AOL-Time Warner Merger," Presentation at the International Communication Association Conference, May
24–27, 2001.

35. See, e.g., Mark A. Lemley and Lawrence Lessig, "The End of End-to-End:
Preserving the Architecture of the Internet in the Broadband Era," UC
Berkeley Law & Economics Research Paper No. 2000–19, Stanford Law
School, John M. Olin Working Paper No. 207, October 2000.

36. See Cisco Systems White Paper, "Controlling Your Network—a Must
for Cable Operators," 1999, available at http://www.cptech.org/ecom/
openaccess/cisco1.html. The paper notes: "The ability to prioritize and
control traffic levels is a distinguishing factor and critical difference between
New World networks employing Internet Technologies, and the Internet."

37. James Love, Comments of Consumer Project on Technology to the Federal
Communications Commission, "En Banc Hearing on American Online,
Inc., and Time Warner, Inc., Application for Transfer of Control," CS
Docket No. 00–30, July 27, 2000, available at http://www.cptech.org/
ecom/aol-tw/enbanc.html.

38. "Nearly three-quarters of AOL members' time and nearly 40 percent of the
time that all Americans spend on the Web is currently spent within AOL's
'walled garden' of content and services...." Editorial, "A Theory of the
Case," *The Economist*, January 15, 2000.

39. Dan Carney, "Whose Net Is It Anyway?" *Business Week*, July 31, 2000.

40. Report by Jupiter Media Metrix at http://www.jmm.com, as reported by
Martin Stone, "Media Concentration Narrows Control of Online Time,"
Newsbytes, June 4, 2001.

41. Companies whose names are used in these domain names have sometimes

sought to shut them down, claiming a dilution of their trademark rights. See Julia Angwin, "Are Domain Panels the Hanging Judges of Cyberspace Court?" *Wall Street Journal*, August 20, 2001.

42. Thomas E. Weber, "Network Solutions Sells Marketers Its Web Database," *Wall Street Journal*, February 16, 2001, p. B1.

43. Leading critics of ICANN include University of Miami professor A. Michael Froomkin, a founder of ICANN Watch; James Love of the Consumer Project on Technology; Jerry Berman of the Center for Democracy and Technology; and Scott Harshbarger of Common Cause.

44. A. Michael Froomkin, "Wrong Turn in Cyberspace: Using ICANN to Route around the APA and the Constitution," *Duke Law Journal*, vol. 50, no. 1 (2000), pp. 17–186.

Chapter 8: The Privatization of Public Knowledge

1. Charles F. Gosnell, Director of New York University Libraries, "The Viewpoint of the Librarian and Library User," in A. Kent and H. Lancour, editors, *Copyright: Current Viewpoints on History, Laws, and Legislation* (New York: Bowker, 1972), p. 63.

2. A useful array of resources about the public domain can be found at the Web site for the Center for the Public Domain at http://www.centerpd.org. For useful background on the public domain in intellectual property law, see Jessica Litman, "The Public Domain," *Emory Law Journal*, vol. 39 (1990), p. 965, and James Boyle, *Shamans, Software, and Spleens: Law and the Construction of the Information Society* (Cambridge, MA: Harvard University Press, 1996), esp. chap. 13.

3. Thomas Jefferson, Letter to Isaac McPherson, August 28, 1813. This quotation was brought to my attention by Professor Lawrence Lessig.

4. Brandeis dissent in *International News Service*, 248 U.S. 259 (1918). This quotation was brought to my attention by Professor Yochai Benkler in his law review article, "Free as the Air to Common Use: First Amendment Constraints on the Enclosure of the Public Domain," 74 *NYU Law Review* 354 (May 1999). Brandeis also wrote: "The fact that a product of the mind has cost its producer money and labor, and has a value for which others are willing to pay, is not sufficient to insure to it this legal attribute of property."

5. See transcript of conference in *Whole Earth Review*, May 1985, p. 49. Also, "Information Wants to Be Free" Web site, http://www.anu.edu.au/people/Roger.Clarke/II/IWtbF.html.

6. The Online Computer Library Center of Dublin, Ohio, claims copyright and trademark rights in the Dewey Decimal Classification system and has sought to collect licensing fees from libraries using the system. Correspondence between Joan S. Mitchell, Online Computer Library Center, Dublin, Ohio, and Paul Jones, University of North Carolina, September 15, 2000.

7. House report on the Berne Convention Implementation Act of 1988, H.R. Report 609, 100 Cong., 2d Session, 23, cited in L. Ray Patterson and Stanley W. Lindberg, *The Nature of Copyright: A Law of Users' Rights* (Athens, GA: University of Georgia Press, 1991), p. 49.

8. An excellent review of the history of copyright right and its current biases can be found in L. Ray Patterson and Stanley W. Lindberg, *The Nature of Copyright*. See also Siva Vaidhyanathan, *Copyrights and Copywrongs: The Rise*

of Intellectual Property and How It Threatens Creativity (New York: NYU Press, 2001).

9. Patricia Schroeder, president of the Association of American Publishers, said, "We have a very serious issue with librarians" over what constitutes fair use of written material. "One librarian buys one of a publisher's journals. They give it to other libraries. They'll give it to others." Schroeder finds fault with libraries and academic instituions that often give away access to their materials rather than charge people to read. Linton Weeks, "Pat Schroeder's New Chapter," *Washington Post*, February 7, 2001, p. C1.

10. A landmark law review that summarizes the literature on the public domain is David Lange, "Recognizing the Public Domain," 44 *Law and Contemporary Problems* 4 (1981), pp. 147–178.

11. I am indebted to David Lange's 1981 article, "Recognizing the Public Domain," for an extended analysis of how vaudeville comics "borrowed" from the commons.

12. James Boyle, *Shamans, Software, and Spleens*, pp. 56–57. This theme is also explored in Jessica Litman, "The Public Domain," 39 *Emory Law Journal*, 965 (Fall 1990).

13. A leading monitor of the public domain is the Copyright Commons at the Harvard Law School Berkman Center for Internet and Society, accessible at http://www.cyber.law.harvard.edu/cc. Examples of works affected by the Copyright Term Extension Act can be found at http:/www.csmonitor.com/durable/1998/06/11/fp54s2-csm.htm.

14. David D. Kirkpatrick, "Court Halts Book Based on 'Gone With the Wind,'" *New York Times*, April 21, 2001.

15. Daren Fona, "Copyright Crusader," *Boston Globe Magazine*, August 29, 1999.

16. See http://cyber.law.harvard.edu/eldredvreno. For a list of copyrighted works affected by the Bono Act, see http://www.kingkong.demon.co.uk/ccer/ccer.htm.

17. To protest the suppression of First Amendment rights, critics have inserted the banned code into a variety of creative works (poems, bar codes, etc.) to dramatize that software code must be treated in the same fashion as other expressive speech. David P. Hamilton, "Banned Code Lives in Poetry and Song," *Wall Street Journal*, April 12, 2001, p. B1.

18 Amy Harmon and Jennifer Lee, "Arrest Raises Stakes in Battle Over Copyright," *New York Times*, July 23, 2001.

19. Julie E. Cohen, "Call it the Digital Millennium *Censorship* Act," *New Republic*, May 23, 2000. See also http://www.tnr.com/online/cohen 052300.html.

20. For more on this phenomenon, see John Gilmore, Electronic Frontier Foundation, "What's Wrong with Content Protection," available at http://www.toad.com/gnu/whatswrong.html.

21. For an overview, see Walter A. Effross, "Withdrawal of the Reference: Rights, Rules, and Remedies for Unwelcomed Web-Linking," *South Carolina Law Review* vol. 49, no. 4 (Summer 1998), pp. 651–691. Professor Benkler writes: "At stake in the linking cases is who will control the context in which certain information is presented.... The right to control linking becomes a right to shape the meaning and relevance of one's statements for others.... As long as one can deep link to publicly accessible information tidbits without anyone controlling access, there can be many ways of access-

ing it, contextualizing it, and thereby understanding it. But once a right is established to prevent deep linking the owner gains the power to condition access to the specifically sought information." Benkler, "Property, Commons and the First Amendment: Towards a Core Common Infrastructure," A White Paper of the First Amendment Program of the Brennan Center for Justice at NYU School of Law, 2001, available at http://www.law.nyu.edu/benklery/whitepaper.pdf.

22. Yochai Benkler, "Free as the Air to Common Use: First Amendment Constraints on the Enclosure of the Public Domain," 74 *NYU Law Review*, 354 (May 1999).

23. An impressive, comprehensive account of the issues raised by e-books can be found in Clifford Lynch, "The Battle to Define the Future of the Book in the Digital World," *First Monday* [online journal], vol. 6, no. 6 (June 2001), available at http://firstmonday.org/issues/issue6_6/lynch/index. html.

24. Felicity Barringer, "Leery of the Web, Olympics Officials Set Limits on News," *New York Times*, September 25, 2000, p. 1. See also Barringer, "Damming the Flow of Free Information," *New York Times*, May 2, 2000 [Week in Review section], p. 6.

25 Statement signed by more than 130 institutions, available at Web site of Digital Futures Coalition, http://www.databasedata.org/statement/statement.html.

26 *San Francisco Arts & Athletics, Inc. et al v. United States Olympic Committee*, 483 U.S. 522 (1987).

27. Kate Silver, "Serving up the McDictionary," *Las Vegas Weekly*, May 22, 2001.

28. Presentation by James Boyle, "Reclaiming the Commons" conference sponsored by New America Foundation, Washington, DC, March 12, 2001. See also Boyle, "A Politics of Intellectual Property: Environmentalism for the Net," 47 *Duke Law Journal* (1997), p. 87.

29. National Research Council, *Bits of Power: Issues in Global Access to Scientific Data* (National Academy Press, 1997), chap. 4, Box 4.2, cited in J. H. Reichman and Pamela Samuelson, "Intellectual Property Rights in Data?" 50 *Vanderbilt Law Review* (1997), p. 121.

30. See, e.g., James Boyle, "Cruel, Mean, or Lavish? Economic Analysis, Price Discrimination, and Digital Intellectual Property," 53 *Vanderbilt Law Review* (2000) 6.

31. See Julie E. Cohen, "A Right to Read Anonymously: A Closer Look at 'Copyright Management,'" 28 *Connecticut Law Review* (1996), p. 981.

32. See, e.g., "Special Report: Geography and the Net," *Economist*, August 11, 2001, pp. 9–10, 18–20.

33. See Julie E. Cohen, "Copyright and the Perfect Curve," in 53 *Vanderbilt Law Review* 1799, (November 2000), at http://www.law.georgetown.edu/faculty/jec/perfectcurve.pdf.

34. Scott Rosenberg, "Assimilating the Web," *Salon*, June 26, 2001, available at http://www.salon.com/tech/feature/2001/06/26/locking_up_the_web/index.html.

35. Seth Shulman, *Unlocking the Sky: The Forgotten Story of Glenn Curtiss and the Birth of the Airplane* (New York: HarperCollins, 2002).

36. J. H. Reichman, "Of Green Tulips and Legal Kudzu: Repackaging Rights in Subpatentable Innovation," *Vanderbilt Law Review*, vol. 53, no. 6 (November 2000).

37. Seth Shulman, *Owning the Future* (Houghton Mifflin, 1999), p. 162.
38. Christopher Stern, "Copyright Holders vs. Telecom," *Washington Post*, May 16, 2001, p. E4.
39. In fact, an Australian court in August 2001 asserted jurisdiction over the United States publisher Dow Jones in a case alleging defamation by an article posted on a *Wall Street Journal* Web site based in New Jersey. See *Glutnick v. Dow Jones & Co. Inc.*, VSC 30, August 28, 2001, available at http://www.austlii.edu.au/au/cases/vic/vsc/2001/305.html.
40. Lisa M. Bowman, "Global Treaty Could Transform Web," CNET News.com, June 22, 2001, available at http://news.cnet.com/news/ 0–1005–200–6345725.html. See also the Web site of the Consumer Project on Technology, at http://www.cptech.org.
41. Lawrence Lessig, "Reclaiming a Commons," Keynote address at the Berkman Center's "Building a Commons" conference, May 20, 1999, Cambridge, Mass., available at http://www.cyber.law.harvard.edu/events/ lessigkeynote.pdf.
42. Presentation by J. H. Reichman, Harvard Law School, May 7, 2001.

Chapter 9: Enclosing the Academic Commons

1. Leonard G. Boonin, "The University, Scientific Research, and the Ownership of Knowledge," in Vivian Weil and John W. Snapper, eds., *Owning Scientific and Technical Information: Value and Ethical Issues* (New Brunswick, NJ: Rutgers University Press, 1989), pp. 262.
2. National Science Foundation figures, as cited by Eyal Press and Jennifer Washburn, "The Kept University," *The Atlantic*, March 2000, p. 41.
3. Karen W. Arenson, "Columbia Leads Academic Pack in Turning Profit from Research," *New York Times*, August 2, 2000, p. A1.
4. Press and Washburn, pp. 39–54. I am greatly indebted to the reporting and interpretations of Press and Washburn, and am grateful to Washburn in particular for her presentation at a conference, "Reclaiming the American Commons," sponsored by the New America Foundation, Washington, DC, March 12, 2001. See http://www.newamerica.net.
5. Kurt Wolff, ed. and trans., *The Sociology of George Simmel*, (Glencoe, IL: Free Press, 1950), p. 387.
6. Robert P. Merges, "Property Rights Theory and the Commons: The Case of Scientific Research," *Social Philosophy and Policy*, vol. 13, no. 2 (Summer 1996), pp. 145–167.
7. National Science Foundation, *Science and Engineering Indicators, 2000*, available at http://www.nsf.gov/sbe/srs/seind00/access/c6/c6h.htm.
8. Ronnie Dugger, "The Struggle that Matters the Most," in Geoffry D. White, *Campus, Inc.* (Amherst, NY: Prometheus Books, 2000), p. 21.
9. The Bayh-Dole University and Small Business Patent Act (1980) dealt with IP rights in federally funded grants, contracts, and cooperative agreements. The Stevenson-Wydler Technology Innovation Act (1980) and Federal Technology Transfer Act (1986) dealt with IP rights at government laboratories. A 1984 Act repealed the five-year limitation on the use of exclusive licenses by nonprofit institutions that held title to inventions that had been developed with federal funds. The Federal Orphan Drug Act is another law by which drug companies sometimes obtain exclusive marketing rights to drugs developed by federal funding.

10. Statement of Rep. Jack Brooks, dissenting views, in report *Amending the Patent and Trademark Laws* (Bayh-Dole Act), Committee on the Judiciary, U.S. House of Representatives, 96th Congress, 2d Session Report 96, 1307, Part I, p. 29.

11. As Ralph Nader testified to Congress in 1993, the 1985 amendments to the Bayh-Dole Act eliminated the "needs" test for federal Orphan Drug Act exclusive marketing privileges on drugs; other amendments have increasingly emphasized *exclusive* licensing of federal research; the Cooperative Research and Development Agreements (CRADAs) are widely used to allocate exclusive property rights to federal research *before* discoveries are in hand; changes made in the Federal Acquisition Regulations (FAR) give corporations exclusive commercial rights to vast federal information resources developed entirely with federal funds; and new secrecy rules relating to public records have prevented the American people from demanding greater accountability from public officials spending taxpayer money. Statement of Ralph Nader before the Subcommittee on Regulation, Business Opportunities and Energy of the Committee on Small Business, U.S. House of Representatives, on "Private Sector Agreements to Market Federally Funded Research," March 11, 1993, p. 92.

12. For an excellent overview of the privatization of public research, see Chris Lewis, "Public Assets, Private Profits: Federal R&D and Corporate Graft," *Multinational Monitor*, January/February 1993, pp. 8–11.

13. Carey Goldberg, "Across the U.S., Universities Are Fueling High-Tech Booms," *New York Times*, October 8, 1999, p. A1.

14. Based on survey data, updated November 13, 2000, by the Association of University Technology Managers (AUTM), available at http://www.autm.net under heading "Bayh-Dole Act."

15. Press and Washburn, *The Atlantic*, p. 40.

16. Press and Washburn, *The Atlantic*, p. 47.

17. Report of the National Institutes of Health Working Group on Research Tools, June 4, 1998, available at http://www.nih.gov/news/researchtools/index.htm.

18. Ibid.

19. Michael A. Heller and Rebecca S. Eisenberg, "Can Patents Deter Innovation? The Anticommons in Biomedical Research," *Science*, May 1, 1998, pp. 698–701. See also Michael A. Heller, "The Tragedy of the Anticommons," *Harvard Law Review*, vol. 111, (1998), p. 621.

20. Heller and Eisenberg, *Science*, p. 698–699.

21. According to Dr. Ana Sittenfeld, associate professor, University of Costa Rica, quoted in Andrew Pollack, "The Green Revolution Yields to the Bottom Line," *New York Times*, p. D1.

22. This statistic is from a 1999 survey by Steven C. Price, director for industry relations, University of Wisconsin, quoted in Pollack, *New York Times*, May 15, 2001, p. D1.

23. David Shenk, "Money + Science = Ethics Problems on Campus," *The Nation*, March 22, 1999, pp. 11–17.

24. Hamilton Moses III and Joseph B. Martin, "Academic Relationships with Industry: A New Model for Biomedical Research," *Journal of the American Medical Association*, vol. 285 (February 21, 2001), p. 933. Also, Liz Kowalczyk, "New Steps Urged on University Research Bias," *Boston Globe*, February 21, 2001.

25. See Mark Clayton, "Corporate Cash and Campus Labs," *Christian Science Monitor*, June 19, 2001.

26. David Blumenthal et al., "Withholding Research Results in Academic Life Science: Evidence from a National Survey of Faculty," *Journal of the American Medical Association*, vol. 277, no. 15 (April 16, 1997), p. 1224.

27. Shenk, *The Nation*, pp. 11–12.

28. Amy C. Crumpton, "Meeting Report—Secrecy in Science: Exploring University, Industry and Government Relationships," *Science and Engineering Ethics*, vol. 5 (1999), p. 419.

29. Thomas M. Burton, "Unfavorable Drug Study Sparks Battle over Publication of Results," *Wall Street Journal*, November 1, 2000, p. B1.

30. David G. Kern, M.D., "A Recent Case Study," presentation at the Secrecy in Science conference, sponsored by MIT and the American Association for the Advancement of Science, March 29, 1999, available at http://www.aaas.org/spp/secrecy/Presents/Kern.htm.

31. Sheryl Gay Stolberg, "The Biotech Death of Jesse Gelsinger," *New York Times Magazine*, November 28, 1999.

32. A detailed account of the Taborsky episode can be found in Seth Shulman, *Owning the Future* (Boston: Houghton Mifflin, 1999), pp. 106–111.

33. Marcia Angell, M.D., "Is Academic Medicine for Sale?" *New England Journal of Medicine*, May 18, 2000, pp. 1516–1518.

34. Mildred K. Cho et al., "Policies on Faculty Conflicts of Interest at U.S. Universities," *Journal of the American Medical Association*, November 1, 2000, pp. 2203–2208.

35. Susan Okie, "Medical Journals Set New Publication Rules," *Washington Post*, September 10, 2001, p. A6.

36. Presentation by Jon F. Merz, Antigone Kriss, Debra G.B. Leonard, Mildred K. Cho, "On the Restriction of HFE Testing for Hemochromatosis: Results of a Nationwide Survey of Clinical Laboratories," Decade of ELSI Research Conference, Bethesda, Maryland, January 16–18, 2001. See also statement of Jon F. Merz to the Subcommittee on Courts and Intellectual Property, Committee of the Judiciary, U.S. House of Representatives, on "Gene Patents and Other Genomic Inventions," July 13, 2000, available at http://www.house.gov/judiciary/merz0713.htm.

37. Press and Washburn, *The Atlantic*, p. 50.

38. Shenk, *The Nation*, p. 17.

39. Jon F. Merz, "Disease Gene Patents: Overcoming Unethical Constraints on Clinical Laboratory Medicine," *Clinical Chemistry* 45:3 (1999), pp. 324–330. Another set of researchers reviewed 37 U.S. patents for diagnostic tests involving genes associated with breast and ovarian cancer and certain hereditary diseases. They found that the patents were often being used by companies to prevent other laboratories from providing the testing services. Anna Schissel and her colleagues concluded that this "may raise costs, curtail access to testing and limit clinical observations, which is fundamental to the practice of medicine." Correspondence, Ann Schissel, Jon F. Merz, and Mildred K. Cho, *Nature*, November 11, 1999, p. 118.

40. Carl Elliot, "Pharma Buys a Conscience," *The American Prospect*, September 24–October 8, 2001, pp. 16–20.

41. Bernard Stamler, "Wooing Collegians on Campus with, What Else, Television," *New York Times*, June 6, 2001, p. C9.

42. Joseph N. DiStefano, "A Campus Debate over Credit-Card Solicitations," *Philadelphia Inquirer*, April 8, 2001.
43. See, e.g., Naomi Klein, *No Logo: Taking Aim at the Brand Bullies* (New York: Picador, 1999), chap. 4, and Geoffry D. White, *Campus, Inc.* (Amherst, NY: Prometheus Books, 2000).
44. David F. Noble, "Digital Diploma Mills: The Automation of Higher Education," *First Monday* [online journal] vol. 3, no. 1 (1998), available at http://www.firstmonday.org/issues/issue3_1/noble/index.html.
45. MIT OpenCourseware Fact Sheet, http://www.mit.edu/newsoffice/nr/2001/ocw-facts.html. See also Jan Newmarch, "Lessons from Open Source: Intellectual Property and Courseware," *First Monday* [online journal], vol. 6, no. 6 (June 2001), available at http://www.firstmonday.org/issues/issue6_6/newmarch/ index.html.
46. Michele Tolela Myers, "A Student is Not an Input," *New York Times*, March 26, 2001, p. A17.

Chapter 10: The Commercialization of Culture and Public Spaces

1. Cited in Eric Barnouw, *Tube of Plenty: The Evolution of American Television* (New York: Oxford University Press, 1975), p. 74.
2. The literature on the commercialization of American culture is burgeoning. Worthwhile books include Gary Cross, *An All Consuming Century: Why Commercialism Won in Modern America* (New York: Columbia University Press, 2000); Juliet Schor, *Do Americans Shop Too Much?* (Boston: Beacon Press, 2000); James Twitchell, *Lead Us Into Temptation: The Triumph of American Materialism* (New York: Columbia University Press, 2000); Thomas Frank, *One Market Under God: Extreme Capitalism, Market Populism and the End of Economic Democracy* (New York: Doubleday, 2000); Naomi Klein, *No Logo: Taking Aim at the Brand Bullies* (New York: Picador, 2000); Michael F. Jacobson and Laurie Ann Mazur, *Marketing Madness: A Survival Guide for a Consumer Society* (Washington, DC: Center for Science in the Public Interest, 1995); Alan Durning, *How Much Is Enough? Consumer Society and the Future of the Earth* (New York: Norton, 1992); Leslie Savan, *The Sponsored Life: Ads, TV and American Culture* (Philadelphia: Temple University Press, 1994). An excellent review of some of these books is Alan Wolfe, "America Consumed by Consumption," *New Republic*, October 23, 2000.
3. A compelling history of the struggle over the public's airwaves is Robert W. McChesney, *Telecommunications, Mass Media and Democracy: The Battle for Control of U.S. Broadcasting, 1928–1935* (New York: Oxford University Press, 1995).
4. *Shaeffer Radio Co.*(FRC, 1930), quoted in John W. Willis, *The Federal Radio Commission and the Public Service Responsibility of Broadcast Licensees*, 11 *Federal Communications Bar Journal* (1950), p. 14.
5. *Red Lion Broadcasting Co. v. FCC*, 395 U.S. 367 (1969), p. 389.
6. *Office of Communication of United Church of Christ v. FCC*, 359 F.2d 994 (DC Circuit, 1966), p. 1003.
7. See, e.g., Barry Cole and Mal Oettinger, *Reluctant Regulators: The FCC and the Broadcast Audience* (Reading, MA: Addison-Wesley Publishing Co., 1978).

8. Under the Telecommunications Act of 1996, licensing periods for TV were extended from five years to eight years, the criteria for FCC nonrenewal of a license were raised, the ability of third parties to challenge license renewals was restricted, and station ownership limits were relaxed. In a separate action, the Fairness Doctrine was formally rescinded.

9. Newton N. Minow and Craig L. LaMay, *Abandoned in the Wasteland: Children, Television and the First Amendment* (New York: Hill & Wang, 1996), p. 11 and p. 22.

10. Alliance for Better Campaigns at http://www.bettercampaigns.org.

11. Paul Taylor, Alliance for Better Campaigns, Testimony before the FCC, October 16, 2000.

12. Benton Foundation, "Market Conditions and Public Affairs Programming," March 27, 2000, available at http://www.Benton.org/Television/lpa.pdf.

13. Alliance for Better Campaigns, "Gouging Democracy: How the Television Industry Profiteered on Campaign 2000" [Washington, DC, report], March 6, 2001.

14. Helen Payne Watt, *Common Assets: Asserting Rights to Our Shared Inheritance* (San Francisco: Redefining Progress, 2000), p. 23. Watt derived these numbers from Congressional Budget Office estimates of the value of analog and digital television licenses, a National Telecommunications and Information Agency methodology for calculating the value of radio licenses, and November 1999 revenue from auctions of FCC licenses.

15. Christopher Stern, "Mixed Signals," *Washington Post*, December 17, 2000, p. H1.

16. Congress forfeited any political leverage in dictating public interest requirements for digital broadcasters, leaving that task to a federal advisory panel, The Gore Commission, which was politically divided and whose recommendations were a mishmash of modest proposals that have gone nowhere. See *Charting the Digital Broadcasting Future: Final Report of the Advisory Committee on Public Interest Obligations of Digital Television Broadcasters* (Washington, DC: National Telecommunications and Information Administration, December 18, 1998).

17. A history of the broadcasting industry's campaign to win control over the "digital spectrum" can be found in Joel Brinkley, *Defining Vision: The Battle for the Future of Television* (New York: Harvest Books, 1998).

18. William Safire, "Spectrum Squatters," *New York Times*, October 9, 2000.

19. Stephen Labaton, "FCC to Approve Low-Power Radio, Seeking Diversity," *New York Times*, January 20, 2000, p. A1. For more on the low-power radio proposal, see the Web sites of the Benton Foundation (www.Benton.org/News/Extra/broad020100.html) and the Media Access Project (www.mediaaccess.org/programs/lpfm/index.html).

20. Jerold M. Starr, *Air Wars: The Fight to Reclaim Public Broadcasting* (Boston: Beacon Press, 2000).

21. Gary Ruskin, "Why They Whine: How Corporations Prey on Our Children," *Mothering Magazine*, November/December 1999.

22. James U. McNeal (professor of marketing at Texas A&M), "Tapping the Three Kids' Markets," *American Demographics*, April 1998.

23. Mike Searles, cited in Brian Bennett, "Uniforms Aid Student Performance, Academics: Not Only Do Uniforms Eliminate Status Wars, They Help

Students Concentrate on Schoolwork," *Los Angeles Times*, December 10, 1989.

24. Bruce Horovitz, "Targeting the Kindermarket," *USA Today*, March 3, 2000, p. 1.

25. Joseph Pereira, "Kids' Advertisers Play Hide-and-Seek, Concealing Commercials in Every Cranny," *Wall Street Journal*, April 30, 1990.

26. Janet Maslin, "Like the Toy? See the Movie," *New York Times*, December 17, 1989, Section 2, p. 1.

27. Dr. Rebecca Moran, cited in Gary Ruskin, *Mothering Magazine*, November/December 1999.

28. Susan Linn, Ed.D., Harvard Medical School, et al., press release announcing a protest of the advertising industry's Golden Marble awards at a conference, "Advertising and Promoting to Kids: The Third Annual Conference about Breakthrough Marketing to Kids," September 14, 2000.

29. Constance L. Hays, "Channel One's Mixed Grades in Schools," *New York Times*, December 5, 1999, p. 13–14.

30. Steven Manning, "Students for Sale," *The Nation*, September 27, 1999, p. 17.

31. Constance L. Hays, "District Rethinks a Soda-Pop Strategy," *New York Times*, April 19, 2000. Kate Zernire, "Coke to Dilute Push in Schools for Its Products," *New York Times*, March 14, 2001.

32. Anne Marie Chaker, "Pitching Saturns to Your Classmates—for Credit," *Wall Street Journal*, January 31, 2000, p. B1.

33. U.S. General Accounting Office, "Commercial Activities in Schools," GAO/HEHS-00–156, September 14, 2000, available at http://www.gao.gov/new.items/he00156.pdf.

34. See, e.g., David Gelman, "Words for the Sponsor," *Newsweek*, December 29, 1975, p. 40, and "Presented by Xerox," *The Nation*, December 27, 1975.

35. Naomi Klein, *No Logo*, p. 51 and 54.

36. Michael Sorkin, "The Big Peep Show," *New York Times Magazine*, December 26, 1999, p. 9–10.

37. Jeremy Rifkin, *The Age of Access: The New Culture of Hypercapitalism Where All of Life is a Paid-for Experience* (New York: Jeremy P. Tarcher/Putnam, 2000); Kalle Lasn, *Culture Jam: The Uncooling of America* (New York: Eagle Brook, 1999).

38. Dean Bonham of the Bonham Group, Denver, cited in Fred Bayles, "Massachusetts Subway Ties into Name Game," *USA Today*, January 16, 2001.

39. Michael Janofsky, "What's in a Stadium Name—Tradition or Money?" *New York Times*, October 30, 2000.

40. Michael Janofsky, "Where All Back Broncos, A Split on Stadium Name," *New York Times*, August 23, 2001.

41. Julie Edelson Halpert, "Dr. Pepper Hospital? Perhaps, for a Price," *New York Times*, February 18, 2001.

42. Verne G. Kopytoff, "Now, Brought to You by Coke (or Pepsi): Your City Hall," *New York Times*, November 29, 1999, p. C17.

43. Robert Weissman and Russell Mokhiker, "City for Sale," syndicated column, "Focus on the Corporation," February 15, 1999, available at http://lists.essential.org/corp-focus/msg00005.html.

44. "Corporate Bail-Out: General Motors Buys a State Sponsorship," on

TomPaine.com, available at http://www.tompaine.com/opinion/2000/06/12/1.ahtml.

45. Leslie Eaton, "And Now, A Balloon from Our Sponsor," *New York Times*, November 24, 1999, p. 1.

46. Robert Johnson, "Ad-Packed TVs May Soon Be Boarding City Buses," *Wall Street Journal*, February 21, 2001.

47. Karl Grossman, "Space to Let: Advertising in the Skies," *The Ecologist*, March 2001. For the time being, the "space billboard" is prohibited by the Space Advertising Prohibition Act of 1993, but that law applies only to "non-obtrusive commercial space advertising," which means that ads on the space station, space transportation vehicles, launch facilities, and other equipment are still legally possible.

48. Lisa Gubernick, "A Night at the Previews," *Wall Street Journal*, October 1, 1999, p. W1.

49. Alex Kuczynski, "Radio Squeezes Empty Air Space for Profit," *New York Times*, January 6, 2000, p. C1.

50. Joe Flint, "Disappearing Act: The Amount of TV Screen Devoted to Show Shrinks," *Wall Street Journal*, March 29, 2001.

51. Alex Kuczynski, "On CBS News, Some of What You See Isn't There," *New York Times*, January 12, 2000, p. 1.

52. Michael McCarthy, "Digital Ads Show Up in Unexpected Places," *USA Today*, March 23, 2001.

53. Stuart Elliot, "Real or Virtual? You Call It," *New York Times*, October 1, 1999, p. C1.

54. Margaret Kohn, "The Mauling of Public Space," *Dissent*, Spring 2001, pp. 71–77.

55. Jerold S. Kayden, *Privately Owned Public Space: The New York City Experience* (New York: John Wiley & Sons, 2000).

56. See Web sites for Commercial Alert, http://www.commercialalert.org, and the Center for Commercial-Free Education, http://www.commercialfree.org.

57. For more on Buy Nothing Day, go to http://www.adbusters.org/campaigns/bnd. For more on National TV-Turnoff Week, go to http://tvfa.org.

Chapter 11: The Giveaway of Federal Drug Research and Information Resources

1. James Love, "Looting the Medicine Chest," *The Progressive*, February 1993, pp. 26–28.

2. Health Insurance Association of America, as cited in Jeff Gerth and Sheryl Gay Stolberg, "Drug Firms Reap Profits on Tax-Based Research," *New York Times*, April 23, 2000, p.1.

3. See, e.g., Merrill Goozner, "Patenting Life," *American Prospect*, December 18, 2000, pp. 23–25.

4. See, e.g., Joint Economic Committee, U.S. Senate, "The Benefits of Medical Research and the Role of the NIH," May 2000, available at http://www.mco.edu/research/nih_research_benefits.pdf.

5. Iain Cockburn and Rebecca Henderson, "Public-Private Interaction and the Productivity of Pharmaceutical Research," National Bureau of Economic Research working paper 6018, pp. 10–11, cited in Joint Economic Committee, U.S. Senate, "The Benefits of Medical Research and the Role of the NIH," May 2000.

6. Public Citizen, *Rx R&D Myths: The Case Against the Drug Industry's R&D Scare Card* (Washington, DC: Public Citizen, July 23, 2001, available at http://www.citizen.org/comgress/drugs/R&Dscarecard.html.

7. Cockburn and Henderson, National Bureau of Economic Research working paper 6018.

8. CHI Research, "Industry Technology Has Strong Roots in Public Science," March 1997, available at http://www.chiresearch.com/nltv1.htm.

9. Ralph Nader and James Love, "Federally Funded Pharmaceutical Inventions," testimony before the Special Committee on Aging, United States Senate, February 24, 1993, p. 7.

10. See http://www.cptech.org/pharm/pryor.html.

11. Daniel Newman, "The Great Taxol Giveaway," *Multinational Monitor*, May 1992, pp. 17–21.

12. According to James Love, Bristol-Myers Squibb quoted $6.09 per milligram as the Red Book average wholesale price for Taxol on September 19, 2000, while a generic producer reported that his costs of making paclitaxel were $.07 per milligram. See http://www.cptech.org/ip/health/taxol.

13. See the Consumer Project on Technology Web site on paclitaxel at http://www.cptech.org/ip/health/taxol.

14. This account draws upon Ralph Nader and James Love, "Looting the Medicine Chest," *The Progressive*, February 1993, pp. 26–28; and Merrill Goozner, "The Price Isn't Right," *The American Prospect*, September 11, 2000, pp. 25–29. See also Daniel Newman, "The Great Taxol Giveaway," *Multinational Monitor*, May 1992, pp. 17–21.

15. An extensive account of Xalatan's development can be found in Jeff Gerth and Sheryl Gay Stolberg, "Drug Firms Reap Profits on Tax-Based Research," *New York Times*, April 23, 2000, p. 1.

16. See http://www.cptech.org/ip/health/aids/gov-role.html. See also James P. Love, "Pharmaceutical Drug Pricing: Hearings before the Senate Committee on Government Affairs, Federal Document Clearing House, July 27, 1994.

17. House Amendment 791, enacted on June 14, 2000. See Sanders' press release, http://www.house.gov/bernie/press/2000/06–14–2000.html.

18. According to a preliminary report by the Inspector General of the Department of Health and Human Services, as reported by Gerth and Stolberg, *New York Times*, (April 23, 2000) p. 1.

19. U.S. Congressional Budget Office, "How Increased Competition from Generic Drugs Has Affected Prices and Returns in the Pharmaceutical Industry," July 1998, Summary, p. 1.

20. "The Stalling Game," *Consumer Reports*, July 2001, pp. 36–40.

21. Sheryl Gay Stolberg and Jeff Gerth, "In a Drug's Journey to Market, Discovery Is Just the First of Many Steps," *New York Times*, July 23, 2000, p. 13.

22. Gardiner Harris and Chris Adams, "Drug Manfacturers Step Up Legal Attacks that Slow Generics," *Wall Street Journal*, July 12, 2001.

23. See, e.g., Gregg Fields, "Brand-Name Drug Makers' Tactics Slow Generics," *Miami Herald*, August 17, 2000. See also Sheryl Gay Stolberg and Jeff Gerth, "How Companies Stall Generics and Keep Themselves Healthy," *New York Times*, July 25, 2000, p. 1.

24. *Consumer Reports*, July 2001, p. 38.

25. According to the Kaiser Family Foundation, drug companies spent three times more on marketing and general and administrative expenses than on R&D, as a percentage of sales, in 1998. See Stolberg and Gerth, "How

Companies Stall Generics and Keep Themselves Healthy," *New York Times*, July 25, 2000, p. 13. See also an April 2000 report by the Consumer Project on Technology which finds that 11 of 19 pharmaceutical companies studied spent the majority of their money on marketing and administration, not R&D. *FDA Week*, April 26, 2000, p. 12. According to *Consumer Reports*, "the 11 drug companies in the Fortune 500 spent just 12 percent of revenues on R&D and 30 percent on marketing and administration; they took 17 percent as profits." *Consumer Reports*, July 2001, p. 39.

26. James Love, "Government Information as a Public Asset," Taxpayer Assets Project, Working Paper No. 4 (Testimony before the Joint Committee on Printing), Washington, DC: Taxpayers Assets Project, April 25, 1991. See also John Markoff, "U.S. Shifts to a Freer Data Policy," *New York Times*, October 22, 1993, p. D1.

27. David Hilzenrath, "SEC Plans Computer Access to Business Filings," *Washington Post*, October 23, 1993, p. C1.

28. Three possible "homes" for the NTIS include the Library of Congress, the Department of Commerce, and the Government Printing Office.

29. See Senator John Warner, "The Growing Crisis in Public Access to Public Information, *Congressional Record*, Senate, February 27, 1997, p. S1730. Also, Robert M. Gellman, "Twin Evils: Government Copyright and Copyright-Like Controls over Government Information," *Syracuse Law Review*, vol. 45 (1995), p. 999.

30. An excellent review of Congress's own information policies can be seen in David Corn, "Filegate.gov," *Wired*, November 2000, pp. 226–236.

31. Testimony of Gary Ruskin, Committee on Rules and Administration, U.S. Senate, Hearing on S. 2288, the Wendell H. Ford Government Publications Reform Act of 1998, July 29, 1998, available at http://www. congressproject.org/infopolicy/gpratest.html.

32. "Info-Corruption," *Roll Call*, June 8, 1998.

33. Dwight Thompson, "A Hill Hearing Aid," *Washington Post*, May 22, 2000, p. A4; Timothy Noah, "Privatizing Congressional Hearings," *Slate* May 24, 2000 available at http://www.slate.msn.com/Code/chatterbox/chatterbox. asp?Show=5/24/200&idMessage=5378.

34. Eve Gerber, "How Congress Resists the Web," *Slate*, November 30, 1999, available at http://www.slate.msn.com/netelection/entries/99–11–30_ 56807.asp.

Chapter 12: The Commons: Another Kind of Property

1. *The Ecologist, Whose Common Future? Reclaiming the Commons* (Philadelphia, PA: New Society Publishers, 1993), p. 12.

2. In posing this question, Sax cited such examples as the razing of a long-established Poletown neighborhood in Detroit to build a new General Motors factory; the removal of the American Indians from their homelands; and the harm to communities in the Owens Valley, California, when Los Angeles seized its water supplies. Joseph L. Sax, "Do Communities Have Rights? The National Parks as a Laboratory of New Ideas," *University of Pittsburgh Law Review*, vol. 45, pp. 499–511.

3. "When numerous individual consumers make minor decisions the aggregate consequences of which they would not have chosen had they been explicitly presented with the larger composite decision, they fall victim to the tyranny

of small decisions. The consumer becomes a victim of the 'narrowness of the contexts in which he [or she] exercises ... sovereignty.'" Alison Rieser, "Ecological Preservation as a Public Property Right: An Emerging Doctrine in Search of a Theory," *Harvard Environmental Law Review,* vol. 15 (1991), p. 424, citing Kahn, "The Tyranny of Small Decisions: Market Failures, Imperfections and the Limits of Economics," *Kyklos,* vol. 19, (1966), pp. 23–28.

4. See, e.g., Daniel R. Coquillette, "Mosses From an Old Manse: Another Look at Some Historic Property Cases About the Environment," 64 *Cornell Law Review,* 761, (1979), pp. 801–803. Also, R. Lee, *The Elements of Roman Law* (London: Sweet & Maxwell 4th ed., 1956), pp. 109–110.

5. Much of the modern-day revival of public trust doctrine, at least as applied to natural resources, stems from a seminal 1970 article by Joseph Sax, "The Public Trust Doctrine in Natural Resource Law: Effective Judicial Intervention," 68 *Michigan Law Review,* 471 (1970).

6. Ibid.

7. The common heritage of mankind principle was first proposed in 1967 by Arvid Pardo, Maltese ambassador to the United States. The concept is discussed in Susan J. Buck, *The Global Commons: An Introduction* (Washington, DC: Island Press, 1998).

8. Carol M. Rose, *Property and Persuasion* (Boulder, CO: Westview Press, 1994), pp. 121–122.

9. Carol M. Rose, "Takings, Public Trust, Unhappy Truths and Helpless Giants: A Review of Professor Joseph Sax's Defense of the Environment through Academic Scholarship," 25 *Ecology Law Quarterly,* 351 (1998).

10. See, e.g., Bruce Ackerman, *Private Property and the Constitution* (New Haven, CT: Yale University Press, 1978).

11. Michael A. Heller, "The Boundaries of Private Property," 108 *Yale Law Journal,* (1999) pp. 1163–1223.

12. See, e.g., Tom Bethell, *The Noblest Triumph: Property and Prosperity through the Ages* (New York: St. Martin's Griffin, 1998).

13. The paradox of rational individualists finding the means to cooperate in creating a civil society is explored in Frank I. Michaelman, "Ethics, Economics and the Law of Property," 22 *NOMOS: Property* no. 3, edited by J. Ronald Pennock and John W. Chapter (1980), pp. 30–31. An interesting critique of rationality in economic theory can be found in Amartya K. Sen, "Rational Fools: A Critique of the Behavioral Foundations of Economic Theory," in Aafke E. Komter, *The Gift: An Interdisciplinary Perspective* (Amsterdam (Holland): Amsterdam University Press, 1996), pp. 148–163.

14. Carol M. Rose identifies the oxymoron quite succinctly: "A property regime, in short, presupposes a kind of character who is *not* predicted in the standard story about property. And that, I suggest, is why the classic theories of property turned to narrative at crucial moments, particularly in explaining the origin of property regimes, where the need for cooperation is most obvious. Their narrative stories allowed them to slide smoothly over the cooperative gap in their systematic analyses of self-interest." Rose, "Property as Storytelling: Perspectives from Game Theory, Narrative Theory Feminist Theory," *Property and Persuasion,* pp. 25–45.

15. Legal realists and institutional economists have developed extensive critiques of this reality. Robert Hale, in particular, detailed "the role of positive legal entitlements in shaping what were supposedly the 'natural' rights of owner-

ship and the 'natural' laws of distribution in a laissez-faire economy." An excellent review of Hale and this literature is Barbara H. Fried's *The Progressive Assault on Laissez Faire: Robert Hale and the First Law and Economics Movement* (Cambridge, MA: Harvard University Press, 1998). See also Cass R. Sunstein, *The Partial Constitution* (Cambridge, MA: Harvard University Press, 1993).

16. Peter Barnes helped clarify these distinctions for me.

17. Frederic W. Maitland, *Township and Borough* (Cambridge, England: The University Press, 1898), p. 18, cited in Martha Hirschfield, "The Alaska Native Claims Settlement Act: Tribal Sovereignty and the Corporate Form," *Yale Law Journal*, vol. 101 (April 1992), n. 96 and 100. Maitland describes municipal corporate charters that emerged from the feudal era as "not the transfer of something, some thing, called ownership from one sort of 'units' to another . . . [but] the crystallization round several different centers and in very different shapes of that vague 'belongs' which contains both public power and private right, power over persons, right in things." Maitland, p. 30. This is an apt description of the authority exercised by the commons as a social regime.

18. Martha Hirschfield, "The Alaska Native Claims Settlement Act: Tribal Sovereignty and the Corporate Form," *Yale Law Journal*, vol. 101 (April 1992), p. 1331.

19. Hirschfield, *Yale Law Journal*, p. 1342.

20. Lewis Hyde examines the tensions between individual ownership and community in *The Gift: Imagination and the Erotic Life of Property* (New York: Vintage, 1999) pp. 74–92.

21. John Frow, "Information as Gift and Commodity," *New Left Review*, September/October 1996, p. 108. People who live "the contractual rationality of the commodity" naively disregard the social and human context which affects how any market functions. The ludicrous results can be seen in software "bots" that are programmed to search for data or conduct market transactions with a strict rationality that fails to take account of social externalities. See, e.g., John Seely Brown and Paul Duguid, *The Social Life of Information* (Cambridge, MA: Harvard Business School Press, 2000), pp. 41–62.

22. The great eclecticism of the commons is well illustrated by the issue of *Whole Earth* (Fall 1998) devoted to "Commerce and the Common Good."

23. *The Ecologist, Whose Common Future? Reclaiming the Commons* (Philadelphia: New Society Publishers, 1993), p. 7–8.

24. *The Ecologist, Whose Common Future?*, p. 6.

25. As Elinor Ostrom puts it: "The differences in the particular rules [of various commons] take into account specific attributes of the related physical systems, cultural views of the world, and economic and political relationships that exist in the setting. Without different rules, appropriators could not take advantage of the positive features of a local CPR or avoid potential pitfalls that might be encountered. in one setting but not others." Elinor Ostrom, *Governing the Commons* (New York: Cambridge University Press, 1990) p. 89.

26. Ostrom, *Governing the Commons*, pp. 88–102.

27. Susan J. Buck, *The Global Commons.*

28. Bonnie J. McCay and James M. Acheson, eds., *The Question of the Com-*

mons: The Culture and Ecology of Communal Resources (Tucson, AZ: University of Arizona Press, 1986).

29. Glenn G. Stevenson, *Common Property Economics: A General Theory and Land Use Applications* (New York: Cambridge University Press, 1991).
30. *The Ecologist, Whose Common Future?*
31. The leading scholarly organization is the International Association for the Study of Common Property, based at Indiana University. See http://www.indiana.edu/~iascp. The World Bank Group sponsors a Common Property Resource Management Network, which publishes a newsletter and hosts gatherings. *Whole Earth* magazine published a special issue devoted to the commons in Fall 1998, as did *Yes!* magazine in Summer 2001. Other groups dedicated to fostering the commons include the Tomales Bay Institute (Point Reyes Station, CA), the Chaordic Commons (Half Moon Bay, CA) and the Creative Commons (Palo Alto, CA).
32. See, e.g., Kevin Kelly, *Out of Control: The New Biology of Machines, Social Systems and the Economic World* (New York: Addison-Wesley, 1994); and M. Mitchell Waldrop, *Complexity: The Emerging Science at the Edge of Order and Chaos* (New York: Touchstone, 1992).
33. E. O. Wilson, ed., *Biodiversity* (Washington, DC: National Academy Press, 1988).
34. David Leonhardt, "Executive Pay Drops off the Political Radar," *New York Times*, April 16, 2000.
35. Jeff Gates, *Democracy at Risk: Rescuing Main Street from Wall Street* (Cambridge, MA: Perseus, 2000).
36. Robert Reich, *The Work of Nations: Preparing Ourselves for 21st Century Capitalism* (New York: Vintage Books, 1992), Chapters 21 and 23.
37. This quotation is taken from Harry C. Boyte and Nancy N. Kari, *Building America: The Democratic Promise of Public Work* (Philadelphia: Temple University Press, 1996), p. 191. Adams also wrote that "Property monopolized or in the Possession of a few is a Curse to Mankind. We should ... preserve all from extreme Poverty, and all others from extravagant Riches."
38. Elinor Ostrom, *Governing the Commons*, pp. 61–88.
39. Quoted in Lewis Hyde, *The Gift*, p. 22.
40. Ivan Illich, "Silence Is a Commons," *CoEvolution Quarterly*, Winter 1983, p. 7.
41. This theme is explored in depth in Nancy Folbre, *The Invisible Heart: Economics and Family Values* (New York: New Press, 2001).

Chapter 13: Strategies for Protecting the Commons

1. Lawrence Goodwyn, *Democratic Promise: The Populist Moment in America* (New York: Oxford University Press, 1976), p. ii.
2. For example, Celera Genomics, the firm mapping the human genome, says it will publish the humane genome map in *Science* magazine under a special arrangement that would allow the company to monitor who accesses the database of gene information. See Kristen Philipkoski, "Celera Maps Out Alternate Route," Wired.com, December 13, 2000, available at http://www.wired.com/news/technology/1,1282,40645.html.
3. A paradigmatic example is the corporatization of independent Web sites devoted to pop culture icons such as *The X-Files* and *Star Trek*. See Sarah

Kendzior, "Who Owns Fandom?" Salon.com, December 13, 2000, at http://www.salon.com/tech/feature/2000/12/13/fandom/print.html.

4. See, e.g., Dee Hock, *The Birth of the Chaordic Age* (San Francisco: Berrett-Koehler, 1999).

5. This principle was famously asserted by the U.S. Supreme Court in the 1892 case of *Central Railroad v. Illinois*, 146 U.S. 387 (1892), when the Court held that the Illinois state legislature could not simply give away most of Lake Michigan and its powers to regulate commerce to the Illinois Central Railroad. That was an inalienable obligation of a public trustee.

6. Elaine Sciolino, "Smithsonian Is Promised $38 Million, with Strings," *New York Times*, May 10, 2001.

7. See Russell Mokhiber and Robert Weissman, "The Real Thing: Democracy as a Contact Sport," *Focus on the Corporation* syndicated column, December 13, 2000, available at http://lists.essential.org/pipermail/corp-focus/2000/ 000050.html. which details the Library of Congress hosting a promotional event for Coca-Cola.

8. Robert W. McChesney, *Telecommunications, Mass Media and Democracy: The Battle for Control of U.S. Broadcasting, 1928–1935* (New York: Oxford University Press, 1995).

9. Two of the leading proponents for using spread spectrum technologies to create a wireless commons are Professor Yochai Benkler and Professor Lawrence Lessig. See Lessig, *The Future of Ideas: The Fate of the Commons in a Connected World* (New York: Random House, 2001), chap. 5.

10. For more information on the Alaska Permanent Fund Corporation, see http://www.apfc.org.

11. The discussion here draws upon Helen Payne Watt, *Common Assets: Asserting Rights to Our Shared Inheritance* (Washington, DC: Corporation for Enterprise Development and Redefining Progress, 1999), p. 16.

12. Sam Howe Verhovek, "Alaskans Know Pockets Are Lined with Oil," *New York Times*, March 18, 2001.

13. For a full exposition of the Sky Trust proposal, see Peter Barnes, *Who Owns the Sky? Our Common Assets and the Future of Capitalism* (Washington, DC: Island Press, 2001). The Corporation for Enterprise Development in Washington, DC, is also involved in producing analyses and studies in support of the Sky Trust proposal.

14. Peter Barnes and Rafe Pomerance, "Pie in the Sky: The Battle for Atmospheric Scarcity Rents" (report), (Washington, DC: Corporation for Enterprise Development, 2000), p. 9.

15. Bruce Ackerman and Anne Alstott, *The Stakeholder Society* (New Haven, CT: Yale University Press, 1999), p. 36.

16. A key information resource for the Land and Water Conservation Fund is the advocacy group, Americans for Our Heritage and Recreation, a coalition dedicated to revitalizing the fund. Its Web site, http://ahrinfo.org, has materials on its legislative campaigns.

17. Jeff Zinn, "Protecting Natural Resources and Managing Growth: Issues in the 107th Congress," Congressional Research Service, August 6, 2001.

18. J. H. Reichman, "Of Green Tulips and Legal Kudzu: Repackaging Rights in Subpatentable Innovation," *Vanderbilt Law Review*, vol. 53, no. 6 (November 2000), p. 1776.

19. Peter Barnes, *Who Owns the Sky?*

20. Henry George, *Progress and Poverty: An Inquiry into the Cause of Industrial*

Depressions and of Increase of Want with Increase of Wealth . . . The Remedy (New York: Robert Schalkenbach Foundation, 1997 reprint edition).

21. There are a number of "Georgist" champions of land value taxation: The Center for the Study of Economics, Common Ground—USA, The Banneker Center for Economic Justice, the American Journal of Economics and Sociology, and the International Union for Land Value Taxation. A foundation devoted to the idea is the Robert Schalkenbach Foundation in New York City, whose Web site is http://www.schalkenbach.org.

22. See Dr. Robert V. Andelson, ed., *Land-Value Taxation Around the World*, 2d ed. (New York: Robert Schalkenbach Foundation, 1998).

23. The endorsements were made in a letter to Mikhail Gorbachev dated November 7, 1990, signed by 30 prominent U.S. economists. See *Incentive Taxation*, November 1991, on the Web site of the Robert Schalkenbach Foundation, op cit.

24. Richard W. Behan, *Plundered Promise: Capitalism, Politics and the Fate of the Federal Lands* (Washington, DC: Island Press, 2001), pp. 172–173. Behan credits Herman E. Daly and John B. Cobb, Jr., *For the Common Good* (Boston: Beacon Press, 1994), for this idea.

25. Margaret Jane Rudin, *Contested Commodities* (Cambridge, MA: Harvard University Press, 1996), chap. 7, pp. 102–114.

26. Sax sought to "liberate" the public trust doctrine from its "historical shackles"—its application only to navigation and waterways—and to make the doctrine a more general-purpose legal doctrine for protecting community resources. See Sax, "The Public Trust Doctrine in Natural Resource Law: Effective Judicial Intervention," *Michigan Law Review*, vol. 68 (1970), p. 471. A wonderful overview of Sax's thinking about the public trust is made by Carol M. Rose, "Takings, Public Trust and Unhappy Truths and a Helpless Giant," in *Ecology Law Quarterly*, vol. 25 (1998), p. 351.

27. Researchers have documented that P2P file-sharing can be plagued by free riders—people who take more than they give. See John Markoff, "Many Take, But Few Give on Gnutella," *New York Times*, August 21, 2000. But some P2P software, such as SongSpy, are designed to thwart freeloaders through a digital script called Karma. See Thomas E. Weber, "As Napster Evolves, Host of Rivals Emerge to Offer Free Music," *Wall Street Journal*, January 15, 2001.

28. Elinor Ostrom, *Governing the Commons: The Evolution of Institutions for Collective Action* (New York: Cambridge University Press, 1990), pp. 103–142.

29. James M. Acheson, "The Lobster Fiefs Revisited: Economic and Ecological Effects of Territoriality in Maine Lobster Fishing," in Bonnie J. McCay and James M. Acheson, eds., *The Question of the Commons: The Culture and Ecology of Communal Resources* (Tucson, AZ: University of Arizona Press, 1996), pp. 37–65.

30. Robert C. Ellickson, *Order Without Law: How Neighbors Settle Disputes* (New Haven, CT: Yale University Press, 1991). See also Dan Dagget, "It's Un-American, or at Best Un-Western, but Cooperation Works," *High Country News*, October 16, 1995, available at http://www.hcn.org/servlets/hcn.Article?article_id=1404. See aslo Dagget, *Beyond the Rangeland Conflict: Toward a West that Works* (Reno, NV: University of Nevada Press, 2000).

31. Meredith Lathbury and Redefining Progress, "Appendix III: The Edwards Aquifer," in Helen Payne Watt, *Common Assets: Asserting Rights to Our*

Shared Inheritance (Washington, DC: Corporation for Enterprise Development and Redefining Progress, 2000), pp. 44–51.

32. Meredith Lathbury and Redefining Progress, "Appendix IV: Alaska Halibut Fishery," in Helen Payne Watt, *Common Assets*, pp. 52–59.

33. Michael M'Gonigle, "Where There's a Way," *Yes!* magazine, Summer 2001, p. 30. For more on "ecosystem-based community forestry," for example, see http://www.forestsandcommunities.org.

34. The Web site for Terra Civitas, an Illinois-based nonprofit, is http://www.chaordic.org.

35. The Northwest Atlantic Marine Alliance's Web site is at http://www.namanet.org.

36. The Web site for the Community Alliances of Interdependent AgriCulture is at http://www.caia.net.

37. Brian Donahue, *Reclaiming the Commons: Community Farms and Forests in a New England Town* (New Haven, CT: Yale University Press, 1999).

38. Ellen Graham, "Community Groups Print Local (and Legal) Currencies," *Wall Street Journal*, June 27, 1996, p. B1. See also the Web site for Ithaca Hours local currency, available at http://ithacahours.org.

39. Ronald Lee Fleming and Lauri A. Halderman, *On Common Ground: Caring for Shared Land from Town Common to Urban Park* (Harvard, MA: Harvard Common Press, 1982).

40. Michael H. Shuman, *Going Local: Creating Self-Reliant Communities in a Global Age* (New York: Routledge, 2000). Another useful book in this regard is Christopher Gunn and Hazel Dayton Gunn, *Reclaiming Capital: Democratic Initiatives and Community Development* (Ithaca, NY: Cornell University Press, 1991).

41. Jeff Gates, *The Ownership Solution: Toward a Shared Capitalism for the Twenty-First Century* (Reading, MA: Perseus Books, 1999), p. xxi.

42. See, e.g., Roger E. Alcaly, "Reinventing the Corporation," *New York Review of Books*, April 10, 1997, pp. 38–44.

43. A nice survey of different types of vehicles for public ownership can be found in Gar Alperovitz, "Distributing Our Technological Inheritance," *Technology Review*, October 1994, p. 30.

44. David Morris and Daniel Kraker, "Rooting the Home Team: Why the Packers Won't Leave—and Why the Browns Did," *American Prospect*, September/October 1998, p. 38.

45. The Creative Commons is being organized by a coalition of faculty at the University of California at Berkeley, Berkman Center for Internet & Society at Harvard Law School, MIT and Stanford Law School. Professor Lawrence Lessig at Stanford Law School is one of the lead organizers.

46. The Web site of the Electronic Frontier Foundation is at http://www.eff.org/IP/Open_licenses/eff_oal.html.

47. The Free Art License is available at http://artlibre.org/licence/lalgb.html.

48. See, e.g., Bryan Pfaffenberg, "Why Open Content Matters," *Linux Journal*, April 11, 2001, available at http://www2.linuxjournal.com/articles/currents/0030.html.

49. Katharina Kopp, "The DOT Campaign: Making ".us" Work for All of US," *The Digital Beat* (online newsletter of the Benton Foundation), October 24, 2000, available at http://www.benton.org/DigitalBeat/ db102400.html.

50. This phenomenon is explored at length by John Seely Brown and Paul

Duguid in *The Social Life of Information* (Cambridge, MA: Harvard Business School Press, 2000).

51. Robert D. Putnam, *Bowling Alone: The Collapse and Revival of American Community* (New York: Simon and Schuster, 2000); and Robert E. Lane, *The Loss of Happiness in Market Democracies* (New Haven, CT: Yale University Press, 2000). See also Jonathan Rowe, "Rebuilding the Nonmarket Economy," *American Prospect*, Winter 1993, pp. 109–117.

52. Amy Jo Kim, *Community Building on the Web: Secret Strategies for Successful Online Communities* (Berkeley, CA: Peachpit Press, 2000), p. xiii–xvi.

53. The Slashdot Web site is http://slashdot.org.

54. The Web site for BirdSource is http://birdsource.cornell.edu. The Web site for Journey North is http://www.learner.org/jnorth. See also Joel Garreau, "Flocking Together through the Web," *Washington Post*, May 9, 2001, p. C1.

55. Lawrence Lessig, *The Future of Ideas: The Fate of the Commons in a Connected World* (New York: Random House, 2001). See also Andy Oram, ed., *Peer-to-Peer: Harnessing the Power of Disruptive Technologies* (Sebastopol, CA: O'Reilly, 2001).

56. Open letter from the Public Library of Science, available at http://www.publiclibraryofscience.org.

57. An excellent refutation of traditionalists can be found in Julie E. Cohen, "*Lochner* in Cyberspace: The New Economic Orthodoxy of 'Rights Management,'" *Michigan Law Review*, vol. 97 (November 1998), pp. 462–563.

58. Bonnie J. McCay and James M. Acheson, eds., *The Question of the Commons*, p. 25.

Bibliography

Abbate, Janet, *Inventing the Internet* (Cambridge, MA: MIT Press, 2000).

Ackerman, Bruce, and Anne Alstott, *The Stakeholder Society* (New Haven, CT: Yale University Press, 1999).

Alexander, Gregory S., *Commodity and Propriety: Competing Visions of Property in American Legal Thought, 1776–1970* (Chicago: University of Chicago Press, 1997).

Barlow, Maude, *Blue Gold: The Global Water Crisis and the Commodification of the World's Water* [report], (San Francisco, CA: International Forum on Globalization, 1999).

Barnes, Peter, *Who Owns the Sky? Our Common Assets and the Future of Capitalism* (Washington, DC: Island Press, 2001).

Baskin, Yvonne, *The Work of Nature: How the Diversity of Life Sustains Us* (Washington, DC: Island Press, 1997).

Behan, Richard W., *Plundered Promise: Capitalism, Politics and the Fate of the Federal Lands* (Washington, DC: Island Press, 2001).

Berry, Thomas, *The Dream of the Earth* (San Francisco: Sierra Club Books, 1988).

Boyle, James, *Shamans, Software and Spleens: Law and the Construction of the Information Society* (Cambridge, MA: Harvard University Press, 1996).

Boyte, Harry C., and Nancy N. Kari, *Building America: The Democratic Promise of Public Work* (Philadelphia, PA: Temple University Press, 1996).

Brown, John Seely, and Paul Duguid, *The Social Life of Information* (Cambridge, MA: Harvard Business School Press, 2000).

Buck, Susan J., *The Global Commons: An Introduction* (Washington, DC: Island Press, 1998).

Cahn, Edgar, and Jonathan Rowe, *Time Dollars* (Emmaus, PA: Rodale Press, 1992).

Coombe, Rosemary J., *The Cultural Life of Intellectual Properties: Authorship, Appropriation and the Law* (Durham, NC: Duke University Press, 1998).

Daily, Gretchen C., ed., *Nature's Services: Societal Dependence on Natural Ecosystems* (Washington, DC: Island Press, 1997).

Daly, Herman E., and John B. Cobb, Jr., *For the Common Good* (Boston: Beacon Press, 1989).

Daly, Herman E. and Kenneth N. Townsend, *Valuing the Earth: Economics, Ecology, Ethics* (Cambridge, MA: MIT Press, 1993).

Dittmar, Helga, *The Social Psychology of Material Possessions* (New York: St. Martin's Press, 1992).

Donahue, Brian, *Reclaiming the Commons: Community Farms and Forests in a New England Town* (New Haven, CT: Yale University Press, 1999).

Echeverria, John, and Raymond Booth Eby, *Let the People Judge: Wise Use and the Private Property Rights Movement* (Washington, DC: Island Press, 1995).

Ecologist, The, Whose Commons Future? Reclaiming the Commons (Philadelphia: New Society Publishers, 1993).

Edwards, Paul N., *The Closed World: Computers and the Politics of Discourse in Cold War America* (Cambridge, MA: MIT Press, 1997).

Ferguson, Charles H., *High Stakes, No Prisoners: A Winner's Tale of Greed and Glory in the Internet Wars* (New York: Times Business, 1999).

Fischer, Frank, *Citizens, Experts and the Environment: The Politics of Local Knowledge* (Durham, NC: Duke University Press, 2000).

Foster, John, ed., *Valuing Nature? Economics, Ethics and Environment* (New York: Routledge, 1997).

Frank, Thomas, *One Market Under God: Extreme Capitalism, Market Populism and the End of Economic Democracy* (New York: Doubleday, 2000).

Fried, Barbara H., *The Progressive Assault of Laissez Faire: Robert Hale and the First Law and Economics Movement* (Cambridge, MA: Harvard University Press, 1998).

Gates, Jeff, *The Ownership Solution: Toward a Shared Capitalism for the Twenty-First Century* (Reading, MA: Perseus Books, 1999).

Hawken, Paul, *The Ecology of Commerce: A Declaration of Sustainability* (New York: HarperBusiness, 1993).

Hirsch, Fred, *Social Limits to Growth* (New York: toExcel, 1999, reprint of 1976 Twentieth Century Fund Study).

Hirt, Paul W., *A Conspiracy of Optimism: Management of the National Forests Since World War Two* (Lincoln, NE: University of Nebraska Press, 1994).

Hock, Dee, *Birth of the Chaordic Age* (San Francisco: Berrett-Koehler Publishers, 1999).

Hyde, Lewis, *The Gift: Imagination and the Erotic Life of Property* (New York: Vintage Books, 1979).

Kaul, Inge, Isabelle Grunberg, and Marc A. Stern, eds., *Global Public Goods: International Cooperation in the 21st Century* (New York: Oxford University Press, 1999).

Kayden, Jerold S., *Privately Owned Public Space: The New York City Experience* (New York: John Wiley & Sons, 2000).

Kim, Amy Jo, *Community Building on the Web: Secret Strategies for Successful Online Communities* (Berkeley, CA: Peachpit Press, 2000).

Klein, Naomi, *No Logo: Taking Aim at the Brand Bullies* (New York: Picador, 1999).

Kropotkin, Petr, *Mutual Aid: A Factor of Evolution* (Boston: Porter Sargent Publishers/Extending Horizons Books, reprint of 1914 edition).

Kuttner, Robert, *Everything for Sale: The Virtues and Limits of Markets* (New York: Knopf, 1997).

Lane, Robert E., *The Loss of Happiness in Market Democracies* (New Haven, CT: Yale University Press, 2000).

———, *The Market Experience* (New York: Cambridge University Press, 1991).

Lasn, Kalle, *Culture Jam: The Uncooling of America* (New York: William Morrow & Co., 1999).

Lessig, Lawrence, *Code and Others Laws of Cyberspace* (New York: Basic Books, 1999).

———, *The Future of Ideas: The Fate of the Commons in a Connected World* (New York: Random House, 2001).

Litman, Jessica, *Digital Copyright* (Amherst, NY: Prometheus Books, 2001).

McCay, Bonnie J., and James M. Acheson, *The Question of the Commons* (Tucson, AZ: University of Arizona Press, 1986).

Mauss, Marcel, *The Gift: Forms and Functions of Exchange in Archaic Societies* (New York: W.W. Norton, 1967).

Mayer, Carl J. and George A. Riley, *Public Domain, Private Dominion: A History of Public Mineral Policy in America* (San Francisco: Sierra Club Books, 1985).

McChesney, Robert W., *Rich Media, Poor Democracy: Communication Politics in Dubious Times* (Urbana, IL: University of Illinois Press, 1999).

National Research Council, *The Digital Dilemma: Intellectual Property in the Information Age* (Washington, DC: National Academy Press, 2000).

Newman, Nathan, *Net Loss: Government, Technology and the Political Economy of Community in the Age of the Internet,* http://socrates.berkeley.edu/~newman.

Olson, Mancur, *The Logic of Collective Action: Public Goods and the Theory of Groups* (Cambridge, MA: Harvard University Press, 1965).

Oram, Andy, ed., *Peer-to-Peer: Harnessing the Power of Disruptive Technologies* (Sebastopol, CA: O'Reilly, 2001).

Ostrom, Elinor, *Governing the Commons: The Evolution of Institutions for Collective Action* (New York: Cambridge University Press, 1990).

Patterson, L. Ray, and Stanley W. Lindberg, *The Nature of Copyright: A Law of Users' Rights* (Athens, GA: University of Georgia Press, 1991).

Polanyi, Karl, *The Great Transformation: The Political and Economic Origins of Our Time* (Boston: Beacon Press, 1944, 1957).

Power, Thomas Michael, *Lost Landscapes and Failed Economies: The Search for a Value of Place* (Washington, DC: Island Press, 1996).

Putnam, Robert D., *Bowling Alone: The Collapse and Revival of American Community* (New York: Simon & Schuster, 1999).

Radin, Margaret Jane, *Contested Commodities* (Cambridge, MA: Harvard University Press, 1996).

Rifkin, Jeremy, *The Age of Access: The New Culture of Hypercapitalism Where All of Life Is a Paid-for Experience* (New York: Jeremy P. Tarcher/Putman, 2000).

Rose, Carol M., *Property and Persuasion: Essays on the History, Theory and Rhetoric of Ownership* (Boulder, CO: Westview Press, 1994).

Shiva, Vandana, *Biopiracy: The Plunder of Nature and Knowledge* (Boston, MA: South End Press, 1997).

Shulman, Seth, *Owning the Future* (Boston: Houghton Mifflin, 1999).

Shuman, Michael H., *Going Local: Creating Self-Reliant Communities in a Global Age* (New York: Routledge, 2000).

Starr, Jerold M., *Air Wars: The Fight to Reclaim Public Broadcasting* (Boston: Beacon Press, 2000).

Steen, Harold K., *The U.S. Forest Service: A History* (Seattle, WA: University of Washington Press, 1976).

Steinberg, Theodore, *Slide Mountain, or the Folly of Owning Nature* (Berkeley, CA: University of California Press, 1995).

Stevenson, Glenn, *Common Property Economics* (New York: Cambridge University Press, 1991).

Wachtel, Paul L., *The Poverty of Affluence: A Psychological Portrait of the American Way of Life* (Philadelphia: New Society Publishers, 1999).

Watt, Helen Payne, *Common Assets: Asserting Rights to Our Shared Inheritance* [report] (Washington, DC: Corporation for Enterprise Development and Redefining Progress, 2000).

Williams, Raymond, *The Country and the City* (New York: Oxford University Press, 1973).

About the Author

David Bollier, an author and civic strategist, is active in a variety of initiatives to promote the commons in American life. He is currently a Senior Fellow at the Norman Lear Center at the USC Annenberg Center for Communication in Los Angeles, and Director of the Information Commons Project at the New America Foundation in Washington, D.C. Mr. Bollier is also the cofounder of Public Knowledge, a new advocacy group that defends the public's stake in intellectual property law and the Internet. He lives in Amherst, Massachusetts.

Name Index

Subject Index